Praise for *Spirography*

"*Spirography* is the rare, wonderful book: as alive with its own weathers as the lake around which Stoddard's childhood life revolves. An elegy to a father lost to cancer; a childhood-cancer-survival memoir that refuses any easy definition of survival; a story of gender and sexuality, of water skiing and downhill skiing, of Michigan and the West, and what it means to be family, this is a radiant, restless search for answers and overlaps, all traced with such grace and intellectual and emotional power. I couldn't put it down."

—Alexandra Teague, author of *Spinning Tea Cups: A Mythical American Memoir*

"*Spirography* is a moving love story, richly layered: a daughter's love for their father spirals outward to include family, friends, lovers, a daughter of their own, and love for place, too—from one small lake in Michigan to the Great Lakes generally to mountains in Colorado and Washington. Cara Stoddard is a generous narrator, ever in motion—skiing, skating, hiking, swimming, boating—with a curious mind, ever searching, questioning. Their voice brims with wisdom and grace and warmth most of all, welcoming the reader at every turn."

—Ana Maria Spagna, author of *Uplake: Restless Essays of Coming and Going* and *Test Ride on the Sunnyland Bus: A Daughter's Civil Rights Journey*

"Stoddard's stunning debut memoir, *Spirography*, strands together their and their father's cancers, his death, and their attempts to rebuild their world. It is written the way herons peer into dark lakes: unflinchingly gazing 'beneath the surface all the way down to the bottom.'"

—Sean Prentiss, author of *Finding Abbey: The Search for Edward Abbey and His Hidden Desert Grave*

"This elegant memoir explores the loss of a father and the rearing of a daughter through the shifting lenses of place and memory."

—Mary Clearman Blew, author of *Think of Horses*

SPIROGRAPHY

Made in Michigan Writers Series

A complete listing of the books in this series can
be found online at wsupress.wayne.edu.

SPIROGRAPHY

A Memoir of Family, Loss, and Finding Home

CARA STODDARD

WAYNE STATE UNIVERSITY PRESS
DETROIT

© 2025 by Cara Stoddard. All rights reserved. No part of this book may be reproduced without formal permission.

ISBN 9780814351901 (paperback)
ISBN 9780814351918 (ebook)

Library of Congress Control Number: 2024943187

Cover art © Adobe Stock. Cover design by Laura Klynstra.

Publication of this book was made possible by a generous gift from The Meijer Foundation.

Wayne State University Press rests on Waawiyaataanong, also referred to as Detroit, the ancestral and contemporary homeland of the Three Fires Confederacy. These sovereign lands were granted by the Ojibwe, Odawa, Potawatomi, and Wyandot Nations, in 1807, through the Treaty of Detroit. Wayne State University Press affirms Indigenous sovereignty and honors all tribes with a connection to Detroit. With our Native neighbors, the press works to advance educational equity and promote a better future for the earth and all people.

Wayne State University Press
Leonard N. Simons Building
4809 Woodward Avenue
Detroit, Michigan 48201-1309

Visit us online at wsupress.wayne.edu.

This is a work of creative nonfiction insofar as the characters, events, and dialogue are rendered from the memory of the author and filtered through the perspective of childhood, adolescence, and young adulthood. Some names have been changed to protect privacy. The opinions and interpretations of specific moments are the author's alone and are meant to depict the mosaic of research, interviews, and lived experience that went into the making of this book.

For Lucia

1

orty miles east of Lake Michigan, a small inland lake, Lake Bella Vista, borders a town called Rockford, built on the Rogue River. Before it was a town, Rockford was just a dam in the river, built to power a sawmill, restraining water destined for the Grand River and Lake Michigan and then, eventually, the Atlantic Ocean. Our house was five miles east of town, a cottage-style home painted yellow with white trim, built on a lakefront lot. I grew up to the sound of water sloshing against the sides of our ski boat, the hum of jet skis on Saturdays in July, and the scrape of our screen door in its tracks. Water, more than air or forest or farmland, was the medium of my youth.

In the basement hung an aerial photograph of Lake Bella Vista in the early 1990s, before the neighborhood was built up. In the photo, the lake looked like an amoeba with a scorpion tail. As kids, my brother, Ryan, and I stood on the old couch in the basement and stared face-to-glass at that photo as if it were a map of our origins. Ryan, two and a half years younger, was my captive audience. *Here*, I said to him, smudging the glass, *this is Bailey's, where we go for ice cream. Where Dad gets gas.* He studied the photo where my finger was pointing. *And here is the dam.* The dam was where we went on Saturdays, where everyone threw out their anchors and played their radios at full volume and sunbathed on the back seats of their ski boats.

When we stood side by side on the couch cushions, his head reached my shoulders, his height lagging behind until he turned fifteen, when all at once I could look him straight in the eyes.

And this is the narrows. The lake pinched off in a section where the scorpion tail met the amoeba, only thirty-five feet wide. When I learned to waterski, my dad had taught me that the narrows was the most dangerous part of the lake to take a fall, congested with boat traffic in both directions and no room for drivers to go around a floating kid in a life jacket. He had said, *Don't go in and out of the*

2

wake through there, his sliver of fear gaping through the cracks of our house on the lake.

Ryan, look. Here is Hanson's. This family friend's house on the other side of the lake was a landmark. In our minds the lake was divided by the narrows into two halves. When my dad asked me where I wanted to ski, I'd say *All the way around*, or *Just to Hanson's and back*, or *Just to the dam and back*, depending on where it was the flattest, which way the wind was blowing.

Bella Vista means "beautiful view" in Spanish, I said to Ryan, perpetually the know-it-all big sister. *I know*, he said. Its name was a slogan, a point of pride we gleaned from our parents. Only later would I interpret this name as a charge, a way of looking at the horizon and insisting on its beauty.

In the photograph, we saw a small white speck in the center of the darkest blue, where the lake was deepest. My brother and I swore each other to secrecy about the white speck. Weeks before this photo appeared in our basement, we had thrown a Styrofoam cup off the dock. It had been an experiment. *Let's see if Styrofoam floats.* But the wind caught it and blew it out of our reach away from the dock, and neither of us was in our suits, so we let it go, watched it bob up and down in our cove, then float out into the middle of the lake until it vanished.

On first inspection of the photo, we saw the speck and swallowed. We jumped simultaneously to the same conclusion, that it was ours, and that we were sorry.

Years later, we saw the speck for what it really was: a lone boat, unmoored from its dock, captured and frozen in the stillness of the photo. But the mythology was already ingrained in us. This lake was sacred, and we were autonomous beings, marring what was meant to be perfect. The map to which we could point and say, *Look, here is our house*, was also documentation of our own regret. Both of us born with lumps in our throats and the acute awareness that everything we cherished was fleeting.

* * *

3

What I knew of Lake Bella Vista as a child had been pieced together from listening to my dad joke with neighbors on our lower deck. *This is Grass Lake, you know*, they'd say, commiserating over the relentless weeds stuck in the props of their ski boats. Summoning the lake's original name as a kind of curse, the inevitable course of what is harnessed and beautified for the sake of suburbia returning to its natural state: a swamp. The chatter of these men, holding sweating Heinekens stuffed in neon koozies, became the background din of my childhood. They had been teenagers in the late 1970s and early 1980s, had learned to waterski behind someone's outboard speedboat on swampy lakes like Grass Lake, and had come to forge their own fantasy dream homes in their early twenties—suntanned wives in bikinis, weekend mornings spent sipping coffee on a deck with a view—then brought their dreams to fruition in the late 1980s after the second of Reagan's tax cuts during the biggest dip in the cost of building a new home since World War II.

Ours was one of the first houses on the north side of lake, our front yard on a cul-de-sac, our backyard spilling out into a small finger of the lake. My parents worked with a builder and designed the shape of every window, the angle of every wall.

In a home video I found in my twenties, one we hadn't watched since it had been filmed, my dad narrates a tour of the half-built house. He is self-conscious about the performance, apologizing for the bumpy picture—*It's my first time with the camera*—the garbage piled in the dirt in our front yard, the cattails overgrown in the back. *We have lots of work to do back here*, he says to the camera.

We found the video a year after my dad died from a glioblastoma multiforme, an aggressive form of brain tumor. He was fifty-two when he died; I was twenty-three. My mom tells me he wanted to make this video for his own mom, who was dying of MS at the time and couldn't travel to see the house. In the video, I am one and a half, toddling over plywood floors, handing my mom bent nails, pressing my finger against the aperture of the camera lens. In one shot, my mom stands in the second-story window of the room

4

that would become my bedroom, holding me in her arms. We are waving at my dad filming us from the driveway.

And that's the tour of 6010 Belinda, he says.

* * *

Today I live with my partner, Ada, and her eleven-year-old, Lucia, in a Dutch colonial house in a suburb of Seattle. Ada and I fell in love when Lucia was nine, and I moved in with them a few months after she turned ten. Lucia is half Brazilian and, I, a constant Midwestern curiosity to her: butter left out at room temperature, ketchup on my scrambled eggs. *Cara, why do they call Michigan the Mitt?* she asked. I explained the peninsula surrounded on three sides by freshwater lakes: a mitten. I held up my left hand, follow-ing the bone of my ring finger south, and pointed to a freckle just to the left of a blue vein. This is where Rockford is. This is where I grew up.

Tourists come to Michigan for the lighthouses, or the National Cherry Festival in Traverse City, or the ferry ride to Mackinac Island, where they can buy fudge and rent a tandem bicycle and ride on paved roads where no motorized vehicles are allowed. We are the Great Lakes State, I tell her, according to our license plates, named by the Ojibwa, *mishigamaa*, meaning "large water."

During a rare June heat wave, we take Lucia to a public beach on Lake Washington to swim. She's a tentative swimmer at first, the weather in Seattle rarely warm enough for anyone to want to get in the sixty-degree water, but I show her how she can turn her hot pink pool noodle into a squirt gun, and she forgets her reticence momentarily. *Cara, watch this,* she says, then dunks under her noodle and comes up on the other side grinning. *When I was growing up,* I tell her, *during the summers when my dad was at work, my mom used to take my brother and me to the beach at Grand Haven on Lake Michigan.* Ryan and I piled plastic buckets and beach towels and inflatable rafts into our minivan, and at the park entrance, we craned our necks to see the rip current rating, hoping for a yellow flag, for big waves, on a beach that could easily be confused with an ocean's.

Unlike Washington, with its two mountain ranges and shrub-steppe scablands, Michigan is flat and marshy and pocked with small inland lakes. Torch Lake, Crystal Lake, Lake Cadillac and Lake Mitchell, Big and Little Glen Lakes, Whitefish Lake, each lake bordered by a Lakeview Drive, carved wooden bear totems, and a party store with Live Worms on the letter board out front. I can see in my mind's eye through the van's back seat windows lakes that are vast and gray and rough in August, during days and days and days of rain, lakes glowing orange with sunset, lakes that freeze solid in late December, kept smooth enough by the wind for pond hockey, peppered with small white and tarp-blue fishing shanties.

But really there are two Michigans. One where water slakes, untreated, through antique pipes and comes from the tap laced with lead seven times higher than the EPA legal limit. And one where people take vacations up north, downhill skiing in the winter and to the beach in the summer. My childhood was devoid of fears about police or drinking water. My family took vacations up north. Up north, every town has an ice cream shop, a pizza place, a La Señorita Mexican chain restaurant, and a tourist shop selling brightly colored fish windsocks and jewelry made out of Petoskey stones.

The kids from my neighborhood all grew up knowing the difference between board shorts and swim trunks with those embarrassing mesh liners, knowing which end of a boat is the bow and which the stern, knowing how to ski in at least one of the seasons, and knowing that there was something magical about sunlight just before dusk that comes filtering through poplar and white pine boughs across a paved two-lane road following the meandering perimeter of some inland, sparkling lake.

Nowadays, I make sun tea in glass mason jars out on our back patio and sit with Lucia as she plows her way through a bowl of cherries, carefully spitting her pits into a small dish I set out for her. I tell her we used to have cherry pit spitting contests off our back deck, and she smiles at me through a mouthful of cherries, motions to me to spit with her, as our dog chases the arc of our pits across the backyard.

6

My dad said we were Lake People. That you could pick us out at a restaurant in October, the only ones still tan, still wearing sandals, still eating outside on the deck. And because we went to the Church of the Lake all those Sunday mornings in August when I would wake to the buzz of my dad lowering the Glastron's propeller into the water, slip out of bed and pull on my suit, take the stairs two at a time to the unfinished part of the basement where wetsuits hung from water pipes and inflated tubes were stacked almost to the ceiling. I would swing my life jacket over one shoulder, burst through the back door, skip across dewy lawn and over the loose boards of our dock, and hop into the rider's seat to be his spotter.

He cut quick zigzags behind the boat while my mom drove, letting go with his outside hand at the apex of each turn, reaching around some invisible buoy, racing back across the wake in a crouch, my chin following him back and forth, a rhythm I kept time to.

*   *   *

The day my mom found out she was pregnant with me she bought a set of red-and-white wooden baby skis, tied together at the tips and tails. They hadn't been trying to get pregnant. My dad came home from work and saw the skis on their waterbed, and he knew.

The summer I turned four, he started pulling me around in the shallow water near shore, making motorboat noises just to hear me laugh. I held tight to the handle, happy to be a skier like he was. When he put me behind the boat later that summer, I stood up on the first try, born already knowing how.

*   *   *

The summer of my seventh birthday, my mom planned a fish party. In the kitchen, she was cutting a rectangular chocolate cake into the shape of a fish. *Mom,* I hollered from the living room, sifting through piles of CDs, *what's that song Dad always plays for my birthday?* We were filling the morning hours, waiting for my dad to come home from work.

It's Paul McCartney, the live album. She returned to her fish cake, spreading the yellow frosting, giving it a gumdrop eyeball.

My mom decorated our house like something torn from the pages of *Country Living*, antiques everywhere: an old spinning wheel, a ceramic pitcher and basin embellished with small pink flowers, a clay butter churn, a wrought-iron rug beater mounted on the wall next to a hundred-year-old rolling pin, one she lifted from its nail on the wall and used every time she made a pie. At the top of the stairs leading up to the bedrooms hung a Regulator wall clock my dad had made from a kit when my parents were first married. The clock had to be wound once a week, with a key he kept inside the door, where he'd return it after winding. Each time, he'd give the pendulum a light tap to set the clock back in motion.

I sat cross-legged before the massive wardrobe used to house our TV and stereo equipment, riffling through the stacks of plastic cases. *Mom, I can't find the CD.* My dad bought her the wardrobe at an antiques dealer in southern Michigan, strapped the thing into the trunk of his Corvette, and drove thirty-five miles an hour for three hours to get it home. He spent weeks stripping the wardrobe and then restaining it, bringing out the hues of the original oak.

She came in from the kitchen with a spatula for me to lick, found the CD in the first stack, and went back to her cake. On the back of the case, I found "Birthday," track seven, and changed the track on the CD player. *It's lucky*, I hollered, *the same number as me*, and turned up the volume, the familiar first few chords blaring. She never told me to turn it down.

I was helping my mom set up for the party—carrying fishing poles from the back room down to the dock, trying to keep the hooks latched, the lines taut—when my dad arrived home from work. He was five feet, eleven inches tall, broad-chested and fit, built the same as when he played football in high school, save for the deep furrow between his eyebrows where the black-rimmed glasses he started wearing at forty sit now, his eyes the only evidence of his aging. Walking down the hill toward us, still in his

8

dress clothes—black pants, ironed shirt, and matching tie, sunglasses. I ran to greet him.

* * *

The fish party went like this: Each kid had to find her own worm and catch her own fish. Then my mom took our fish off the hook for us and carried it across the yard to the cement stoop by the back door and hit it over the head with a hammer, killing it instantly.

My dad hated fishing, never baited hooks. Never helped Ryan or me when we'd pull in a fish, clumsy and careless, the fish writhing on the dock. As the older sister, I was supposed to be the brave one, but I was afraid to touch it, afraid I'd cut my hand on its spiny dorsal fins, afraid of the heaving blood-red muscle inside its slit of gills. My mom told us that our dad had gone pheasant hunting once with his Uncle Bob but that he never shot anything. I imagined him carrying a gun and dressed entirely in camouflage and hiking boots, and I knew those were not things he had in his closet. I wondered who else he had been before we were born.

At the party, each of us sat fidgeting at the picnic table covered in a plastic fish-patterned tablecloth, waiting for my mom to return with our fish. Our catch was mostly spotted sunfish and yellow perch, all of them bug-eyed and frowning. Already their iridescence was muted by being brought from water to air. Gone also was their animated displeasure from earlier down on the dock. When my mom brought each of our fish to the table, they lay still, their pectoral fins gone limp, glued with their stress-slime to the sides of their bodies. We each painted our fish with fabric paint and then stamped it, paint side down, onto a plain white tank top, then outlined it with puff paint. We gave our fish sequin eyes.

I don't think any of us really knew that the fish we were painting were dead. I know we watched my mom at the back stoop, not really out of sight or earshot, but none of us went over with her to watch our fish die.

* * *

Lucia is small for her age, muscular, fastidious, her tiny hot pink sneakers placed neatly by the door, her brown hair curling past her shoulders. She and I had no warming-up period. The day we met, she asked me my favorite color, then asked if I'd have a Nerf war with her, gave me her best gun. Later we walked my dog around the neighborhood, and she reached for my hand. Watching TV with her mom and me in our bed, she insists on being in the middle, bony knees against my thighs, bony shoulders against her mom's chest, a wiggly sack of sharp corners. Here, she is biting her nails. Here, she is looking up memes on my phone. Here, she is writing messages in Portuguese on our fogged-up bathroom mirror: "*Te amo mamães.*"

One summer night, the three of us sleep in a tent in our backyard. Our neighborhood butts up against Highway 99, the state highway that runs north–south from Everett to Tacoma, but the backyard is surrounded on three sides by hundred-year-old Douglas firs, red alder, and a youngish western red cedar, and we sometimes forget that we're in the city. The tent is the same tent Ada slept in with her parents as a child, but backyard tent camping is a reenactment from my childhood. We have a bonfire and scavenge for long, straight sticks under the cedar tree to roast marshmallows. Rod Stewart sings the first cut is the deepest. We sit in rapt attention, enthralled by the embers, the music. Decades later, everything is the same. When the fire's burned itself out, we crawl into the tent. Ada and I zip our mummy bags together. The neighbors light firecrackers, and Lucia comforts the dog. I read aloud from *Roll of Thunder, Hear My Cry*, a book my mom read to me when I was Lucia's age, until I fall asleep.

Reading with Lucia before bed; grocery shopping with her at Trader Joe's; watching her water the garden, toggling the hose nozzle between shower and jet; cajoling her into doing the dishes as she neglects all the pans on the stove—I am simultaneously her and not her. I have a prerecorded voice box of my dad in my chest. I am looking down from above into the dollhouse that is our house, with the roof removed. Layered over our house is a hologram of my

10

childhood house. In both houses there is a girl asleep in her bed, half in half out of the covers, her arm curled around her stuffed animal. The parents pressed each other up against the counters in the kitchen, sneaking a kiss. The distinction between past and future falls away. She has none of my genes but all of my antics. I harvest snap peas from our garden, put two on her plate for her to try, and she makes a face, chases each bite with a sip of orange juice. *Go put your napkin in the washer*, I tell her after dinner, then watch her toss it in the dryer with the clean clothes. Each wind of the clock, I am ten again, begging my parents for quarters to play air hockey. I fall asleep in her bed reading. I wake up and realize this time it's me playing Paul McCartney for her birthday. How much of this repetition is purposeful, willed, and how much is instinctual? Is this belief that I am uniquely myself, a composite product of all my lived experiences, an individual, a myth I invented?

I remember mosquito bites and my mom telling me not to itch them, sunblock like a second skin, and sand in everything. In my mouth, in my hair, in my crotch, in my sheets. French braids, keeping my hair out of my face. Great blue herons fishing off our dock at dawn, leaving huge four-pronged bird prints in our sand like pterodactyls, lurching their necks and lifting their knees high when they walked, pointing their toes, not creating a ripple. Kingfishers perching in the neighbor's cottonwood tree, studying the movements of fish beneath that sparkling sheen of glass. Killdeer, permanent residents on all the empty lots, running ahead of us on our bikes, calling frantically their own names. And mallards and Canada geese bobbing like buoys, sometimes a pair of swans, once a set of coots, all these waterfowl mating for life.

In summer, we wore only pajamas and bathing suits. We had Rice Chex at the pink Formica counter in the kitchen, then spent the rest of the day outside. After breakfast, we'd burst through the screen door, onto the deck with the giant umbrella shading the table, and down the steps to the wet grass of the backyard. From April to October, we ate every dinner on that deck, staring out at the lake sparkling like a mirage, slouching in our white wicker deck chairs, our legs draped over their sides, propping our bare feet on each other's chairs, dripping watermelon down our bare stomachs.

We lived on that beach those summers, each of our dispositions completely dependent upon the weather. My dad teaching us the patterns: *See those cirrus clouds, the thin, wispy ones, way high up there? That means it's going to rain in the next day and a half.* On partly cloudy days, he'd count down for my mom, sunbathing in her bikini, *Three more minutes and the sun will be back out.* We had a thermometer on our deck with a caricature of a waterskier at three different temperature ranges. Anything seventy or hotter, he was in his swim trunks, sweating and happy. From thirty to seventy, he wore his shorty wetsuit, his fist held out in front of his skinny body, brandishing a thumbs up. From negative thirty to thirty degrees, he was in his long-sleeved wetsuit, blue skinned and shivering. Above the thermometer, my dad hung a wind chime, five hollow metal pipes, each a different note, with a wooden knocker strung down the middle. It had been a Father's Day gift from when I was in high school but hangs now in my memory as something that had always been there. The thermometer and the wind chime, situated directly below my parents' bedroom window, were the instruments of his navigation, what we bound our lives to. When I was in high school, he was always the one to wake me up, gently, from the doorway, to ski. *Cara, the wind chime's at a standstill.* Code for, *Let's go.* Code for, *The lake is glass out there.* Code for, *I love you more than there are words to say.*

* * *

Waterski ropes are seventy-five feet of braided polypropylene. Waxy, plastic to the touch, but sixteen strands strong. All those years, I watched my dad splice old ski ropes with his blowtorch, melting one strand into the other, then melting the ends so they wouldn't fray.

After fusing the two old ropes into a new one, he would toss me the handle up on shore, tell me to pull tight, up in the grass, to make sure it was strong enough. And I would arch my back and dig in my heels, putting all my weight into pulling away.

12

There was something umbilical that flowed through that rope from him to me. And as twisted and tangled as those ropes became when limp and unused under the passenger's seat of the boat, his calloused hands and mine would always untangle them, find our way to each other.

* * *

Here is a family portrait: A hot morning in July, two parents and their teenage children, two ski ropes tied to the pylon. The girl is floating in the water fifty-three feet away from the boat, port side, the tip of her ski barely poking out of the water, black and shining like a whale fin, her dad and his ski identical, floating starboard, seventy-five feet away, out at long line. Their ropes make a perfect thirty-degree angle from the back of the boat. The boy is sitting in the passenger's seat, spotting. The mom is driving, hand on the throttle.

The girl looks to her dad and whispers from six feet away, *You ready?*

Yeah.

Hit it, she shouts, and the mom guns it. They hold on tight, fight the water with their quads, the motor groans, and soon they are up, skimming the surface. This is a practiced routine, and he calls all the shots because his rope is longer. She knows when she hears him say *Now* to cut in toward the wake, ducking under his rope, watch him for the turn, and then cut back. And this is their rhythm, their pulse, their lives crisscrossing through time, becoming something tightly woven, a braid that could never unravel.

Later: A summer storm is gathering late in the day, the rain like bullets on their faces as they speed the boat back into the dock. The boy and his mom gather beach towels, racing toward the house. There is thunder now, rolling deep and low, and she knows about electricity, how water carries the current. The girl and her dad stand knee-deep next to the dock—she is at the bow, he is at the stern, snapping carabineers into eye hooks to secure the boat. She runs up on shore, grabs the canvas boat cover in her two arms, tossing him the end, doing this together until it's done. She hooks the pointed end over the nose of the boat, and he pulls his end over the rub rails, tightening it into a knot at the stern, their hands quick with familiarity. Lightning strikes a mile or two away, and the whole world roars.

The girl's mom stands at the kitchen window, watching them work, knowing it is faster with two.

* * *

I read somewhere once that blue herons' eyesight has evolved so that when they look at water, they don't see their own reflections but rather can see beneath the surface all the way down to the bottom of the lake. I watched them out the kitchen window, their yellow eyes set on either side of their heads beneath their black caps, their long beaks poised, ready to dart at anything that moved. They stood on our dock for hours, perfectly still, full of dignity, gazing into that slate-gray water as if by looking long enough they might see into and through whatever it was they were wanting.

* * *

In retrospect, so many memories look like foreshadowing. A spring morning. My mom walking me to the bus stop. A cedar waxwing dead in the driveway.

The dawning of understanding came slowly: The waxwing flew into the clear glass of our basketball backstop and died on impact. I remember its soft yellow underwings, the way its feathers looked more like fur, and how, in death, the bird appeared suddenly fragile and precious, its colors more vivid. My mom was afraid to touch it, used a shovel to scoop it into the trash bin. This was before my dad's diagnosis, before our six long years spent knowing he would die. I thought then: This is how a life stops, suddenly, with a thud.

2

I was diagnosed with a pediatric germ cell tumor when I was seven. What I remember best from that day: the fish in the waiting room. *Mom, what kind of fish is that?* I said, pressing my finger against the glass. *A tiger barb*, she said without elaboration. *What about that one?* I tried again. *A neon tetra*, she said. I watched its small body, following that bright blue stripe of color across the tank. *It's see-through*, I said finally.

My pediatrician didn't know what was up but suspected something serious. Appendicitis? He called ahead and got us in for ultrasound imaging at Butterworth Hospital. I spent so much of my childhood riding in the car with my mom across town, running errands, being schlepped to soccer practice, to flute lessons, to the mall. How can one errand, like any other errand on any other day, change an entire lifetime's trajectory? I rode the twenty minutes from pediatrician's office to hospital, the seat tipped all the way back, curled on my side, sucking my thumb. Not knowing, really, what it meant to go to the hospital.

Besides fish, I remember the wet deodorant stick of the ultrasound. *This won't hurt at all. Just a bit cold*, the woman in the white lab coat warned. And that my mom called my dad from the waiting room. *Something's wrong*, she said. *We're spending the night.* I squirmed in my chair, nervous at her open crying in this public place. *Bring her blanket*, she reminded him.

My mom worked as a lab tech in a hospital lab. She spent six days a week staring through the eyepiece of a microscope, peering at the blood samples of strangers, running strep tests, preparing pathology reports. Earlier that day, she had answered a call on the plastic corded phone mounted to the wall in her lab. After she hung up the phone, she traded in her white lab coat for her purse and left work early. Something about the tone of the babysitter's voice on the phone, the way she said *I picked her up from school before lunch*,

16

made my mom worry. She was a parent with the dread of a microbiologist coursing through her.

Unshackled from context and experience, I had a heightened attention to the sensory: the snap of latex gloves, the smell of rubbing alcohol that preceded the needle, the way the plastic cover on the thermometer felt too big in my mouth, under my tongue. Being cold.

I can only guess at my mom's thoughts that afternoon, her daughter, bare-chested and too small for the ultrasound table. Seven years earlier she had turned toward that glowing screen and caught a glimpse of me for the first time, black and white and sucking my thumb. Now, in the ultrasound, a white bulge of cells growing where a child might have grown, a monster kept secret inside the belly of a child. Maybe she didn't need to look. She was already beginning to read the stony faces of hospital staff, a nuanced language she would learn fluently in the months and years to come.

The day after the ultrasound, I sat still and attentive as my pediatric oncologist drew a sketch of a uterus and ovaries—a frontal view of an ant's head and antennae. She drew a tumor attached to the right ovary, doubling its size. She explained that they were going to remove one of my ovaries and fallopian tubes, maybe both, that my hair would fall out but would eventually grow back, that this was the best she could do. *Yes, I understand,* I said that day, stoic. I watched my dad's face redden as he left the room.

When I was in college, home for summer break but working at a sleepaway camp in northern Michigan, my dad would tell me that the neighbor kids came over asking my whereabouts. They were a trio of towheaded beach bums, their parents ten years younger than mine. I had babysat for them occasionally when I was in high school, and apparently they wanted me to come over and play ghosts in the graveyard. My dad looked me in the eye and said, with the same pride he beamed with at my cross-country meets or band concerts and when dropping me off at my high school dances, *I know you're going to make a good mom someday.*

I had had my period since age twelve, and, as much as my fertility was a looming question in my mind, it was not something my parents and I ever talked about. None of the adults I knew in my parents' circle of friends were childless. Plus, I liked kids. In college, I was minoring in education. Whatever disappointment I might have felt for this traditional expectation he had for my future, it was overshadowed by feeling beloved, awash in his approval.

At age seven, my pediatric oncologist's drawing embarrassed me, this acknowledgment of organs unique to being born a girl, words like "uterus" and "ovary" even less familiar than "cancer." This sketch seemed like something secret and off limits, my child's psyche mixing up what was anatomically correct sexuality with what was supposed to be an explanation of my own mortality.

They said the tumor on my ovary was the size of a grapefruit. Recalling this now, I think of a boa eating a mongoose. It had been growing inside me for at least six months, then ruptured and was causing infection as slivers do when they fester. How did I not notice? It was hard not to feel duped.

* * *

That winter, I did three rounds of chemo, inpatient for a month at a time, each in my corner room in the pediatric ward on the ninth floor. On a gray day like so many others that winter, my mom sat in the window seat, holding a needle between her pursed lips. With her orange-handled scissors, she followed the perimeter of a tissue paper triangle pinned to the black-and-white checked fabric. Her slender hands were unwavering; her narrow shoulders hunched over the work in her lap. Outside it was snowing, a short-lived Michigan flurry, the streets below etched in black-and-white stripes from so many cars tracing their individual arcs through the snow in the intersection, like a Spirograph drawing, wildly cyclic in its mathematical logic. The outline of my mom's body blurred to blue in winter's low light. She didn't see me propped up on one elbow in bed and watching her. Everything was still, quiet, save for her careful shearing.

I was playing the part of the harlequin for Odyssey of the Mind,

18

an extracurricular theater club. She'd explained the character as a court jester, a silent jokester, pantomiming with overexaggerated gestures. I imagined kings and queens hysterical with laughter atop velveteen thrones. I sensed something sinister about this setup, that only royalty enjoyed the luxury of boredom, and that a harlequin was probably not a very respectable job. My part in the skit was to carry the Act I, Act II, and Act III signs across the stage, silently, like a joke.

Earlier that day I had been practicing my entrances. My mom said a harlequin was supposed to act absentminded. She suggested I carry the Act II sign upside down, an intentional accident. My mom read the lines at the ends of Acts I and II, then nodded to me as my cue. From the doorway, I moved toward her, half skipping, half galloping.

In the pediatric ward, each patient had their own room. Among the muted gray hospital furniture and fixtures, there were colorful signs of a children's play world: the tiny pink soccer ball, brought from home after my first surgery in an attempt to help me regain my strength by kicking it around the nurse's station, IV in tow. Crayola markers I hooked end to end with the girl in the room next door, enough markers to stretch the length of our entire hall. An arts-on-a-cart tornado-in-a-bottle project on my bedside stand. The soundtrack of *E. T.* emanating out of someone else's room. But, for the most part, it was a solemn place.

The harlequin costume is long since gone now, but I remember the feel of the inside-out sweatshirt I wore, its fleece worn thin, balled into the same texture as the baby blanket I ran across my upper lip every night as I fell asleep. My mom hot-glued black felt diamonds in neat columns up the front of the white sweatshirt. The sweatshirt hung to my knees, and I wore black-and-white houndstooth leggings underneath, a black sneaker on my right foot and one of my white Keds on my left. The hat she made from those triangles of checked fabric had three prongs she stuffed with newspaper so they bent in their middles, and she sewed a tiny red bell to the end of each prong, so when I skipped across the stage, the audience could hear their quiet tinkling.

My dad wouldn't stand for me to miss the event, and he arranged a plan with my head oncologist that none of the nursing staff would have approved. The day our skit was to be performed at the district competition was sunny. I was dozing with the sun glinting off the pouch of bleomycin, a photosensitive chemical, its plastic bag coated in brown wax paper to protect the contents. When the hour came for us to leave for the school, he quietly unplugged me from my IV, flushed and capped the two tubes of my port as he had done so many times before, taped the tubes inside a Ziploc baggie to discourage infection, and held my hand as we walked nonchalantly past the nurse's station and onto the elevator to meet my mom and brother in the minivan they'd pulled into the patient pickup lane.

It's better to ask for forgiveness than permission, he said when we made it to the van, smirking at me conspiratorially in the back seat. I was sick to the bone from the chemo, breaking out of the hospital to play a nonessential role in a children's theater production, and my dad was teaching me civil disobedience. Recounting this story now, I see that my parents were grasping at whatever remaining shreds of control they still had, willing a normal childhood to play out, even when creating that fiction required extreme, forced choreography on their parts. Brought to the edge of the abyss every parent eventually comes to, they had gone into crisis mode, their personalities warped into exaggerations of what they had been before. My mom became hyper-involved in my care, suspicious of all medical personnel save for my team of three oncologists, demanding a full explanation for every decision the nurses made. My dad turned into a determined comedian, hell-bent on keeping everything light. But the origin of his foolheartedness lay in his anticipation of combat. Underneath his too-loud jokes and stunts, I sensed, even then, something seething.

When we arrived at the school, my mom herded me to the bathroom, sat me in front of a wall-to-wall mirror, and painted my face two-tone. I watched as the black and white paint turned me unrecognizable. This was my first public appearance since my hair had fallen out. *Mom*, I asked, *do you think anyone will notice?*

20

No, she said, Velcroing my jester hat under my chin and pulling her red lipstick out of her purse.

Don't forget to smile, she said.

I think of Lucia spreading an egg wash on a loaf of challah we'd made together, asking me in all earnestness if an egg could have turned into a baby chick. I deflected the question, said something about how not all eggs are fertilized, that in fact, most store-bought eggs, like these were, are not. Childhood is riddled with these opportunities: behind door number one, a sugar-coated lie; behind door number two, an ugly truth most adults have forgotten because they entrenched it so deep in euphemism. I can understand the protective urge behind door number one. I knew the question arose because I'd told her the purpose of the egg coating was just to make the bread shiny, and she saw it as a kind of frivolous step, a waste of an egg, a life. Perhaps we have shifted culturally since the 1990s, and parents today have an easier time with an eyes-wide-open approach to parenting than they did then. Maybe my mom just intuited I'd reached my maximum of ugly truths for the year. Or she wanted as badly as I did for no one to notice my baldness.

Either way, it felt surreal to be out of the hospital and with my friends. I sensed that they regarded me differently, but I didn't have words to name it. My mom had pinned her black-and-white drama mask pin to the breast of my sweatshirt, one face smiling, the other frowning. I made each of my entrances on cue, held the Act II sign upside down, acted absentminded, stayed silent. Now, I understand that the two faces are inverses of each other, necessarily linked. I take solace in what poet Khalil Gibran has written, "The deeper that sorrow carves into your being, the more joy you can contain."

* * *

To this day, my grandmother writes daily, religiously in a one-by-two-inch rectangle of her five-year diary. She grew up on a dairy farm, the third born of five, though one of her older sisters died from scarlet fever in infancy. She taught first grade in Jackson Public Schools for twenty-five years. Retired the year I was born to have more time to be a grandma. Ryan and I loved her, and she spoiled us. Whenever she and my grandpa spent the night at our house, we would wake up before dawn and run down to the guest room in the basement to sleep in with her. When we were older, she bought us sugar cereal, took us for long hikes in the woods, played dominoes and rummy cube with us for hours, taught me how to watercolor, taught Ryan how to play bridge.

In the style typical of her generation, her diaries are part phenological observation, part listing of the day's occurrences.

November 18, 1993
Cold sunny day. Went to breakfast with group. Then to Butterfields bought history of Jackson book. Looked at suit at Silvermans. Spent afternoon at home. Jeanne called. Cara has a mass in pelvis and admitted to hospital.

November 19, 1993
Rain this morning. Got off to Jeanne's. Picked Ryan up at Arlene's at 10:20. Took him to the hospital at noon. Things aren't good. Took Duane home and Ryan with Val after I fixed lunch. I went back to the hospital started surgery on Cara at 7:45. She got out about 10:30. Not good—Cancer—.

November 22, 1993
Rain and cold. Jeanne came home for a few or one hour. Her car broke down and the police brought her to the hospital. We had left for the hospital. Bought some groceries and then got to the hospital about one. Left at 4:30. Made supper. Still not eating much. Nothing tastes good.

My grandmother has no use, and no space, for reflection in her journaling. But the physical and psychological toll of her worry is recounted in these fragments. What strikes me most poignantly, reading her diary now, is that everyone's lives had been turned instantly to chaos—with the high medical drama that fueled

22

twenty seasons of *Grey's Anatomy* and fifteen seasons of *ER*—and yet the weather persisted, indifferent.

December 6, 1993
45,000 oil, filter green van. Snow this morning on the road. Little sleep last night. Got to Denise's at 8:30 for Ryan. Jeanne called they are going to do surgery again for Cara about 10:00. Jeanne called about 1:00. There were two kinks in the bowel and adhesions causing the pain. Gave Val the baby shawl.

December 7, 1993
Cloudy cool day. Ryan went to preschool. We went to the hospital to see Cara. She was doing well but really didn't want to see us. She was happy with her dad. Went out to lunch and did errands for Jeanne and Rick. Ryan went to play with Ross. Duane has a bad pain in his back. Got better with Motrin.

December 12, 1993
Beautiful clear cold day. Cara was worse this morning and we had a worried day. Later they figured out it was an antibiotic that made her sick. We went up to see her after 5 P.M. Came home and got Ryan in bed by 8 P.M. Called Claribell and Faye.

December 13, 1993
Beautiful sunrise. Took Ryan to hospital. He was bad at lunch so brought him home at 1:00. Cara came home at 4:00 P.M. A furnace man came for their furnace and they need a new one. Cara slept with me all night. She had a very restful night.

December 18, 1993
Cloudy, Rainy. Went to see Cara at the hospital today. Jeanne went to work. She was very upset and I talked with her that life had to go on. I didn't go to the hospital to stay with Cara tonight. Jeanne and Rick both stayed. She is to come home tomorrow.

December 23, 1993
Sunny. Quite cold. Ground white. Got hair fixed. Went to
Jacobsons for breakfast. Then drove to Jeanne's. Started to snow
about 4:30—we all went to the Amway for an elegant dinner
and then a carriage ride in the city with the snow falling. Kids
were extra good. Even Ryan.

How hard it must have been for my grandma to bear witness to all this, the gutting of her daughter and beloved son-in-law, the worry for her granddaughter, the thankless task of caring for a toddler behind the scenes who had had his entire stable world turned on its head. It's December in Michigan, and my parents' car and furnace are both broken, they are trading off shifts spending sleepless nights with me at the hospital, something catalyzes my mom to return to work (out of family medical leave days?), and her mother consoles her in her even and stern way: *Life has to go on.*

I don't remember the constant intake and discharge from the hospital, three different stays all within that first six weeks. And I don't remember anything about the pain. I remember the toys.

My uncle brought me a giant plush Saint Bernard. The stuffed animal sprawled across the bottom of my bed where my feet didn't reach, spanning the entire width, as large as the real dog, with a mouth that opened to reveal a pink felt tongue. I named the dog Big Bernard. This dog was a part of some sort of plan among the adults, at least that's how I conceived of him, a guardian meant to scare away strangers and the long line of curious doctors and researchers from other disciplines sent to see the girl on the ninth floor with an endodermal sinus tumor, something new and different. DeVos Children's Hospital in Grand Rapids was the best-resourced pediatric hospital in the state of Michigan, funded by the DeVos legacy. But the hospital had only ever successfully treated one other instance of my type of cancer at the time I was admitted as a patient. We were a spectacle. In a matter of days, hours, I'd become the centerpiece of the room, and even then, I disliked being fussed over.

24

In high school, I gave the dog to my first boyfriend as a kind of collateral for the gray Ferris State hoodie I had stolen from him, then told him the whole story of the uncle and the parade of unwanted visitors. We were both sixteen and had a lot of non-sex in his parents' hot tub, our bodies tangled and pale under the slate-gray sky, the moon ambient behind a curtain of clouds. I didn't know what to do with my limbs, and I suppose he didn't either, both of us too shy to ask what the other wanted. I kept tracing the outline of his ear with my pointer finger. Whenever he was turned on, I hated the way his face went flat, his hands too eager, the way they pressed against my breasts, like a vice pinning me to the plastic walls of that hot tub. Christian radio blared the five miles between his house and mine. I had a midnight curfew.

I told him everything about the year I'd been sick, an obligatory explanation for my naked body. I thought maybe in telling him the parts of myself I held secret, I could replicate the intimacy of sex, that laying bare my narrative was more meaningful than anything I could do with my body. I told him about the day in February when my second-grade teacher came to visit me in the hospital to drop off a new packet of homework. How I had been in the bathtub when she came, how I had walked into the room dripping and naked, not knowing I had a visitor, how my mom had shouted my name in surprise, and I sat on the floor in the bathroom crying until my teacher left. I told him about the girl in the room next door, the hemophiliac, how we traded wristbands, pretending to take on each other's illnesses, trying to trick our impersonal nurses, who insisted on checking our names every time our IVs beeped, into giving the chemo drugs to the girl with a full head of hair.

But my telling him just made him tentative, his movements more measured. *Are you still sick?* he asked, unsure if that was the right thing to say. *Do they know if it will come back?* He pulled on his T-shirt over his bare chest, sending waves across his waterbed, the sloshing between us punctuating my silence. He said nothing about his own childhood in return. His silence in this moment was its own kind of grace that I didn't yet have the wisdom to pick up on. I resented him for not being able to empathize, for not at least trying. Somewhere along the way, I had scrambled the vulnerability that comes from speaking my truth with the vulnerability of actual nakedness. In the ways that firsts imprint on us, I began to believe in the impossibility of reciprocity, and that that was my unique burden to carry. Who, at sixteen, had known the non-negotiability of life-threatening illness? Who, at sixteen, had known their bodies to be dramatically altered, had lain awake under so many glow-in-the-dark stars, trying to find the words for loss, when nothing in particular had been lost? In reality, he was the first person I told this to who didn't pity me. Both of us were just trying, within our separate bodies of nerves and muscles and flesh, to figure out how to love and ask for love, when some huge pieces of our lives happened before we ever knew each other.

I broke up with him nine months later, in the parking lot after a football game, told him I needed to *figure out some stuff with God.*

The dog, the story of the dog, was a stand-in for my body, for all my insecurities at that age. *Here, you can have this.* I figured the inertness of my body against his body was the awkwardness of every teenager, that the shame I felt overpowered all my nerve endings, and that I might as well stay single until I could reconcile the dissonance between my raging hormones and my desire to be a good kid, to wait until I was older. I never gave him back his sweatshirt. He never returned Big Bernard, but he did come over to my house in his truck once, after we broke up, to deliver a pile of wood to my dad. He had a surplus from a tree he took out, one of his landscaping gigs, and thought we could burn it that winter. My dad and I stood in the driveway and watched him drive away. After he was gone, my dad taught me how to split wood, how to gently tap the wedge in to balance it, how to hold the mallet with two hands. He said, *You have to work with the grain of the wood, Cara. Like this. Look. You're making it too hard on yourself.*

* * *

26

In the six years that followed 1993, I had regular checkups: every month, then every other, then four times a year, then biannually, then annually, then not at all. Each time we went to the hospital, a nurse gave us a new white bottle of barium, my name printed backward, last name then first, on the label. We kept the barium in the back of the fridge behind the glass bottles of 2 percent milk and the cardboard cartons of Tropicana. I dreaded the barium more than I ever feared needles or phone calls or doctors' cold hands.

Eight years old, past my bedtime, and my dad started singing me a drinking song from when he was in college, *Drink chug-a-lug-a-lug-a, drink chug-a-lug-a-lug-a. Drink.* My mom gave him a sideways look, and he said, *Just pretend it's a chocolate milkshake.* I was stalling.

My mom promised they would take me out to breakfast after all my tests in the morning before they took me back to Mrs. Althizer's third-grade classroom. My dad had canceled all his morning meetings so he could come too. I sat at the counter pressing my cheek against the crook of my arm, staring sideways at the half-drunk glass of barium. *Look,* my mom said, *you're more than halfway. See. The cup gets narrower at the bottom.* I looked at her but didn't lift my head. I could tell she was getting frustrated, that I was making this worse for her. She said, *Just drink it, Cara,* pleading. *The longer you take, the harder it is.*

In the morning, waiting in the radiology waiting room for the CAT scan, a nurse brought me more barium to drink, this kind flavored cherry with ice and a straw, the wrapper left at the end of the straw for me to remove myself. *Drink your drink,* my dad said halfheartedly, reluctant to take on the role of enforcer.

When the lab tech in the white coat called my name from the doorway, mispronouncing it *Care-a,* my dad went with me into the dark room. They hooked up an IV in the crook of my elbow, pumped me full of a liquid dye. I was suddenly aware of the way my blood circulated in rhythmic surges—the liquid dye, a warmth that coursed through me, so metallic I could taste it—and I felt like I was falling through the narrow gurney, through the floor, through however many cement floors were beneath that floor. The falling was like a dream I'd had so many times before, but the CAT scan roared to life, emitting a sliver of green light across the inside arc of the donut, the same line of green reflecting off my abdomen, and I knew I was not asleep. My dad took my small hand in his rough one and gave it a hard squeeze, rolling the bones over each other.

The lab tech told me to close my eyes, and kaleidoscopes bloomed behind my eyelids. I know now that this hand-holding was just as much for him as it was for me. Had I opened them, I might have seen how terrified he was.

3

It was January, my third round of chemo. It had snowed six inches over the past six hours. My dad and I played backgammon in our corner room on the ninth floor, directly below the helicopter landing pad. He was teaching me addition—*Move one guy six and one four, or this one ten.* The click-drip of an IV and the ding of elevator arrival were the only other sounds.

I loved our backgammon set for its corduroy compact case, the muted rattle of dice in felt-lined cups, the tall triangles in contrasting colors, a mouthful of brown and tan teeth. The way my dad's calloused fingers, careful and patient, plucked the tiny round pieces, and the way he counted aloud, skirting the perimeter of backgammon's felt and leather stage. These are the moves of brown and ivory stones kept in neat rows, progressing in semicircles from one corduroy cradle to another, his stones and mine, moving in opposite directions.

Under those fluorescent lights, my skin was raked raw and reptilian, white whispies poking out from beneath my jean hat, the only feathers of hair left. His body next to mine in between the plastic rails of that robot bed. Trying to maintain some semblance of order, he scolded me for itching out my eyebrows. *Pick out mine instead,* he said, as if he wished he could take my place, or that we all might end up unchanged. Doesn't every parent wish, futilely, they can protect their kid from wanton hurt and suffering? For all I know, he made some desperate deal with the devil in those doldrum hours between two and four in the morning, sitting at my bedside, that whatever ill was to befall me might pass from me to him.

* * *

In the years that followed 1993, my family rarely spoke of what happened, as if we all wished we could unremember. When I was eight, on a visit to the Pediatric Hematology-Oncology clinic for one of my checkups, I sat in the center of an exam room on an exam table, wearing my Save the Manatees T-shirt and white Keds, my knees pulled into my chest, shredding the paper sheet pulled down over the table. My parents were engaged in a cross-examination with my doctor—*Does she ever talk about it with you? No. At school? No, she thinks it was like having the flu, that she is just like every other kid in her grade. Normal.* I stayed silent. None of them commented on the confetti accumulating on the floor beneath my sneakers.

Two years later, when I was ten, my mom asked if I'd give a survivor speech for a benefit for DeVos Children's Hospital. I said, *Sure*, tentative, compliant. She pulled blank notecards out of her desk and handed them to me. *This is supposed to be a celebratory event*, she said, *so make it a hopeful message.* I sat down at the kitchen counter and picked at the eraser of my pencil, at a loss for what to write.

I have no recollection of that speech now, no memory of what I said, no memory of being nervous, though I'm sure that I was. I know I wore a dress and that the benefit was on a Friday, that I missed the first half of the school day when my classmates had to do the mile run on the soccer fields behind the playground. And when I returned to school, it was lunchtime, and my PE teacher asked if I wanted to make up my mile during recess. I said that I did and ran the whole distance in my dress and some sneakers from the lost and found, my teacher standing on the corner of the field in her sweats, calling out my splits on her stopwatch. I know that my time was the best I had in elementary school, despite the dress, and that it felt good running in rectangular laps on one of the first sunny days of spring. I was hopped up on some kind of adrenaline from that morning, looking out into that audience of adults and having the courage to name aloud this thing I rarely talked about. My mom had dressed me up, braided my shoulder-length hair, and stood me behind that too-tall microphone, so I could say the words, *I survived*, an attempt to convince us all that this was over.

We were stuck inside an endless loop of relief and anxiety, more than half expectant that cancer would return, knowing full well it could return without any notice.

* * *

Were our two cancers a coincidence? At age seventeen, I had had so few major life events that when I found out my dad had a tumor in his brain, I instantly suspected correlation and became obsessed with rooting out both of our etiologies.

Squeeze my hand, my dad said as I lay face up under that raging CAT scan machine. The technician pressed the power button from inside an anteroom, behind radiation-proof glass. In that transference from my hand to his, both of us tracing over and over the mantra *Please don't let there be anything*, maybe the propensity for relapse passed from me to him. Cancer is a disease of recurrence, copy-paste ad infinitum, the repetition taking hold in his body instead of mine, the burden of caretaking changing hands. We were stuck in an endless, repeating loop, the teeth of my Spirograph set winding along the inside perimeter of its spiral template.

* * *

Growing up, I fought with my parents about their so-called overprotectiveness. As a teenager with an exacting sense of injustice, I argued that none of my friends had a midnight curfew, that no one else's parents had a rule against riding with other teenage drivers in their first year of having a driver's license. Or against taking passengers other than family in their car. Of course other parents had these same rules. But my parents, sensibly, did not take that approach. They reasoned, deadpan, *none of your friends' parents nearly lost their kid to cancer*. But for as much as we had braced ourselves for cancer's return, and as much as we believed, superstitiously, in the power of our own collective wills—that we could protect against cancer's return by anticipating it at every turn—all our psychic energy was laser-focused on me. So, when cancer did return, quietly, unnoticeably, none of us realized until it was too late.

On an unimportant night when I was sixteen, I was sitting at

32

the kitchen counter doing my calculus homework, when my mom handed me a printout of a journal my dad kept for me, roughly stapled at the top left corner. I had no idea my dad had ever kept a journal, let alone one written as a series of letters addressed to his daughter. *What's this?* I asked. My mom said he found the file on an old computer at work and that he wanted me to have it. I scanned the document and noted the journal was comprised of five entries from 1994, the first from February, not even a month after I'd been discharged from the hospital.

Every entry opens with a statement of where he was going, what was on his mind, then returning to the chronological narration of the year I was sick.

> *February 6, 1994*
> *I am on the plane on my way to Dallas after you, Mom, &*
> *Ryan left me at the airport.*

I remember taking him to the airport that day, standing in the gate with my hands pressed against the window, watching him board the plane from the tarmac, staying to watch the plane take off. I can revise this memory now, picture him buckled into his seat, wearing his dress clothes, his laptop splayed open on the tray table in front of him, typing this to me.

> *May 3, 1994*
> *I'm now on my way to Erie and I hope you, Ryan, & Mom*
> *are still sleeping. We made it out of Butterworth, I believe on*
> *a Saturday for the first time, after the first round of chemo. You*
> *seemed to be doing OK, but not too active. We attributed that to*
> *the chemo.*

To hear him retell it was validating, shattered a silence that had been lurking around our house. That day, I abandoned my calculus homework and read and then reread the whole document in the privacy of my bedroom, welling up at his bare and honest account.

33

When we got home, I remember you and Ryan playing together on the floor and I remember thinking that all of us depend on each other tremendously.

We were a private family, displaying our affection for each other in small, understated ways. The goodnight ritual with my dad: *See you later alligator. / After a while crocodile. / Not too soon baboon.*
I wonder now what prompted him to archive his thoughts in this journal. He wasn't a lettered man. In my parents' bedroom, the bookshelf on his side of the bed contained his childhood Bible and a few Dean Koontz novels, the only books that belonged to him in a whole house full of books. He was a tool and die engineer, liked patterns, liked precision, spent his second date with my mom on a picnic teaching her logic so she could pass her math class.

I do not remember the nurse's name that we had the 1st night of chemo, but I did not like her. The chemo drugs did not make it up to the room until late in the day and I was apprehensive all day. As she was starting the 1st bag of chemo, she seemed very nervous, which was making me crazy. I finally lost control and told her to get someone more competent. She did not like that at all, and left. She then replaced herself with someone else, and sent her supervisor after me. I did not give a shit what that nurse thought of me; I only wanted the best for you. That was the worst experience that we had with a nurse. Others were maybe not as good, but I was slightly more at ease with the process.

According to my mom, my dad was "type A"—ambitious, impatient, competitive. In reality, both my parents were driven, liked being in control. They often sparked against each other for this reason. Reading this then, it was fascinating to hear him talk about being at the mercy of his own emotions in front of this nurse. At sixteen, I was just beginning to see my parents as human. The pediatric ward, it occurred to me then, was a kind of public-private place, the nursing staff saw us all stripped to

34

our barest, worst selves. Reading this now, hearing him recount his own composure cracking at the sham authority the nurse held over him, makes me see him as he must have seen himself during that time: a full-grown force of a person, stripped of his dignity.

Home, after my first round of chemo, I remember visitors coming by to see me as I slept off a fever in my parents' bed.

> *By Sunday evening, you were not doing so well. We again thought chemo related and tried Mylanta etc to get you more comfortable. Nothing worked. Off to Butterworth . . . That night Dr. Xxxx was the resident (again a person that we immediately connected with, later in mid January, he helped me throw a SuperBowl party in your room!).*

I could tell Dr. Xxxx had befriended my dad and that my dad probably intended to ask my mom if she remembered the doctor's name. I imagine Dr. Xxxx as another man in his thirties on that pediatric floor full of women, and that he and my dad had forged a fast friendship. My dad, desperate to keep everything light, clung to this friend, part medical expert, part partner in crime. The same entry continues:

> *It was the night from hell. They had to place another NG tube in before surgery to view your stomach/bowel. I could not be in the room. Your Mom went with you. She also went into the testing room and I sat in the lobby with the fish. I had also called Grandpa S at 1:00 AM to tell him something was seriously wrong again. While sitting with the fish I read a sign that said you should not be pregnant in the room you were in. At that time we thought your Mom might be, so I asked a nurse to replace me with her. We did, and you were in extreme pain. I was having a difficult time staying composed, but I had to. Dr. Xxxx was helping me. Grandpa S. showed up at 3:00 AM to be with us and he stayed with Mom.*

There was always talk of how they wanted three children, how the timing had been bad. At sixteen, reading this, I likely took on some undue responsibility for this unborn sibling. But what weighs the most to me is his commentary on the potential risk of secondhand radiation exposure and his insistence at putting himself in harm's way if it meant sparing my mom. Ionizing radiation is a known risk factor for brain tumors.

My mom spent December making miniature Christmas trees for all the nurse's stations, hot gluing tiny ornaments, pine cones, and red and green bows to plastic boughs, straightening their wire branches. She hemmed tiny tree skirts for each and sewed a miniature sound box into the skirts that played "O, Christmas Tree" when you pressed the button through the tree skirt. Each tree: a tiny offering to tradition, to the repetition of seasons, keeping her hands busy despite everything else crumbling around her.

I had stopped believing in Santa that year because a boy on the playground told me the whole thing was a sham. But when Santa called on the in-room landline asking what I wanted for Christmas, I played along, for Ryan's sake. *I want to go home.*

And I did, a week before Christmas, our van piled to the roof with balloons and stuffed animals.

Sometime the next week, you asked to go Christmas shopping for Mom. I took you after work one night to the Country House, and then out to dinner at Shelde's at your request. You were such a lady and I was so proud. You had been through allot in the last month, and were so mature.

His words capture a snapshot of a girl, seven years old, eating french fries dragged through ketchup, in the process of becoming an adult. None of us was ever willing to say that the ordeal of having had cancer would force me to grow up fast.

* * *

36

That spring all four of us returned to our yellow house on the lake. We woke up feeling as though we'd been drawn to the edge of something, forced to look down, and backed away trembling. My mom's parents returned to their winter home in Florida. We were quiet, unsure of what to do with ourselves. The white light of winter sunshine angled through the front windows, spotlighting tall parallelograms across the living room carpet. The lake was melting into pieces. My mom had quit her job when her boss wouldn't give her any more sick days to be with me at the hospital, and she began, slowly, tentatively, to look for a new one. I returned to the second grade weighing less than when I started kindergarten.

Each night over dinner my parents spoke to each other in hushed voices. The tone, from what I could decipher, was one of humility, of owing a debt. Maybe my parents thought that the less they dwelled on it, the less power it would have over us. But I think now that I was probably the one who didn't want to talk about it, that I became silent and shy whenever someone mentioned it. I spent much of my childhood and adolescence trying to prove my own physical strength and show my illness hadn't been a setback, that I could outsprint any of the boys in my PE class, and that I could do a hundred sit-ups, enough to pass the fitness exam despite the incision across my abdominal wall. My parents were probably honoring my wish to ignore it, all of us learning to tiptoe around it.

* * *

The day we were released from the hospital for what we hoped was the last time, my mom put away the syringes she'd used to flush my port in the drawer of kitchen utensils, using them for years to pipe *Happy Birthday* onto cakes or for the care packages of sugar cookies she sent me when I was in college, the six points of a snowflake perfectly outlined in a thin line of blue frosting.

She had saved all of my hair as it fell out too, and, on one day that spring when I was seven, we ventured out into the yard. The snow had melted, and the grass was matted down in clumps, the earth a sponge beneath our boots. In one hand my mom held a plastic grocery bag full of blonde curls, in the other she held my hand, small and cold in the brisk morning wind. The hair was lifeless in the bag, wadded as though someone had saved a lifetime's worth of hair from the bathtub drain. She whispered to me about baby birds coming into this world cradled by the softness of my hair and pointed to a chickadee already gathering straw. She reached into the bag and pulled out a small handful of curls, draping them on the budding bushes. A few blew away, but most lingered, white and fuzzy against the dark twigs. She held the bag out to me. I hesitated, afraid to touch what was once mine, to finalize the detachment. The hair was softer than I expected, and as I pulled out a handful, it separated like a cotton ball. I thought about mother birds, working hard to prepare a place for their chicks.

That entire spring I watched through the kitchen window as the birds built their nests, wondering if they ever found my hair. I imagined that they did, that they carried it strand by strand and lined the insides of their nests, insulating their eggs against the cold.

* * *

My mom was thirty-five and my dad thirty-six the year I was sick, only two years older than Ada and I are now. I think of the four-paragraph email I sent Lucia's teacher in response to some minor injustice. What parent doesn't feel fiercely protective in the face of any threat, large or small, aimed at their child? If anything, the frustration my dad felt at the futility of his protectiveness fueled his proclivity for going to bat for me. I missed much of the second-grade curriculum, but I remember learning the food groups. In the hospital, my dad's job was to get me to do my homework. From his journal:

> *School wasn't the greatest for you since you had to be away so much. Working at Butterworth was hard to do, for you and for me to make you. Why bother? January was ugh! Counts were down. Your body was being pounded by the Chemo. It was overwhelming for your Mom and me.*

38

His abbreviation of that time period triggers a deeply buried memory, one I never would have excavated without his prompting. Inpatient for round three, a good day, he and I looked up "tomato" in the encyclopedia from a closet designated Pediatric Library. The worksheet had us drawing lines from clip art images of produce in the left column to its correct classification on the right. *Dad, is a tomato a fruit or a vegetable? What about watermelon?* Maybe I only remember these two because I got them wrong, had missed some in-class announcement about vines and seeds on the insides. Whatever the encyclopedia said, I put down. In January, my teacher wrote a handwritten letter to my parents:

> *Dear Mr. and Mrs. Stoddard, I want you to know that Cara is doing great. Please don't feel any pressure as far as Cara's Academics is concerned! All the work Cara has completed so far is excellent. Take your time on completing the Lit Logs. We will postpone Cara's Progress Report until after January 17th. We'd like to have Cara with us for more than a couple of days in a row to do our assessments. Again, we will work as a team to be sure Cara continues to progress and be ready for the third grade.*

I had been absent for more days of school than I attended that year, and that spring, my teacher convinced the principal that I should be held back a year. My parents never let on to me that this was a concern. I went to second grade when I was seven, and third grade when I was eight, just like everyone else. But years later, I learned that my dad had gone to parent-teacher conferences that spring, enraged about the insignificance of school in light of his child's cancer, at the stupidity of categorizing fruits and vegetables, at the suggestion that a second grader should be held back a grade.

When I went back to school that winter, I wore my favorite jean hat, hoping it would disguise my baldness, hoping it would revert everything back to status quo, grant me the anonymity of a normal childhood. *Are you a boy or a girl?* the kids on the bus teased, their faces wild with the thrill of stealing my hat. *Timmy's farting on your hat*, they said. I bore their teasing in silence, embarrassed they'd been so quick to notice what I thought I could hide. I stamped my clenched fists against the fogged-up windows, making baby footprints, painting in ten toes with my pointer finger. *Sticks and stones*, my grandmother said, and I wanted to believe her. *Just ignore them, and they'll quit*, my mom said.

That year, my mom broke her own rules and let me get my ears pierced when I was seven instead of seventeen because some soccer mom asked if that was her son on defense. To school, I wore leggings patterned with purple roses. I wore a sweatshirt my mom embroidered with a heart, embellished with lace at the cuffs and waistline, a ballerina charm stitched to the apex of the heart. I wore my leopard print winter coat, cinching the waistband to make it into a skirt. Waiting in line for bus forty-two, I stomped frozen-over puddles into chocolate slush. *A girl*, I said finally, caving to their taunts. The day my best friend's older brother stood in the bus aisle and punched the kid who took my hat, my friend's mom called my mom. I stopped riding the bus for a while after that, my parents resigned to the harsh ways kids make a big deal out of difference.

I learned that year what it was to be conspicuous. With each discharge from the hospital, I had been wheeled in a wheelchair to the elevator bank, wishing in the interminable silence of waiting that everyone would stop staring. When I was well enough to return to school, I wanted badly to fit in. My parents, witness to my wanting, wished fiercely for the same. And if that meant using my body as performance to play out a narrowly defined version of femininity, we were all in.

It was the year of the dual unraveling: of a childhood of assumed health and vitality and a body free from its self-conscious antennae.

4

t is winter 1978. A young couple drives a two-lane road in southwest Michigan. At the periphery, deer chew silently in fields of buzz-cut corn. The sun hangs low in the sky casting long blue-gray shadows on wet road, turning asphalt to ice. He has tallied too many points from too many speeding tickets, had his license revoked, so she is doing all their driving. The brown Camaro rides low, locked into the ruts carved by the passage of thousands of other cars. This is their commute.

Home is a double-wide with a view of Lake Michigan. He has a childhood of two brothers and a sister behind him, farming his grandfather's corn and working for his dad at the trailer park. She is the only child of a two-income household: her mother a first-grade teacher and her father a machinist in a machine shop.

Balding tires on black ice, and the Camaro slides into the ditch. Twenty minutes pass, the sky inks out all the remaining daylight. Then, red and blue lights in the rearview mirror. The officer runs both their licenses, shines his Maglite on my dad sitting in the rider's seat with his hands folded in his lap, says, *Sir, were you driving when the car went in the ditch?*

My dad at twenty-one is thin and muscular, an avid long-distance runner and racquetball player. His hair in his eyes is almost blond. Sarcasm bred into him by his own dad. *Sir, if I'd been driving, we wouldn't be in the ditch.*

The way my mom tells it, she and my dad met at her cousin's wedding in college. Her cousin was one of his best friends. After, he asked her on a date. He drove too fast, and when he dropped her off back at her dorm, she told her roommate she would never get in a car with him again. For their second date, they walked.

* * *

In 1995, my dad and I drove a 1929 Ford Model A across the southern half of Michigan, from Grand Rapids to an old car show in Greenfield Village just outside of Detroit. The drive, which would have taken us three hours on the expressway, took us six on back roads. It was fall, the sumacs and maples and ash leaves changing their colors. Time marching perennially forward, and my dad and I winding it backward, as if we could stay forever father and daughter, caught in the orbit of each other. The Model A, a four-cylinder engine in its most rudimentary form, set in motion by the technology of a spark, driving a steel arm up and down.

My maternal grandfather had restored the car himself, made from more than 5,500 interlocking parts. He had a strict rule for using only original parts, this before eBay or Craigslist. When he couldn't scavenge the authentic part from somebody's garage sale or swap meet, he'd make it himself in the machine shop across town where he worked. The finished product he named "Anabelle," a shining dark green box with a water-cooled engine, three-speed transmission, and a manual clutch. In his lifespan, my grandfather restored five vintage cars. Anabelle was his second, a sister for his Model T, Nelliebelle. Anabelle was supposed to be a gift for his daughter when she turned sixteen, but she never learned to drive it—neither of them had the patience for that. So, my grandfather gave it to his son-in-law, a quick study, the son he never had. My dad kept it in our garage under a protective cover next to our bikes, sleds, rakes, brooms. We were given strict orders to walk, not run, inside the garage and watch where we were going, to give Anabelle a wide berth. Under its protective cover, the car shone from all the wax my dad rubbed into it.

On the back roads on our way to Detroit, my dad let me ride up front because there weren't any airbags. There weren't any seat belts either, and the windows rolled down hard, with a crank. Riding in Anabelle was a whole-body, kinesthetic experience. My dad and I were not merely peering into the past, we were reenacting it. The car smelled like my grandpa, like moth balls and oil and gasoline, and sputtered in first gear, a good sign, *the sound of a kitten purring,*

43

my grandpa used to say. The entire car shook violently, my body its tuning fork. I'd hum a single low note just to hear my voice chatter. The windshield was on a hinge so you could angle it open to let in air, rudimentary defrosters. And the radiator on top of the engine sprayed water whenever the car overheated. The red line of the mercury thermometer was visible only from the passenger's side, so it was my job to watch the line and tell my dad when it crept up into the circle. Then, we would pull over into the gravel on the shoulder, and I would get the water jug and his rag out of the back, and he would yell for me to stand back while he unscrewed the lid. Sometimes he burned his hands, swore under his breath, and I would ask him if he was all right and he'd mutter something I couldn't make out, and then we'd get back in and drive some more.

It felt nice to be close to him, just the two of us, driving the old east–west highway across the state in the low light of the setting sun, a breeze coming in through the open windows, following the meandering path of the Grand River through alternating stretches of forest and corn. Without a radio tuned to *Car Talk* or NASCAR or a Detroit Tigers game, we filled the car with our own talk while I did another tracing in my *Lion King* coloring book. Every other page in the book was a transparent sheet of onionskin paper I drew on with my mechanical pencil, outlining Simba standing beside Mufasa, finding satisfaction in the mindless duplication. I glanced up from my workbook. *Dad, the red line is almost to the circle again. We should pull off.*

* * *

Twelve years later, we make a similar trip. Our destination was Henry Ford Hospital, just ten miles from Greenfield Village, except this time I drove. We were in my dad's Corvette on the interstate instead of Grand River Drive. It was the summer between my junior and senior years of college, my dad three years into an illness that would take six years to run its course. Henry Ford was the only hospital in Michigan with the trial drug he needed. Because of his frequent seizures, he'd had his license unofficially revoked by his doctor, which

44

was, perhaps, the biggest loss of dignity, even more so than any of the bodily failings that would come later.

He was the de facto driver of the car. I was a puppet with my right foot on the gas. He tuned his MP3 player to the Dixie Chicks as we merged onto the highway. *Get off at exit 164*, he said, before we'd even hit the hundreds. And, *Stay in the left lane through here, because all that merging traffic comes on slow*. And, *Don't let that blinker blink so long when you're just changing lanes. Just press it half-way like this*, as he reached over to do it for me.

His red Corvette was falling apart, 315,000 miles on Michigan roads, potholed the nine months of the year when they weren't covered in snow. He had been calling it the Rumblin' Red Wreck since long before I was old enough to drive it. The gas gauge had stopped working years earlier, and he had trained me to trip the odometer when I filled up. When it rained, the driver's side window leaked, staining my jeans red from the dye in the leather seat. Useless windshield wipers smeared long streaks of dead bugs across my field of vision, and I had grown accustomed to not using them at all.

He spent much of the drive working, making calls, propping his laptop open on his knees, the wires of his phone charger and his tape deck converter and his portable mouse tangled in the passenger's seat beside me. I drove ninety, ninety-five miles per hour because nothing felt like speeding that low to the ground. Occasionally he would look up, glance over at the speedometer, say, *Check your speed, Carly. There are always cops through here*. He knew exactly where there would be construction, where there would be a coffee shop he would want to stop at, feigning a coffee addiction neither of us believed, because the pre-treatment drugs he was on made him have to use the bathroom every twenty minutes. He had made this trip a hundred times before for business meetings, and now I was here, a foreign component to his ritual, the distance between work and home life getting scrambled.

The Corvette had been his car since before I could remember. It had bucket seats like a racecar and headlights that somersaulted awake. My dad had two successive red Corvettes during the last twenty years of his life, both of them bought used, the only cars he ever drove. My mom teased him about the Corvette, said it wasn't a practical family car and that it wasn't safe to drive in the winter. But he drove it anyway. When we were small, Ryan and I rode in the hatchback next to his briefcase. He would tell us to watch our heads, then shut the glass hatch inches above us, his right arm heaving down like a piston. The closure of that hatch sounded like a vacuum displacing the air, and Ryan and I felt like astronauts ready for takeoff. We watched the clouds, our faces to the sky, ears against the mesh covering the speakers, Bob Seger blaring, and traced the defroster lines with our fingers, smudging the glass.

Lucia is obsessed with cars. On our evening dog walks, she points out the similarity between the quarter glass on a Honda Accord parked in front of our neighbor's house and a Honda Civic, the futuristic angular shape of the window trim. She looks up the new Civic on my phone to show me. She has every 2020 make and model memorized. When it's her turn to choose for movie night, she picks *Ford v Ferrari*. She knows by heart the story of Ayrton Senna, the F1 racer, his fatal crash. Refueling was banned at pit stops the year she was born, the same year my dad died. When she tells me of this ban, it is news to me. I tell her, *In all the NASCAR I watched with my dad, they were always refueling*. She says Americans are all obsessed with NASCAR, but F1 racing is what the rest of the world cares about. She and my dad would have had a lot to talk about.

I think my dad liked cars because his dad was a classic car collector. And because driving made him feel in control. Though I have inherited none of his mechanical sensibility or aesthetic taste for sports cars, I do my best thinking when I'm alone in a car, driving. After his first seizure, Ryan and I began driving him to business meetings. Ryan was fifteen, had his learner's permit, and I was eighteen, on the brink of leaving for college. The few memories Ryan and I have of being adults with our dad are from driving him to treatment for those six years, each of us taking turns in the driver's seat of his red Corvette.

* * *

Maybe memory is just a euphemism we use for what it means to be haunted. Every time I'm in the city, trying to park on the street. His voice, as vivid as the clear, sunny day in July when I was fifteen and he was teaching me how to parallel park.

My dad took me out in his Corvette to a church parking lot near our house. I had logged over a hundred hours of driving on my permit with him and had my driving test the following week. At the edge of the lot, he got out of the car, said, *Okay, you drive.*

I rolled down the windows so I could hear his directions: *Turn the wheel all the way to the right. Okay, now crank it left, halfway. Wait, go slower, just barely ease off the brake.* He was standing like a pylon behind his car, marking off the spot. *I'm not moving, so if you run me over, that's a car you just crunched.*

We did this eight or nine times—*Pull up farther, almost even with the car in the spot in front of you*—practicing until I could do it without his directions. All the while, he stood unflinching on the blacktop in his jean shorts and sandals, unmovable as a 4,000-pound car.

* * *

I worked for my dad the summer before I graduated from high school, the summer before his first seizure. The auto industry was outsourcing jobs, and my dad's company needed to sell their office building, downsize to something with half the rent. Also, his secretary had a new grandkid she wanted to be able to spend more time with. So, I learned to open mail with a fancy silver non-knife and answer phone calls and fill out "While You Were Out" Post-its. But mostly, that summer I packed bankers boxes, then unpacked them in the new office. Every day, I had a task: *alphabetize these files, pull out everything from pre-1995 and shred it, make a spreadsheet and enter these quotes.* Some days I delivered prints.

The back room in my dad's office housed the giant printer and reeked of ammonium so strongly you could taste it. One of my dad's two employees would fold the prints into neat bundles wrapped in plastic binding twine, or sometimes they would roll them into seven-foot cardboard tubes, capped on both ends. This was the summer of my first cell phone, the summer of my black S-10 pickup, the summer of "Red Dirt Road" and "The Impossible" on B-93, Grand Rapids' country music station.

This was also the summer of getting lost. I'd stuff the prints in the jump seat of my S-10 or squeeze them diagonally across the rider's seat, then find the address of my destination, plug it into MapQuest, and print the directions on my dad's desktop printer. I clenched my steering wheel through the S curve tracing the perimeter of downtown Grand Rapids, letting semis pass me on the left, trying not to be intimidated by the cement walls graffitied in rub marks. Then: huge fields of nothing but alfalfa and two asphalt stripes down the middle.

When I noticed the mile markers getting smaller and farther away from my exit number, I pulled over and called my dad. This was the rule: *no driving and using the cell phone.* The S-10 only inches from cars passing at eighty miles an hour.

Perhaps these independent errands were perfectly calculated by my dad, the slow release of responsibility, like so many parents give to their teenage children, meant to build confidence, orchestrate relatively safe circumstances to practice decision-making skills, laying a foundation for college when I would be living on my own. Neither of us knew then that he was preparing me for an adulthood without him.

When I called his office that day, he didn't answer. No answer at his cell number either. It was their lunch hour. He and his coworkers were at the gym.

In the years since his death, I have been lost in my hometown. I have hit a rock on a high mountain pass and punched a hole in my oil pan, draining the car instantly of oil. I have had flat tires, dead batteries, bad catalytic converters. Always I pull off onto the shoulder, my whole car shuddering, tires planted in gravel, the check engine light illuminated on my dash.

In the driveway of my house where I live now, the hood of my car propped open, owner's manual splayed open on the bumper, my right blinker burned out. How do I dislodge the bulb socket? I still have his cell number saved in my phone under "D." I still have his office number, too, even though it's been disconnected.

* * *

On the drive home from Detroit, I get a speeding ticket for doing fifteen over on the expressway. My dad was sleeping, drowsy from the drugs they'd given him, a smudge of drool at the left side of his mouth. The officer who pulled me over was on a motorcycle, hiding under an overpass. I slowed to a stop and reached across the console to get the vehicle registration and insurance out of the glove compartment, waking up my dad. He looked through the glass at the officer, knowing already what this was about, told the cop I was his daughter.

I didn't say we'd been at the hospital, that we were headed home. I didn't want that kind of pity. Void of emotion, I took the ticket, went home, wrote the check, and put it in the mail. The smallest price I'd pay for any of this.

5

s a kid, I visited my dad's first office in downtown Grand Rapids only a few times before they moved closer to our suburb when I was nine, but those few visits were enough to create a setting in my child imagination for how my dad spent his days. Surrounded by drafting boards eight feet tall and fifty-some feet long, mechanical pencil in his mouth, my dad needed to concentrate. He ran the L-shaped ruler up and down and left and right, making tiny hash marks, then connecting the dots with one of his circle stencils. For most of my visits to his office, I came with my mom to drop off lunch or to pick him up at the end of the day. But I remember spending, on occasion, whole afternoons in my dad's office alone with him. He kept me busy with highlighters of every color and geometrically precise stencils. I colored pictures of our yellow house, my mom and dad, me and my brother and the dog, all of us glowing.

After my dad's diagnosis, when I picked him up from work, his desk was littered with invoices and highlighters and huge drafts of plastic injection molds labeled "drawing not to scale," and atop the mess: a model 1950s red Corvette with white side wings and doors that really opened, tires with real rubber, sticky with friction. A Corvette clock behind his computer ticked over the classic rock station on the office-wide speaker system. He was his own boss, a small-business owner who founded this company with one of his coworkers from a different tool and die group the month before I was born.

I learned more about my dad's career from the speech his business partner, Steve, gave at his memorial service than I ever knew while he was alive. As a teenager, busy with my own morning routine, I hardly noticed my dad tying his shoelaces in the laundry room, leashing the family dog, Maggie, a German shorthaired pointer, and leaving the house to run four or five miles with her before work. My mom laid out his clothes for him each morning, hooking the tie around his pants hanger while she ironed his shirt. Some mornings I watched him come down the steps with the corner of a Kleenex stuck to his chin, a tiny speck of congealed blood holding the tissue in place. I knew his work was in an office building with air-conditioning, a boring place where grown men sat quietly staring into the glass faces of computers.

What he actually did at work was a mystery to me. Work was a place he went five, sometimes six days of the week. He and my mom talked about his job over my brother's and my heads at the dinner table, a conversation where I learned new vocabulary like "stress" and "conference call" and "payroll." Our family told time by his arrival home at the end of the day. We knew by the sound of the garage door opening. The whole house shook.

In high school, for a career interest inventory, we had to fill in info about our parents' jobs. *He's a tool and die engineer*, I typed. We had monogrammed pencils at home, smooth and painted silver, with mahogany lettering: *Infinite Concepts Inc.* and in smaller, cursive lettering underneath their business name, *tool and die.*

To my friends, I explained my dad's job as *drawing the molds for car parts*. I'd learned that he and Steve designed the headlights for the 2003 Cadillac Escalade. They did the design work for the hardtop roof for the Jeep Wrangler. But in the late 1980s, when they were first starting out, they also did non-automotive designs. They did all the drawings for Kenner's Stretch Armstrong and for the original Bubble Tape container. These were the years of Everything Plastic. My whole childhood playroom filled with plastic play food, a hot pink Barbie Mobile, sippy cups gnawed down to nubbins, a Fisher-Price picnic table outside on the deck.

My mom, the microbiologist, bought Ryan and me a Creepy Crawler set in the early 1990s, fostering a love for science in her two children. One day, while my dad was at work, the three of us sat at the kitchen counter making bugs. The set came with a miniature oven and several metal trays of different bug molds that we filled with colored glues that solidified into slimy, floppy, quasi-realistic looking insects while they cooked in the oven. The neon-colored dye came in plastic tubes that constantly caked at the tips. *Mom, I can't get the blue to come out*, Ryan said, handing her the bottle to unclog with a safety pin. *Look, Mom*, I said, *the scorpion's tail is a C, like me.* I squeezed glow-in-the-dark dye into the tip of its tail, purple into the rest of the tail, green for the body, the whole mixture bleeding out into the tiny legs of the creature. My mom said the trick was to fill the mold almost to the surface, but not over, because the waxy dye expanded in the oven.

After we pulled our bugs out of the oven and let them cool, my dad—just home from work, still in his tie and dress shoes—trimmed the flabby edges of my scorpion with an X-Acto knife. *This is the flash*, he said, teaching me the jargon of his work.

He was an expert in plastic injection molds, spent his whole adult life thinking in negative space, thinking what the container would look like.

* * *

In middle school, I went to a Wednesday night youth group with my friend Danielle. My mom gave me my dad's suede-covered Bible to bring. She said it had been a gift from his mother when he turned sixteen. The page edges were painted red, and it had his full name stamped into the lower right-hand corner of the cover. In class, the pastor took two volunteers to stand at the front and hold up a string. He said that time was linear and stretched out infinitely, that our earthly lives were a mere dot along the string. But if we believed in God, our souls would go on living infinitely after we died. He gestured to the string spanning the width of the gym.

The idea of something called a soul was not a new idea for me, but the idea of the body as a container for the soul was new. I figured that someday, when my body fell away, no longer useful, that the essence of who I am would cease to exist. But according to this pastor, the body was just a vessel, and that the important part, what made me *me*, was intangible, not a part of the physical realm, and would go on existing after I died, not in this world but in the next.

52

After my dad died, I resented all condolences rooted in this rhetoric. I did not care if my dad's soul lived on in some other realm. I was still stuck in this one.

* * *

My maternal grandpa is taller than my dad ever was, even in old age, and wears baby-yellow and forest-green sweaters my grandma knits for him. The cardigans have neat, ribbed bands around their edges with four wooden buttons up the front and pockets on the sides that he stuffs candy wrappers and used tissues in. He has one sweater he wears to church and to bingo at the clubhouse in their mobile home village in Florida, and one he wears to work on old cars in the garage. When it gets too dirty or when he snags the corner picking blackberries in the bushes behind his garden, my grandma says, *It's okay. I'll just make him another one.*

My grandma likes to tell the story of her husband, before she met him, walking a mile down a dirt road to the town's junkyard and scavenging bike parts, piecing together a bicycle from discarded scraps, one he rode for years. This was during the Depression. My grandpa is retired now, watches his stocks on the ticker tape religiously every day. He worked thirty-three years at a die factory, spent the first five making dies and the rest in the tool room, repairing dented and damaged dies, singled out for his resourcefulness, precision, and attention to detail. On his last day of work before retirement, he was asked to fix the die for a Pontiac water pump. *We had been using the die for a while,* he explains to me, *taking trips to Detroit twice a day with the parts to keep up with demand.* As I understand it, the one die was used to make twenty or thirty water pumps a day; then, someone would drive them to Detroit, an hour and a half in one direction. When the die broke, my grandpa repaired it. This was 1979. The Pontiac die was a design of my dad's. *I repaired Rick's die,* he continues, *then I cleaned off my tools and packed up. That was the last day I had to go into work.*

My dad grew up in what my mom calls an *Ozzie and Harriet* family. I know very little about his childhood, but the handful of details I do know mostly have to do with food. Over dinner out on our deck, my brother and I whine about no buns for our hamburgers. Ketchup is bleeding through the pieces of sandwich bread my mom gave us instead, and my dad retorts, *We never had any money for buns when I was a kid. My mom always used bread.* I heard a story once about how he and his older brother used to throw overripe tomatoes at their sister on his grandpa's farm. When I called home from a mountain town in Colorado, laughing at a customer who came into the coffee shop where I worked and asked for a piece of cheddar cheese on his apple pie, my mom said, *Oh, your dad's mom always served it that way. He loved it like that.* I was twenty-two years old and that was news to me.

My dad's dad owned a mobile home park, and my dad and his siblings grew up working for him. It was a family business, one my dad was slated to inherit with his brothers. But my dad preferred spending his boyhood free time with his Uncle Bob, his mom's brother. Uncle Bob taught my dad to waterski, took my dad pheasant hunting, gave him a set of hockey skates and taught him to play pond hockey. Uncle Bob favored my dad over his three other siblings, and my dad began to see himself apart from the rest of his family, apart from small-town Chesaning. He went to Ferris State, a tech school in central Michigan, to become a tool and die engineer, and met my mom there.

When my parents were first dating, my dad took my mom to a family funeral for his Uncle Bob, who died of lung cancer. Five years later, my dad's mom, Uncle Bob's sister, died of MS. A black-and-white photo of my dad's mom and Uncle Bob as kids hangs in the studio where I write now. They are standing in front of their farmhouse, barefoot, squinting into the sun.

After my dad's death, my mom told me his mom was who held him and his three siblings in close orbit. But after she was diagnosed with MS when my dad was in high school, what had once held them together frayed. His dad dated other women while his wife was in a nursing home. The degeneration of family as he knew it mirrored the degeneration of her health. I wonder if this is some

54

kind of parable. My dad was seventeen when his mom got sick, the same age I was when he had his first seizure.

* * *

In the weeks after my dad died, my mom and I went to another funeral. A family friend with a different cancer. The friend was an artist, did big cartoonish drawings for billboards, mostly environmental advocacy ads, political cartoons, and caricatures for local radio personalities. I'd job shadowed him in middle school for a language arts assignment. He took me out to lunch, asked me, *What do all the kids say these days? What's the new slang?* wanting to incorporate some of the hip language into one of his billboard designs. I didn't know what was hip. I was unpopular in school, a band geek. I stared at my shoes, moved around some fries on my plate, said, *Cool?* After he died, huge billboards of his were still up around town to remember him by, along with photos of billboards online, a website, all this legacy of his mind at work living beyond the grave.

After my dad's death, I searched for evidence of his existence everywhere. I studied the headlights of American-made cars in parking lots, tried to visualize the shape of each plastic shell as its inverse, two steel pieces carved into intricate caverns, clapping together. I was overcome with the feeling that all of the two-dimensional drawings of molds he'd created during his lifespan were a kind of cryptic treasure map I had to decode in order to know who he was. I emailed Steve to ask him to send me some PDFs of one or two prints and, if he had it, the transcript of the eulogy he read. He sent some photos of prints instead of print files themselves, the prints laid out on a tabletop with their corresponding part set on top of them, as if maybe this were all I needed to know: this chart, a constellation of dots and lines, led to the production of this hunk of plastic, end of story. But he sent the eulogy, too, and I studied it like a literature student, underlining and taking notes.

In the eulogy, he told the story of a man I recognized as my dad but in a setting completely foreign to me, as though my dad had existed in three dimensions, and all these years, I had had access only to two.

In the first paragraph of the eulogy, Steve described my dad when they first met, wearing a mullet, polyester pants, and platform shoes. I wanted to object. I had never seen any evidence of my dad as trendy. But then he went on to say my dad introduced himself as a *country bumpkin*, and these are words I had heard him say, and I started to trust this document as an authentic representation.

They had been working together since 1979, had been business partners since 1985, would have celebrated the twenty-fifth anniversary of their company had my dad lived one month longer. In all those years, my dad never said anything negative about Steve. He and his wife were married the same year my parents were married, his kids the same age as my brother and me, but Steve and my dad rarely did anything together socially outside of the office other than lunch breaks at the gym. Perhaps this was a decision they came to mutually, for the good of the company. All I could think about, reading this eulogy, was that they were each other's biggest allies through all those years. I was reminded that the person I knew as a dad had been an adult long before I was born, had been a kid before that, the line of his life stretching far beyond mine, out of range.

They met at a GM plant, both working as rent-a-pencils, investing in what they thought would be a highly covetable career with GM. This was before computer-aided design, and the industry was booming. But they were temps, and there were twenty-five or so other guys with the same job they had. Steve says my dad was already fed up with working under someone else, sensed they were not secure there, and so my dad left, went to work as branch manager of a small design group that had all their employees working in-house. Within the year, Steve started working for my dad. After a year or so as branch manager, my dad confided in Steve his plans to start his own business and asked if Steve would come work for him. Steve said he'd come as his partner, and so they made a deal.

56

Steve went on to describe my dad's wardrobe: "Rick emerged as the only guy in the office with any sense of personal style. He mixed in a variety of sport coats, creative neckties, stopped buying socks, and bought that first red Corvette."

Reading Steve's eulogy, I was struck with validation that the person my dad had been to me rippled out beyond our family unit, that the kind of person he had been, his life, had in fact, left a legacy. Steve was someone who spent nearly every day of his adult life with my dad, both of them working fifty-to-sixty-hour weeks, because that was the expectation in this industry. He could hardly bring himself to begin his speech at my dad's funeral. Halfway through the first paragraph, he was crying openly.

He remembered that my dad, soon after he was married, started making more intentional decisions. "It was at this time that Rick began to focus on becoming more serious about his health. He modified his diet and began running. He did, however, allow himself one indulgence. On Friday afternoon work break he would enjoy a Coke and peanut M&Ms."

Perhaps I was most drawn to these details because they had absolutely nothing to do with the automotive business, sales, or two-dimensional representations of three-dimensional concepts. But also, I felt a jerk of recognition that, on a long drive, these are the two vices I beeline for at any gas station: the M&Ms in their yellow wrapper and a regular Coke.

My dad was two years gone when I finally got up the nerve to read this eulogy, and I had no memory of Steve saying any of this at my dad's funeral. I had spent the two years frantically trying to cling to every detail I remembered of him, opening a new document in Microsoft Word, typing a few cryptic sentences, then saving it as "Dad," a bunch of these files with the same title in different folders on my laptop. Thinking, maybe if I put words on the screen, backed them up to my external hard drive, his legacy would be preserved somehow. This was recorded. This was tangible. As if even though his life's work wasn't hung up on billboards around town or downloadable off some website, here he was in my memories, rendered somewhat lifelike through my words, living beyond the grave.

* * *

Steve's eulogy was itself a kind of blueprint, a map to what my dad was like at work, how he left his imprint on the people he worked with. I knew my dad liked his job, was good at what he did. In the last years, when I drove and he worked, I listened to him talk to customers on the phone. Before any negotiations about pricing or hours he estimated it would take them to complete the job or clarifications about the design, my dad first asked about their kids, about a fishing trip they'd just returned from, how their ski boat was running, if they'd put their dock in yet. He knew them each by name or nickname, knew their kids' names, knew their hobbies.

He lost much of his capacity to remember these details after his first surgery, but he kept diligent notes for himself, dedicated pages of his planner to profiling his customers in his scrawling all-caps handwriting, took verbal notes on a tape recorder when writing became hard.

My dad kept going into the office until six weeks before he died. He had worked from seven a.m. to five p.m. for most of his career, but, in the last few months, my mom talked him into just going in for half days. I was living at home at the time and took him in most mornings when it was still pitch-black outside, drove through the Starbucks across the street from his office, our morning ritual. *Grande latte extra hot and a grande mocha no whip*, I told the barista. I had worked the previous winter in Colorado as a barista in a privately owned coffee shop across the street from a Starbucks and had lectured my family on the transgressions of patronizing such a corporate chain, but none of this mattered anymore.

When I came to pick him up at lunchtime, he was asleep on his keyboard. *Dad*, I said from the doorway, and he startled awake. *It's time to go*, I said. He began packing up his things into his briefcase, still in the habit of bringing work home, then hobbled down the hall to the bathroom. He had a limp from the tumor growth

58

in his brain, weakening his left side. I asked Steve, *How was he?* and he said, *Oh just fine*, protecting my dad's dignity to the end. Eventually, my mom convinced Steve in an email to join her in a united front and broach the idea with my dad of taking some time off, *to stay home and rest*. All of us knew he wouldn't be going back in, but none of us were calling it what it really was. And still, Steve and their two employees kept coming by the house on Fridays with some sort of takeout: Chinese, pizza, subs. Blow-the-diet Fridays, an office tradition.

* * *

Two years after he died, I flew home to visit my mom, and I emailed Steve again. *Can I come by the office and ask you a few questions?* Steve and the two other employees had moved into a new office shortly after my dad died, perhaps in an attempt to downsize or, for a reason similar to my mom's selling of my childhood home, to escape his ghost. The new place was a few blocks from where the old office used to be, and I thought I knew how to get there, but I got lost, asked some construction workers in fluorescent-yellow shirts working a forklift for directions. They shrugged and pointed, and eventually I found it sharing a parking lot with a storage unit facility. I had to drive through the gate for the storage unit facility, thinking maybe this was a metaphor, all the good years of the American automotive industry gone into storage, what was left hiding out in a windowless office that could be confused with a bunker. The face of the business was two years dead, and who needed a conference room anyway, who needed a sport coat and dress shoes and a daughter to deliver prints when there was email?

Steve shoved some papers and metal hunks of junk, a new design he was working on, out of the way for me to sit, clearing only one small patch in a table covered in stuff. His office was also the entryway, and he made some sort of joke or apology about the mess, computer and phone and printer cords coiling around my legs as I sat. He had a print pinned up on the bulletin board behind his desk, and he was punching away on his calculator, a skinny thing from the 1980s, the same model my dad gave me to put me through high school calculus. The office was markedly bare of personal effects save for a framed photo of my dad on his cell phone in front of his laptop, wearing a dressy button-down shirt. My mom gave Steve this photo and frame, I know, because I have the same one in my own office. My dad, in a pose we all knew well, working.

I said, *I am trying to figure out some things about the tool and die industry. I spent my whole childhood not knowing what my dad did at work every day.* I asked, *Do your kids get what you do here every day?* He said, *No,* and laughed, and somehow this laugh put me at ease, made me feel like my curiosity was okay.

He explained plastic injection molds like this: *They're basically complicated Jell-O molds. It starts with a machine. Small pellets of plastic resin are dumped into the machine, and then heated up to a liquid, the consistency of Elmer's glue, and then the machine squirts that hot resin into a hole in two pieces of steel.*

That's what you draw, right, those two pieces of steel.

Yes. The hot resin is shot into the cavity between them, and once it cools and solidifies, the two pieces of steel pull apart, and the part drops out. He pulled out a piece of paper, drew a 2D sketch of a Bundt cake pan. He said, *So if you have these two pieces of steel making a bundt pan, or a cup, the part would just fall out. Easy. But if you add some ornamentation*—he drew rectangle wings on the sides of the bunt pan—*the cake would get stuck, wouldn't be able to drop out.*

This was his explanation of one of the design constraints in this line of work. He was slow and methodical in teaching me, used some of the same turns of phrases my dad would have said—*The automotive industry started getting ugly around 2007. 2009, that was the absolute bottom*—and I wondered if my dad picked up these phrases from Steve, or if Steve said them now because he had heard my dad say them so often.

I thought then of hollowness, of what it would be like to crawl inside one of my dad's molds and be held for years inside that dark space. Protected by a steel shell, all of my cells turned to liquid.

The playground of my elementary school was dragon ship

themed, constructed entirely of wood and old tires, all of it plopped down in a sea of pea gravel. Along the spine of the dragon was a six-foot tractor tire buried into a half-moon in the gravel. At recess, I would crawl inside, pull my knees against my chest and press my back against the inside of the tire, completely invisible from the outside, held by the smell of warm rubber and the knowledge that no one in the entire world knew where to find me. Maybe it wasn't so much the darkness and secrecy that I craved but the feeling of being held.

Steve said their company was considered *a third-tier supplier*, that in the early 2000s they did a lot of work for Hella, a German company, the first-tier headlight and taillight provider for GM and Ford, that they *were doing the small components that go into the main appliance.* I thought then that a third-tier company was where the essence of a thing, its shape, originates, and that companies like my dad's drew the molds for the parts made at a second-tier design shop that would send those hunks of plastic and metal to Hella, where someone else would do all the wiring, plug in a bulb, toss it in a box full of packing peanuts, and send it to Detroit. Talking with Steve, I begin to think that to make a blueprint of a mold is to imagine something in all of its intricacies, how it will fit together with adjacent parts, how all of its edges will retain convexity, how it will fall out of the two steel hemispheres without getting stuck. The thing itself exists most wholly as idea. And maybe our soul doesn't really live "inside" our bodies and only gets "released" when we die but exists before we are even conceived. Its essence blueprinted into our parents, and their parents before them, in their memories and modus operandi. And maybe a portion of my dad's soul had already been released the day I was born.

I wonder about my own mold and the mannerisms and habits of his I cannot shake, how maybe in this way I am him, have always been him, his legacy living on inside each of my cells, each of my thoughts.

* * *

The first winter Ada and Lucia and I spent together, a vagrant snowy owl took up residence in the Queen Anne neighborhood of Seattle not far from where we lived. It wasn't unheard of for snowy owls to overwinter in latitudes this far south, but most did not select urban environments. I could see the appeal, though. We had seen rats the size of gray squirrels scurrying along our fence at dusk, not to mention the squirrels themselves. This high concentration of nonnative rodents was here because of humans and our birdseed and sewers and refuse.

The first time we went to try to see the owl, we walked up and down the grid of the residential neighborhood for over an hour, pointing our binoculars at every chimney, before a couple walking their dog showed us the owl's encampment: a shit-streaked turret of an unassuming two-story house at the top of the hill. No owl.

The dog-walking couple seemed nonchalant, as if to say, *Oh yeah, the owl. We've seen it a thousand times.* But for us, newly in love, a snowy owl in Seattle was a miracle. In our searching, we had spotted a bald eagle on a different rooftop, getting dive-bombed by crows, and Ada turned to me and said, *Who knew we had eagles in the city?*

Lucia wanted a pet rat. All the talk about owls and their diets fueled her campaign to convince us. She explained that rats were clean animals, and very smart, and had big personalities that outsized their small statures. *They are basically the perfect pet*, she said.

What about Skronk? I asked her, referring to her nickname for my eleven-year-old lab mix, Scout, who had begun preferring Lucia over me as soon as I'd moved in. *How are you going to let your rat out of its cage with Skronk around?*

Skronk would like a pet rat, too, Ada teased, taking Lucia's side but smiling at me over the top of her head.

If I had a pet rat, I would name him Ratatouille, Lucia said, content for the time being. She had said her piece.

Being a parent, I was beginning to learn, was spending all your time curating new learning experiences to expose your child to, only to discover, again and again, their uncanny ability to turn that dynamic on its head, invert the roles of learner and teacher. Lucia did not care about seeing an owl, snowy or otherwise. I was becoming a student again, field notebook splayed open, observer of my own heart. Even though Lucia was old enough to be aware of all of my not-very-graceful fumblings through being a new parent, she never held any of them against me.

Like all stepparents who arrive on the scene of a childhood a bit late, part of me wondered if I'd been around since Lucia was a baby, would she be wired differently, say, more curious about wildlife and the natural world. But in that impossible parallel universe, I would not have come to be as I was in this exact moment, shipwrecked with love for the two people on the sidewalk in front of me, exactly as they are, one of them in a pink sweatshirt with a kitten wearing glasses on it, the other with my binoculars around her neck. For Lucia's alarm each morning, Ada played "Sucker" by the Jonas Brothers. "We go together / Better than birds of a feather / You and me." There was a ferocity to the love between them, and it glowed with eminent light, in total defiance of a world that reminded them at every turn that to be just mother and daughter—a solo parent and a child of split custody—was less-than. As if being a parent can be represented by any kind of fraction, no matter how many days a week your child spends apart from you.

The second time we went to try to see the owl, Ada said we should stop at the taco truck first and pick up dinner. Back into the car, I carried a plastic bag full of grease-streaked cartons, rice and beans and steak and chicken tacos, a horchata for Ada and me to share, and a grapefruit Jarritos for Lucia.

We drove the fifteen minutes from our house to the Queen Anne neighborhood and parked across the street from the house the owl had staked out on. New this time was a lady in a fishing vest on the corner, the owl's ambassador I supposed, handing out flyers that warned against putting out poison for rats. *He's in his roost*, she said, when she saw our binoculars. Ada and I craned our necks. What appeared to be just a chimney, when we studied it more closely, was a white fluff ball, or rather a bird of prey, sleeping. *Lucia, do you see him?* I asked. In the back seat of the car, Lucia was picking the chopped onions out of her tacos, pouring on hot sauce.

Part of my initial attraction to Ada was that she was a parent. Predating anything to do with me, she had lived. At twenty-one, she had delivered Lucia in her bathtub at home, had breastfed and potty-trained and built a hundred different figurines out of MEGA bloks. Surrounded as I was by childfree thirty-year-olds who had energy enough to exact their rigid ways of making do in the world—bringing their own glass jars to the bulk food section, boycotting bananas because they were a monocrop—I liked that Ada had grown fatigued of all of this hand-wringing, had found a middle way. Parenting, with its thousand-and-one microdecisions a day, had made her more flexible. She put down clover seed instead of grass seed on the bare patches of her backyard, *for the bees*, she said, and chose not to buy all-natural peanut butter with the impossible-to-incorporate oil at the top of the jar. More than all of that though, her having a kid upped the ante of our dating. When we met, it had been nine years since my dad died. I was tired of dating people who had never known real loss. Ada had experienced a different kind of loss. She knew, in a way I never had, what it felt like to open herself up to the potential for total ruin.

Ada rolled down the windows of the Rav, and I passed the binoculars back to Lucia, said, *Look*. She put the binoculars up to her eyes and adjusted the focus. *Looks like an owl*, she said, and handed the binoculars back up to us.

Ada was exuberant. *Do you see, his eyes are open!* Through the binoculars, I could see him looking at us, blinking one eye at a time, then turning his head 180 degrees to look the other way.

We sat in the bird blind of the car for who knows how long, eating tacos and waiting for the owl to do something, anything, that might impress Lucia. Finally, mercifully, the owl began to preen himself. *Look*, Ada said, *he is stretching out his wing.* The owl continued this sort of preflight owl yoga, pacing back and forth on the roof ridge and, eventually, grotesquely, arching back his head and

64

ejecting a pellet. It felt voyeuristic, watching the owl this intimately, the way he was keenly aware of us in our car but continued with his crepuscular ritual no matter how many car doors slammed or dogs on leashes walked by. Eventually, silently, with no notice, he stepped off the ridge of the roof, opened both wings, and was gone.

Lucia, from the back seat, *The meat on the tacos was overcooked, but the rice and beans were good.*

I think of the things my parents exposed me to when I was a kid that I didn't appreciate at the time: visiting my great-grandfather in his assisted living home, going to an Al Gore campaign rally in downtown Grand Rapids, seeing Ray Charles perform. I know now that the point had little to do with whether I enjoyed the experience in the moment. And, in any case, at Lucia's age, I also didn't take much notice of birds or any other wild animal's comings and goings. I loved manatees because of a nature documentary I'd watched, and sea otters because of the Beanie Baby, and was hell-bent on convincing my parents to get a dog. What awed me most about Lucia was that even though she knew I wanted her to be a mini me, a naturalist in training, or any of the hundred other long-ings I projected onto her, she never tried to bend herself into any of my prefab molds. I knew that sure-footedness and self-confidence was something she had gained from her mom's parenting, and it made me love the both of them all the more.

There was a heartbroken part of me that grieved the nine years that I missed and wanted, desperately, to be able to recognize something physical and concrete of myself in Lucia. Ada intuited this deep sadness in me and was generous in her revisionist history of how the three of us had become a family. When observing the meandering way Lucia told stories, or the way she grew uncom-fortable in the spotlight of attention from others on her birthday, or her musicality, and the way all animals felt at ease around her, Ada joked, *She gets that from you.* In fact, it was never fully a joke. Tongue in cheek, sure, but Ada knew that my presence in Lucia's life was shaping her, and she was trying, in her subversive way, to both mock the family-values rhetoric of blood-only models for kinship and reassure me that my backdoor way of becoming a parent was just as valid as any of the other parents we met on the sidelines of Lucia's soccer games or at back-to-school night.

Ada had the Sally Mann book *Immediate Family* on her coffee table. With that same protective fervor she had for her kid—who had been singled out since day one of preschool for speaking Portuguese, not English, at home and having, in fact, two homes, not one—she extended to include me. She knew that losing my dad had unmoored me, that I craved, perhaps more than most people, some deep sense of belonging. And that becoming simultaneously lover and beloved, on the approved after-school parent-or-guardian pickup list, was cracking open something inside of me that I hadn't realized was there: a desire to be a part of something that would outlast me and a way to bring my dad back to life, not as some phantom benevolent force watching over me, but within me, as charge for who I wanted to be and how I wanted to order the priorities of my life.

*   *   *

I think I went to visit Steve at his office that day wanting to know if I could count the 2003 Escalade as my dad's legacy. That even though his company just did the molds, just did the plastic parts of that headlamp, that maybe it mattered. I wanted public recognition of the life my dad led to verify he was here, that he'd left his mark on this world.

I look at a photo of my dad from before he was sick, and I see that the man opening his eight-year-old daughter's orange soda after a soccer game is the same man who taught her to parallel park, standing like a pylon in the church parking lot, his instructions echoing in her head. He is both gone and not gone.

In the year before he died, I had decided to move back home. My mom told me she wanted to sell the house, downsize to something more manageable, and I had interviewed for four teaching jobs in Colorado but didn't get any offers. I felt like I could attribute my decision to move back home to my dad, to myself, as career related instead of because of his declining health. We didn't know it at the time, but my dad had only four months left to live when we sold the house. I was trying to make an effort to help my mom pack up the contents of the twenty years we had lived in that house. We started in on the dining room, wrapping an entire wall of photos of my ancestors in antique frames in Bubble Wrap. When we finished, we stood in the center of that square room and stared at the blank wall. The floral wallpaper had faded over the years but remained vivid behind where each framed photo had been. Thirty or so dark rectangles, preserved by the photos, shadows of my lineage, all of them coming with us to the next house.

6

There's a steaming dark bar built under a dining hall in the pop-up book of my memory, concrete floors and concrete walls, and wooden cubbies painted in primary colors for purses and coats, like something familiar from kindergarten. It's winter in Ohio, and Jessie and I are both underage, bold black Xs staining our hands.

Earlier that night, she'd taught me to shotgun a beer in the shower before we left our dorm. The bathroom at the end of our hall had four shower stalls, each separated by a white plastic curtain and a tiny tiled step. From inside the stall closest to the frosted windows, Jessie cracked open the can of beer, then punctured its bottom with her car keys, handing it to me through the curtain, then letting me pass it back to her when I couldn't empty it.

In the underground bar, it's loud and there are bodies pushing to get the bartender's attention, bodies rubbing up against each other, wall-to-wall dancing bodies, acid-washed jeans on jeans. In the corner, there's an old arcade game. Jessie gives the bartender a quarter, and we can play until we lose. Someone we know, an upperclassman, gives us a warm beer, sloshing it over the top of its plastic cup, and we share it. No one is watching us. She picks Babes instead of Dudes on *Erotic Photo Hunt*, and this is a game we are good at, noticing missing spaghetti straps, missing areolae, missing thong lines. Touching thighs, touching breasts, touching asses on the touch screen.

When we finish our beer, we gather our coats and go out, past the bouncer, up the sticky concrete steps, through the metal door that scrapes on the salted sidewalk. Outside is freezing, the night overcast and backlit. She pulls me close, smoking a Black and Mild, the woody sweet smoke lingering in the air. She tells me about growing up in Kansas, about youth group and Jars of Clay and her close family friend from church who died at eighteen from leukemia.

There are words neither of us says aloud, ghosts of moisture that linger somewhere above our heads, as if our breaths, invisible against the sky glow, are apparition enough of the child selves we carry inside us.

* * *

When I asked my mom, *How old was I when I started giving you lip?* she says, *Four.* I was surprised, expecting something about turning twelve, hitting puberty. I thought of myself as a compliant child through the stories she'd told: I was an easy baby, came home from the hospital and slept through the night. She liked to tell the story of herself as a new mom, nudging me awake in the afternoons just to see if I'd move or cry, to make sure I was still alive. My dad would be at work, and the neighbor would come over and say, *Look, all you have to do is hold your finger right here below her nose to see if she's breathing.* But my mom said, *No, I can't tell,* and called my pediatrician in a panic. *My baby never cries. She just sleeps.* He said, *For every call I get about sleeping babies, I have ten more from moms whose babies won't stop crying.* He said, *Your baby is fine.*

This was a parable too, I learned, for how she was a worrier, and everyone around her told her to stop worrying, that babies turn into toddlers and then into kids and then into teenagers, and *The easiest day of parenting is the day you bring them home from the hospital.* I think she wanted desperately to believe them that life was perpetual, children resilient. She had my brother two and a half years after me. We both passed our swim lessons, listened when she said, *Only ride your bike on Belinda; Buckle your seat belt; Wear your life jacket in the boat.*

And then everything was for naught. The same pediatrician who said, *Your baby is fine,* was the one who told my mom, seven years later, to take me to the hospital for an ultrasound, said, *I think she might have appendicitis.*

From that year on, my mom was on edge, as if my cancer had been the greatest possible deception, a mockery of her ignorance. Her eyes, interrogating, *What else don't I know?*

* * *

That June, Jessie and I drove from Ohio to her parents' house in Kansas, a Styrofoam cooler of RC Cola and string cheese in the back seat of the Buick. Outside, the Midwest glowed with new growth. I had come to think of interstate driving as sliding from fret to fret, a kind of bending of one note, scooping into the arrival at the next. But I was never the one who played guitar. Jessie was. In the first week we met, she sat on the edge of my bed and played and sang, "Blackbird singing in the dead of night." She was wearing a Rolling Stones baseball T-shirt, her hair falling onto her guitar, a Save Darfur bumper sticker on her guitar case.

As we drove, I told her about album night, a family tradition, my mom, Ryan, and me sprawled out on the navy-blue Berber carpet in the basement, crowding around the turntable, shouting requests, while my dad deejayed. Pulling a beloved record out of its sleeve—Fleetwood Mac, Rod Stewart, Elton John, Paul McCartney—he was completely in his element, radiant. In my memory now, he was most alive when he was sharing some part of his individual self—who he had been before he met my mom or became our dad—with us.

In Missouri, Jessie and I drove through a wind farm, the white turbines standing erect like great three-armed tube men whirring in veneration to their god. It was late in the afternoon; thunderclouds brewed over the highway. On the stereo, Indigo Girls' "Closer to Fine" blared. Jessie knew all the words and sang along. I looked over at her in awe, trying to hide my grin.

Don't we all come to know ourselves only when brought into the context of another?

Eventually we traded in the interstate for state highway numbers circled in sunflowers. Growing up, Jessie wanted to play professional football, wallpapered her walls with posters. Her mom taught in the public schools, and her dad was a hospice chaplain. They were both deacons at their church. Starting in middle school, she and her sister were each responsible for planning and cooking family dinner one night a week. As she filled in more and more of the pieces of her childhood, I began to see Jessie as having the same

70

Protestant origins that I had, the same emphasis on humility above all else, the same casualness in her body, the same openness. But instead of all the Christian rhetoric leaving her full of seriousness and self-doubt, she carried herself with aplomb.

Jessie told me about the summer before college, working at gas station convenience store with her best friend, that she started smoking menthols, came home drunk from a party, and, as consequence, her dad made her write a research paper on the adverse health correlations of underage drinking. Each story she told added to the French braid of what I already knew about her. On her canvas book bag that she brought to our first-year seminar every Tuesday and Thursday, she had an embroidered patch: "War is not healthy for children and other living things." I was magnetized by her maximalism, pulled into her orbit.

* * *

Bodies, I have come to understand, can keep their secrets for only so long. The day we dissected dogfish sharks in fifth grade, they gave us X-Acto knives. Outside was cool and sunny, and we stood, an anxious group of five, around the small gray shark in the center of our picnic table. The boys in my group were squeamish, so I held the knife, performed the incision. We were instructed to find and identify the heart, lungs, liver. But when we opened her up, there were babies inside, exact miniatures of the adult shark, like Pound Puppies born out of a Velcro womb. My fingers smelled like formaldehyde, placing the babies, all five, in a line on the metallic tray.

* * *

As a child I had a recurring dream that my mom was dying. The first time was shortly after my class took a field trip to the Michigan State Capitol building in Lansing. My mom had been a chaperone for the trip. Each time, in the dream, I was standing at the bottom of a shadowy spiral staircase, the same one from the Capitol building, the dark oak shining from so many hands run down the railing. In the dream, my mom was calling for help from the

71

top of the stairs, but every time I replayed the familiar setting and events leading up to her calls, I would jolt awake before I could go to her rescue.

One night, when I was in fourth grade, I could hear my mom calling my name in the dream, but when I jolted awake, I still heard her voice, calling from the kitchen below my bedroom. I could tell by the tone of her voice she was angry. Then I heard her footsteps on the stairs. When she opened my bedroom door, I pretended to be sleeping.

In the doorway, my mom flicked on the light. *Cara Nicole, do you have something to tell me?* I clutched my teal blanket to my face. Never before had my mom woken me up like this. I had no idea what I was supposed to confess.

Get up!

Downstairs, I stood barefoot on the kitchen linoleum under the fluorescent light, wearing one of my dad's running shirts that hung to my knees. My mom had emptied the contents of my *101 Dalmatians* backpack onto the kitchen counter. I could see crumpled parent notes on colored paper I had forgotten to give to her, a half-eaten peanut butter and jelly sandwich in its Ziploc bag, my red folder with this week's spelling words, the crossword puzzle partially completed. None of these items were out of the ordinary; none would have prompted my mom to reprimand me. I searched her face for a clue.

Why haven't you been buying milk at school? she said.

There, under the spelling folder, I could see the baggie of nickels and dimes I'd been hoarding. My mom picked up the baggie to show me, then set it back down on the counter. I watched as the coins spread to cover the largest surface area possible, weighted down by the gravity of being found out.

I said, *The milk at school is warm, Mom*, already crying. I said that the lunch lady would make me drink it all because it made the trash bags heavy. And that all that unwanted milk would cause the bags to tear, would drip and spill across the gymnasium floor when she hauled them out to the dumpster.

Already I knew this wasn't just about the milk money. I wasn't used to being in trouble. I was used to pizza parties and orange pop in the principal's office for the students with perfect report cards and Nutty Bars after soccer games and sitting up front on the car ride home because I was the oldest.

My mom asked, *Why didn't you just tell me?*

I thought you'd be mad, I said.

Sweetie, I wouldn't be mad at you for not buying milk. I am only disappointed because you didn't tell me. You know sometimes not telling me something is the same thing as lying. You shouldn't keep secrets from your family.

Ever since I'd returned to school after missing most of second grade, I'd been a bit of a loner. As often as not, I spent recess alone in a part of the school grounds dubbed The Quiet Area, sometimes thinking, sometimes brooding, sometimes building mouse houses. I hated the way adults who were not my parents treated me differently than they treated my peers, had begun to nurse an identity that no matter how much anyone disguised their pity as feigned compassion, I was on my own.

Come here, my mom said, pulling me in to her hip. I rubbed my face into the rough fabric of her sweater, my shoulders heaving. She took me to the bathroom sink and washed my face with a warm washcloth. That was the beginning of what would take twenty more years to understand: that my interiority was permeable and not entirely my own, that my face gave me away. I had scars on the sexually charged parts of my body that, as a teenager, I did not want anyone to notice or know about. As a young adult, when I first started to perceive my attraction to certain women, I carried around my desire like some clandestine thing, something to be embarrassed of. No matter how much I thought I was masking my thoughts, I always looked furtive.

* * *

In the months after my dad died, I replayed the milk money scene over and over in my mind, like a nightmare I couldn't shake, the clock across the room glowing two a.m., my naked body tucked under the heavy down comforter of another woman's bed, in grad school in Moscow, Idaho. My mom lived two thousand miles away. Whatever intimacy my lover and I allowed ourselves in this bedroom, we denied in public. I was ashamed of the secret but helpless against the indulgence: her head on my shoulder, her hair on my breasts. I tried matching my breathing to hers, tracing the triangle on the palm of her hand like a metronome set to three-four time—losing myself in the lilt of that silent waltz—and watched as the LED segments in the clock's number display rearranged themselves.

Everything about Kayla was illicit. She smoked cigarettes out her apartment window, had a boyfriend who didn't know about us, spilled red wine on the carpet and never bothered to clean it out, used at-home hair dye to dye her cat pink. But her utter disregard for convention felt calculated, eclipsing my own earnest nondisclosure. She lived above a bar. I'd wait until after the bar closed, then text her. There was a wall phone at the back door to her building, and I would call her room number, whisper, *It's me*, and she'd punch some series of numbers on her end and the door three floors below her would unlock. The door was steel, painted green, with a pane of wire mesh glass. I was already on edge, and every time the magnets clicked, loosening their grip on each other, I jumped.

She tasted of vodka and Camels. Her warm tongue against my earlobe, a passkey. There was never any reluctance between us, just the invisible flooding of a canal lock. In each other's arms, in the bunker of her bedroom, both of us urgent and insatiable. My skin, awash with her scent, trembling underneath her hand.

In the morning, she'd be on the other side of the bed, her back turned toward me, and I'd move to fill the space between us where the sheets had turned cold, my body against hers, the fronts of my kneecaps pressed against the backs of her knees. *Hey*, I'd say, *I have to go.*

* * *

74

I came out to my mom in an email, on a Wednesday, in a month that has more hours of darkness than daylight, ten months after my dad died. I was still practicing, with some trepidation, saying aloud the word "lesbian," how those three syllables buzzed at the apex then lost their momentum. I didn't know how she would react, but I had keyed into the growing tension between her gifts of frilly and feminine clothing and my complete eschewal in favor of a folksy grunge aesthetic, and I ballooned this tension into wholesale impending disapproval. I worried that she might see my queerness as unsavory, something better kept private, or that she might think my having had cancer turned me gay, that gayness is a perversion of traumatized childhoods.

A day after I sent the email, we talked on the phone. She said she had bought a flight down to Florida for her spring break the following week so that she could tell her parents. She said she was going to start seeing a therapist. She was unhappy that I had kept it from her for so long and that I hadn't told my dad when he was still alive. *Most of all*, she said, *I am sad for you because I know your life is going to be hard because of this.*

It was 2011, the year the Senate voted to repeal Don't Ask Don't Tell, the year marriage equality passed in New York, the year Hillary Clinton stood up at the United Nations and gave a much belated speech about how gay rights are human rights. But Michigan is not New York, and my mom had come of age in the late 1970s.

I didn't know until college, until Jessie. Though I am sure I had inklings earlier than that, I didn't let myself try on the possibility. In hindsight, I see the affinity I felt with a girl in my ninth-grade gym class for what it really was. She was one year in remission from leukemia, the scar from her bone marrow transplant white and hollow as a celery stalk, running elbow to wrist. Her hair growing back thick and curly like mine did, her whole body shy when people made a fuss about it. She wore Doc Martens and baggy boy's jeans. She was butch, before I had the language for butch.

In third grade, we learned lines of symmetry in math by holding a mirror to geometric shapes printed on the page. We held our mirrors to faces, cutting lines between eyebrows, bisecting noses, lips, chins. We learned if you cut an apple around the equator, the seeds make a five-pointed star. We painted then stamped our apples on construction paper and found that even stars made from seeds have lines of symmetry. We learned symmetry to be naturally occurring, existing in nature of its own accord.

What I felt most after my dad died wasn't hollowness or regret or even that something was missing but an overwhelming desire to be held, intimately, by a lover. Not a longing for sex, although there was that too, but to be fully contained by the circle of two arms, bunkered.

At the mercy of my body: the synapses for grief running adjacent to the synapses for desire, I craved physical intimacy. Only in fulfilling that fantasy, I believed, would the world stop fumbling past me as so much noise, out of my control.

* * *

While my mom was in Florida, she emailed me twice. One email was a photo she took of a paper nautilus shell she'd found on the beach walking with her parents. "There were no shells for the most part except I saw just this one. . . . it is big . . . about 3 or 4 inches in diameter and paper thin. . . . I have never seen one before. . . . I had determined that I did not need any more shells or rocks and so was not taking any home and then ran across this one . . . they are very rare."

Her second email had a link to the Marianne Moore poem "The Paper Nautilus" that her friend had sent her when she told her about finding the shell. The poem is typical of Moore's style, an ode to a specific animal phenomenon that serves as metaphor for an aspect of humanity she wants to laud. In this way, the poem is a love poem, equal parts awe at the fractal precision of the nautilus shell and homage to a mother's love as a fortress of protection. In describing the way the nautilus carries her eggs inside her shell until they hatch:

as Hercules, bitten
by a crab loyal to the hydra,
was hindered to succeed,
the intensively
watched eggs coming from
the shell free it when they are freed

At the time, I was twenty-four and did not have much appetite for complicated midcentury poems laden with allusions to Greek mythology. I resented my mother for making my coming out into some major incident, a great reveal, something she had to endure rather than minimizing it or reassuring me that it was nothing for me to be ashamed of. I knew nothing of Hercules and his twelve labors. I never responded to either of my mom's emails.

But going back to these emails now, I see what my mom was trying to tell me, in the forum she thought I would be most comfortable. That, as a parent, she wanted to believe her love would be enough to protect me from life and all of its offerings.

round which the arms had
wound themselves as if they knew love
is the only fortress
strong enough to trust to.

By epistolary gesture and an invitation to literary analysis, she was communicating in the only way she knew how to her English-major daughter that even though she had wanted to imbue me with protection by having loved me, she saw then the nautilus shell for what it is: fragile and beautiful.

*   *   *

On an early June trip to southern Utah, Ada and I woke up naked in the back of our rental SUV to a sunrise flush across the horizon. We'd crunched into this deserted trailhead parking lot after midnight the night before, black-tailed rabbits sprinting across the road in front of our headlights the whole way, their upright ears like some sort of last-minute costume. The night had been nothing but crickets and then nighthawks and then the absolute silence of the Milky Way, and now, the periwinkle sky split open with daybreak.

The desert transformed Ada. Gone was the responsible businesswoman in a suit, who, for our first date, had shown my dating app photos to the front desk clerk in her high-rise office building and told him to call her when I arrived. In her place was a braless tomboy following lizard tailprints in the sand, finding snakeskins hidden in the shadows of a coyote-sized alcove, climbing up and over near-vertical slickrock like it was mere sidewalk. We'd come here to do a sort of Greatest Hits tour of a road trip she'd taken with her grandmother a few years prior. She said she wanted to show me the touchstones of everything she considered holy, by which she meant: she wanted to show me each individual chamber of her heart.

We'd come to this particular trailhead to hike into a slot canyon and eat pie, brought with us from Capitol Reef the day before. The hike started as an unassuming wash, juniper and pinyon pine, and, pretty quickly, turned from red-walled, open-roofed canyon, bright with sunlight, into a narrow serpentine corridor. The different layers of rock were on a tilt in most places, and the walls were pocked with oval and rectangular holes where water had worried a pebble around and around. I was struck by the obvious presence of water in this bone-dry place. *All that momentum,* I said to Ada, *makes it move at a sashay.*

Flash flood, she said. *It's like an orgasm.*

I noticed then that we were whispering. A raven passed overhead, and we could hear each of its wingbeats like they were coming from inside us.

Ada paused, reached for my hand. We'd skinny-dipped in the Fremont River at dusk the day before, swallows swooping at gnats in the dwindling light. Then Ada had driven the graveyard shift while I dozed, her hand across my knee, Townes Van Zandt on the radio. Neither of us could stand to be in each other's presence for

78

very long without touching, tethered as we were to the land of the living. At the trailhead, we'd opened all the car's windows, brushed our teeth, then curled into each other beneath sleeping bags. The whole world, it seemed to me then, was held in stasis by the press of her skin against my skin, all the daily uses for a body winnowed down to this.

Eventually, somewhere deep in the canyon, a retired Mormon couple from northern Utah caught up with us, and Ada offered to take their photo. In Utah, more than in Seattle, the tension hung thick in my psyche when I felt we were being stared at by strangers. But whatever the political leanings of our early morning hike companions, their disapproval was dispelled by Ada's small talk. She knew Utah. And with an earnestness that had built her book of business, she let them enumerate each of their favorite places to visit.

After the couple was out of sight, Ada nodded at a steep pour-over spot with good holds leading up the middle, said, *Climb up there and I'll take your picture.* As I was climbing, I noticed all along the walls had what appeared to be dark brown marbles lodged in them like pimples, each with a rust-colored ring around it. I thought then about water and rock, how I favored privacy, discretion, while Ada found comfort in the company of others, and how seldom it is that we stand nose to nose and really consider the dramatic forces that shaped a thing.

* * *

My mom said she remembered the first time I gave her lip as plainly as the day I was born. She said, *You came home from dance practice. We were standing in the foyer just inside the front door, and you stamped your little foot on the wood floor and said, "No more dance."* She said, *I was so surprised, I said, "Okay. No more dance." You finished out that month, had your recital, and were done.* She said, *I didn't know anything. I thought little girls did dance, so I signed you up for dance.*

It had been a year since I'd come out to her when we had this conversation. I was on break from grad school and had decided to spend the summer with my mom in Grand Rapids. We were having coffee in bed together. Since coming out, I had dragged my feet a bit on coming home to visit my mom, not sure if everything or nothing would be different between us, not sure which would be more disappointing to me. Maggie, the dog of my childhood, hopped up onto the bed and curled up at my mom's feet. She was nearly twelve years old, a kind of surrogate child since Ryan and I had moved out. She let out a sigh, more human than dog.

My mom points to this day after dance as if to say, *I think I've known since you were four*. And as much as I wanted to correct her, to say, *No, Mom, just because a girl doesn't like the frills or makeup or performance of her body on display for parents with camcorders doesn't make her gay*. I said nothing. Because I knew in this moment that my mom, too, had a revisionist eye, had been forced, since I'd come out, to look back on everything and say, *Oh, that makes sense now*. And in her telling this dance story I felt some semblance of approval, recognition. That she thought of my queerness not as my ultimate act of defiance but rather as something that had always been. And in knowing that she, too, had made a habit of replaying her memories, lining them up chronologically like dominoes, as a coping strategy, a way of forgiving herself for the inevitability of their falling like they did, I was relieved.

7

There are memories that come back to me hermetically sealed, the path to their access well worn, polished smooth from all these years of replaying. From a young age, I learned to consciously conjure a memory, to hold it in my mind like holding a lemon drop on my tongue.

It was hot, too hot to run barefoot across the black tar sealing our driveway, so hot Ryan and I were dressed only in bathing suits, spent our days taking long, frantic gulps from the green garden hose, and were sent to bed hours before the sun set, where we'd flop listlessly, turning our pillows over and over to press our faces against their cool undersides.

In July our screens were full of white puffs from the neighbor's poplar tree. The mayflies molted their exoskeletons all along the railing of our lower deck, leaving transparent containers of their adolescent selves behind—a whole life lived in the span of a day. Orange and yellow and maroon daylilies in the backyard opened each morning in the full sun, curling their petals like singed plastic baggies set too close to the stove, then withered at sunset, replaced by morning, a new flower on each stem. My mom hated the daylilies but said they were the only thing she could keep alive in that kind of heat. By August, each week began to blur into what felt like one long day, marked only by the rituals of garage sales and the neighborhood's annual block party.

I had a pink bike with white tires, white pom-poms sprouting from white handlebars. The day of the block party, all thirty or so neighborhood kids decorated our bikes for a bike parade. Our moms gave us rolls of crepe paper and helped us weave the orange and pink streamers between our spokes. We fastened jokers from a deck of cards to the forks on the front of our bike frames so they clicked against our spokes when we pedaled. One girl's bike had neon beads on every other spoke that went up and down as she

82

pedaled, like a child's wooden abacus, and a bell she rang with her thumb. My bike had a horn that honked when I squeezed its balloon. We made circles around our cul-de-sac, admiring our newly improved bikes, honking our bike horns, happy at the slapping sounds the jokers made against our spokes. Our brothers chased us, teetering from one training wheel to the other.

A crowd gathered in a neighbor's driveway. I was giddy, wearing tennis shoes and my two-piece swimsuit, my skin tanned, my hair held back in a thick ponytail with a neon scrunchie. A dad I knew stepped out in front with a megaphone, pressing all the buttons, one for a siren and one for "Twinkle, Twinkle, Little Star" and one for "Happy Birthday" and one for the baseball theme prompting everyone to shout "Charge!" and the race was off. In my memory, it is the cocooning that stands out most, the sensation of being surrounded on all four sides by bodies and bikes, the collective noise of horns and bells and parents talking above our heads, all of us engaged in a uniform motion, progressing around the block en masse.

The first time I thought about my own mortality was in the back of my mom's car, the center seatbelt strung loose across my small body. I was decidedly not feeling well, lying down on the bench seat. It was the winter of the harlequin costume, sometime between treatments. On an errand to a doctor's appointment, the store, the pharmacy. My mom's eyes kept glancing from the road into the rearview mirror back at me. Up until this moment, the terror of death had been an abstraction to me, an impossibility, meaningless in its lack of definition. I could spell "death," could pronounce it, but lacked the concept to pair with the word, the signifier rendered hollow without the signified.

In my mom's car, at seven, without meaning to, I'm struck with this memory of the bikes. And coupled with the bikes is an overwhelming feeling of melancholy, of ruin. The decorated bikes, each with a child standing over the crossbar, one foot on the asphalt, one foot on a pedal, ready to push off. Words came to me then, like an incantation, *I don't want to lose this.* The flutter inside the cavity of my chest, the sensation of falling, and then a frantic clinging to this memory of the bike parade.

I called home from Idaho, where I lived the three years after my dad died, and my mom asked me, apropos of nothing, if I remembered our neighbor ice fishing. *He used to tie one end of a ski rope to a tree on shore*, she says, *and the other end to his ankle.* I didn't remember the rainbow of ski rope against a backdrop of all that white, but the impulse to tether oneself to the land of the living was one I knew well.

That moment in the car became a dawning of what it would mean to be unalive as a distinct cessation of movement, unable to ride my bike, unable to decorate the bike again next August, unable even to know I was missing out.

The memory of the bike parade became a touchstone, something I conjured purposefully, before bed, before cross-country meets, believing doing so would protect me from slipping out of life into the frightening non-life. By adolescence, years into remission, it had hardened into an impulsive, indulgent tic. A superstition based entirely on the mythology that catastrophe hits only when we are most unsuspecting, so its inverse demanded of me constant vigilance, gratitude. A child's egocentric concept of consequence morphed into an adult belief that death is somehow logical, precisely timed, an event that I could make meaning of. This superstition became the catalyst for my obsession with the question of etiology.

* * *

At age seven I was beginning to read chapter books: *The Boxcar Children*, Beverly Cleary, *Amelia Bedelia*. I'd been an eager reader, reading the text on street signs aloud for months before my mom, weary of my ceaseless chattering, suggested: *Read it in your head.* Then I imagined the letters and words making silent sounds against the backstop of my forehead, moving my lips in a whisper and then a pantomime and then not at all. Thrilled by the way meaning was preserved in this kind of reading, words strung together like beads into sensible phrases: *no turn on red*, *pass with care*, *right lane must turn right*. The onset of silent reading coinciding with the realization of the privacy of my own mind.

Each night before bed, my mom read me to sleep, this ritual spanning as far back as I can remember until middle school, when I picked up where she left off, lulling myself to sleep. Those nights, my body pressed against hers beneath the covers, I'd follow her voice as it traced the words left to right, turning pages for her, fully absorbed in the richness of being held this way, her captive audience. I lay curled against her skin in that low light, my head on her chest. I had my own bedroom across the hall from my parents, pink carpeting, a bay window looking out onto the cul-de-sac, a twin bed, antique wrought iron painted white, a closet with two oak doors spanning nearly one whole wall, a mural of animal faces, fodder for so many childhood dreams. Together we experienced the suspense in *From the Mixed-Up Files of Mrs. Basil E. Frankweiler*, the fear of aggressive dog fights in *White Fang*, the devastation at the end of *Island of the Blue Dolphins*, her back pressed against a pillow, reading in the lamplight only to me.

These stories were as good as real to me, and it became a familiar and pleasant act of voyeurism to allow my mind to travel from that bedroom into some other place. But when I read *Where the Red Fern Grows* to myself in the fifth grade, finishing the final chapter in the front seat of my mom's minivan, trying not to cry, ashamed to have her see me, I began to recognize a cheapened performativity in the kinds of emotions I allowed myself in the presence of others, and the magnitude of those emotions when I experienced them privately. *That's a sad book*, I eventually said. To which my mom replied, *Yeah, but remember, it's only fiction*.

I felt, for what was maybe the first time, that I experienced something she hadn't, had raked through a hundred and some pages with Billy and those hounds, and it didn't matter if the story really happened or not—my emotions were real.

* * *

The Swiss linguist Ferdinand de Saussure calls thought without language "a shapeless and indistinct mass," "a vague and uncharted nebula."

The year I was sick, my mom bought me a picture book called *My Book for Kids with Cansur*, authored by a nine-year-old. I took his spelling for the correct spelling, his candid description of his own illness as the stand-in for how all cancers played themselves out. He narrated his leukemia and remission and relapse with a tone of understatement. On the last page, he ended with a dedication to a friend he'd met in the hospital and the words, "We're both waiting to see if our cancer comes back." One reviewer called this the "purgatory" of living with cancer. Before reading the book, I had never considered relapse. I thought cancer was like chicken pox. Something you could only get once.

So much of my experience of being sick at seven was a "vague and uncharted nebula." I lacked the language to articulate it. I spent much of my adolescence and young adulthood retroactively assigning emotions to that year, but most of the specifics are lost now, unremembered. What is left is murky. The lack of a word to name something results in the dullness of its meaning.

In tenth-grade biology, the words "malignant" and "benign" appeared on a vocab quiz, and even then, despite all I already knew, I kept mixing them up, their definitions crossed somehow. The night before the quiz, too embarrassed to ask my mom which was which, I looked them up in the dictionary: "malignant," from the Latin *male* and the suffix *-gnus*, "badly born."

Later in high school, a kid in my youth group brought his best friend to our Wednesday night prayer circle. We had been praying for this friend for months. Now, here he was, sitting among us, his jaw yellow and puffed from chemo. Looking at him, I saw myself all those years ago, blue veins visible behind his ears, the signified come to life, sitting on the worn-out couch across the circle from me.

At the end of his life, my dad took comfort in the fact that I had had cancer, that this, like waterskiing, was something we shared, that I knew, intimately, what it was like, and in this way the disease that makes so many patients strangers to their own families brought us closer together. I didn't want to tell him that I hardly remembered what it was like. I willed myself to remember. I wanted the closeness he felt to me to be real. As I watched his body wrung through the post-chemo fatigue, the fogginess, his performative cheeriness, some of what I'd forgotten, or never really gave shape to in the first place, came back, fuzzily, in monochrome. Like a lover whose bed I crawl into again and again in the dark, learning by touch where my body ends and hers begins, my understanding of the disease came only once I was able to see myself in the third person.

* * *

In our junior year, Jessie and a mutual friend organized a Relay for Life on our college campus. The American Cancer Society fundraiser was designed to be an overnight walk, each team pledging to raise a certain dollar amount for cancer research and then coordinating a schedule for their team so that at least one representative from each team would be walking laps on the track throughout the night. The walking was supposed to serve as a metaphor for the so-called long and arduous journey it takes to eradicate cancer at both the individual and global levels. Privately, I scoffed at the loftiness of this find-a-cure goal. *This nonprofit preys on the Ambulance Chaser inside well-meaning people*, I thought. *Their entire premise is built on making sure the masses don't actually understand how complex this disease is.* When I was in high school, I had been invited by a family friend to the "survivor dinner" for a Relay at the college where my mom taught, and, at the time, I felt the entire event—the asking for donations based on sympathetic storytelling—was designed to further entrench the disease with a connotation of victimhood. The infield of the track was picketed in signs "Finish the fight!" and "Celebrate Hope!" The signs embarrassed me. The whole twenty-four-hour event embarrassed me. Survivors were given a yellow T-shirt, while everyone else wore green. The shirt, the survivor lap, the special dinner in our honor, all of it made me feel conspicuous, overly visible, a feeling I associated with being in the hospital. More so than my own personal discomfort, though, I felt Relay for Life made the whole private agony of having had cancer, the most sobering, serious ordeal of my life, into a kind of Mardi Gras charade. But still, I felt some nebulous, abstract obligation to "give back" in some way, to make my experience not for naught—what exactly I was giving back, or to whom, I wasn't sure.

Jessie delegated me to the Survivor Committee, in charge of contacting cancer patients and survivors in the area and organizing a dinner in their honor. Up until then, I'd recoiled at the word "survivor"—more for its association with words like "miracle" and "fighter"—than its actual, naked definition "to go on living" or "to live longer than" someone else. I felt I had somehow evaded death and that my doing so was accidental, the result of random chance, not anything I had done proactively, psychologically, to fend off cancer cells from my body. But when all these survivors showed up at the football field on that sunny night in April, they seemed so pale and delicate, slow moving, pushing walkers, many of them the grandparents of college kids. I handed out our yellow T-shirts and corralled them onto the track for the opening lap, hundreds of white paper bag luminaries outlining the perimeter of the infield, Crayola-markered with names of the survivors, our names, and the names of the dead. Jessie had bought a survivor luminary for me and one for my dad, and something about the gesture made her feel more family than friend.

I was slated to give a speech to kick off the first lap, the survivor lap, one that I'd asked her to help me practice in the week leading up to the event.

As the sun set beyond the western horizon, the festivities—a wing-eating contest, a Relay's Got Talent show, a nearly naked run, root beer pong—commenced under floodlights run by generators, and Jessie was the emcee for all of it. Earlier that afternoon we had set up my tent on the field behind the long jump pit. As the night wore on, all I wanted was for her to come to bed. There comes a point where the number of times I imagined her skin on my skin, the weight of her arm over my arm, my back against her chest in a nest of pillows and sleeping bags and quilts, that I no longer remember if it is a real memory or one I fabricated from wanting. At dawn, I was scheduled to walk my shift. I unzipped the dew-coated rainfly, slipped on my sandals, and let her sleep.

On the track, all but a handful of the luminary candles had burned out. The Ohio sky streaked pink as I walked in circles. Sunlight sparkled through the lowest branches of the trees surrounding the football stadium and there was no wind. The whole world, it seemed, was holding its breath.

* * *

When I was seven and in the hospital, I listened to *Charlotte's Web* on cassette tape. I was mostly bedridden; spent my days in the company of my parents and one friend, the hemophiliac next door. Every adult I knew had turned helpless, had pushed their chips all in on the chemicals that hung from a metal tower above our heads. To keep my mind busy, my mom showered me with books.

Charlotte is the heroine, *a true friend and a good writer*, complex in her resignation about her lot in life. When Wilbur balks at her taste for blood, asks her not to speak of such gore, Charlotte says, "Why not? It's true, and I have to say what is true. . . . A spider has to pick up a living somehow or other, and I happen to be a trapper. . . . My mom was a trapper before me. Her mom was a trapper before her. All our family have been trappers. Way back for thousands and thousands of years we spiders have been laying for flies and bugs."

Wilbur concludes that Charlotte has a "miserable inheritance."

Rereading this book as an adult, I am struck by this line, its nudge toward genetic predisposition, the helplessness of us all, the inheritability of habits. When I opened my pre-algebra textbook to the center, my eyes caught on the two-column tables riddling every page, each with a narrow yellow stripe running along the left margin of the table. After class, I asked the teacher, *What are these?* and he smiled in understanding. *It's a game*, he said, *guess the rule. They're input/output charts.* And instantly I saw a pattern: the correlation between the numbers on the left and right. Input 3, and you get 11; input 5, and you get 17; input 6, and you get 20. The rule: triple any number, then add 2. Input daughter. Input father. The pattern here, a kind of prophecy.

I never took a genetics class, but I did take tenth-grade biology. I learned about Gregor Mendel and his peas and that a white flower crossed with a red flower doesn't come out pink.

In a hotel room in Traverse City on a rainy summer vacation, my dad sat across from me, my permanent euchre partner. I threw a trump card on my mom's ace, and she said, *Okay, Ricky Junior*, calling me by my dad's childhood name. He swept in the cards I'd won for us, organizing them into a neat stack with his hands, then laid them beside the tricks he'd won himself. Our teams were fixed from the beginning, a given.

In hindsight, it's easy to presume there is a rule—some kind of genetic propensity, environmental insult—but maybe this is just me looking at the most formative events of my lifespan as if they were inevitable.

In the barnyard, when the old sheep tells Wilbur he's going to be made into bacon come winter, Wilbur behaves as any sentient creature would once informed of his impending death: he bawls. In his soliloquy, he says, "I want to stay alive, right here in my comfortable manure pile with all my friends. I want to breathe the beautiful air and lie in the beautiful sun." I wonder now if *Charlotte's Web* was what provoked my meditation on my own death in the back seat of my mom's minivan or if it just gave me the language to recognize within myself what my nostalgia for the bike parade was all about.

* * *

To live in a community that crooned over me at every social gathering, to be inundated with compliments from adults who were impressed with my "bravery," adults who believed in the power of "psychic strength" to "fight" a "battle" against cancer, was to grow up ashamed. Every Easter when I was a kid, we would attend church with my mom's parents in Jackson, two hours south of Grand Rapids, and each year I would shake their pastor's hand as we left the sanctuary, a plush toy bunny under one arm. *I remember when you were on our prayer request list,* the pastor would say, ignoring Ryan entirely. *How you doing these days?* I would stare at my feet and let my mom answer for me, *Oh, she's doing well, thanks,* shuttling us out the front door. It felt dishonest to be made out to be a hero for something I didn't have any agency over. From an early age, I learned to deflect all praise. Like all children, I gained my sense of self by paying attention to how people around me saw me. In their eyes, I was a victim.

I am still trying to unlearn that self-definition.

In high school, I invited my flute teacher and two of her other students to play Christmas carols in the pediatric ward at Butterworth Hospital. The caroling had been my mom's idea, one my flute teacher supported in earnest. But when we walked off the elevator and set up our music stands in front of the nurses' station, my flute teacher and the two other students grew suddenly quiet, averting their eyes as a small balding boy in a red wagon passed, IV in tow. Most of the nursing staff had changed in the ten years I'd been gone, but a few still recognized me and made a big fuss in between "Bring a Torch, Jeanette, Isabella" and "Rudolph the Red-Nosed Reindeer." They said, *Cara, is that you?* and *Look how long your hair is!* and *I can't believe how healthy you look.* My flute teacher knew I'd been a patient here, but the other students did not, and my face flushed red in embarrassment. Their hurried gestures to look away confirmed my long-standing suspicion: a child bearing signs of their own mortality is an aberration we fear. I knew too well the rhetoric of healing, that we live in a mastery-oriented culture that is uncomfortable with people suffering through no fault of their own; we want people to move quickly toward a solution, to not dwell too long in the negative. In short, we want stories of survivors, not victims. I was caught by a contradiction. To let my illness define me was to embody fragility, to be cherished simply out of preciousness, a conflation of frailness and my feminine body. But to reject cancer as the most formative component of my identity was to undermine its significance.

* * *

In those six years of checkups that followed 1993, my parents would take me to the hospital cafeteria afterward for breakfast, and I would sip coffee from a white mug, setting it carefully into its saucer alongside my parents' coffees. I would be allowed some kind of forbidden sugar cereal, Froot Loops, Lucky Charms, Crunch Berries. That strange chimera, part child with the stoicism of an adult growing inside her, the cavern of her abdomen hollowed out, then stuffed full again with something my dad called "maturity."

My dad, after one of my surgeries, per my request, brought me a chocolate milkshake from McDonald's. I hadn't been allowed to eat for a day leading up to the surgery, and, as my mom tells the story, my dad was harassed by the Burger King attendant across the street from the hospital, who mistook his dirty clothes and disheveled hair for homelessness and refused to serve him because he was walking instead of driving through the drive-through, the only part of the restaurant open at that hour. So my dad walked the three blocks down to McDonald's instead, brought me my chocolate milkshake.

I came to hate chocolate ice cream after that year, my doctor explaining it as a side effect of one of the chemo drugs I'd been given.

Perhaps I can use that same line of reasoning to explain my aversion to the word "cancer." We used shorthand around my house, calling 1993 "the year I had CA," shrouding it with even more baggage than it already had.

In sixth grade, the five elementary schools in my district fed into one middle school. I conceived of my identity then as monolithic; thought of myself with a sticky note on my forehead: The Cancer Survivor. Thought, maybe now, in this new year and new school, I could avoid being a spectacle. A boy in second period, sneering over my desk. *Did you have cancer? No.* Then, two years later, sleeping over at a best friend's house, each of us in our separate twin beds watching *Annie* on VHS, I was bloated with the secret. During the credits I started clanking the handle on the dresser drawer between us. *Hey, can I tell you something if you promise not to tell?* I was situated within the paradox of wanting to fend off all attention that stemmed from my cancer and craving desperately to be fully seen.

Afterward, I stood in her bathroom brushing my teeth. The bathroom had two wall-to-wall mirrors facing each other, and I was captured by the reflection of myself infinitely repeating itself in smaller and smaller iterations. Whatever the story I tell of myself, this is what I become. Whatever I am to become, this is the story I have to tell.

8

I t's August in southern Michigan at dawn, and the air hangs heavy at the water's surface. The lake is smooth as glass in this morning stillness, the string of houses doubling in its glare. At the end of the dock, my dad's silhouette heaves, coiling a ski rope, the thick straps of muscle up his back flexing with each arm's length as he reels in the rope. I linger at the water's edge, watching him. He is barefoot, wearing swim trunks and a white T-shirt that says "If You Can't Ski with the Big Dogs Stay on the Dock," his skin tanned dark, his nose red and peeling.

I wade into the water, warm as bath water, my left foot held snug inside the rubber ski binding. I'm wearing a life jacket over my two-piece bathing suit, and around my wrists I Velcro neoprene ski gloves, stiff from drying in the sun. My dad says my name quietly then tosses the handle of the rope to me, and I catch it in midair. The only sounds are the hum of our inboard ski boat and the scrape of my slalom ski's fin dragging through the sand beneath the water's surface as I wade a little farther out until the water is up to my knees. I hold the handle in my hands like a baseball bat and bury my right foot in the sand to steady my balance while my dad puts the boat in gear, tightening the rope between us. I float the ski on my left foot to the surface, and, just as the rope gets taut, I yell, *Hit it*, and count to three silently, out of habit, then jump, catching the tug of the rope with my back arched, as the boat, with me behind it, roars to life.

Across the lake, a great blue heron, startled by our noise, lifts into the air, its wings as wide as my own two arms. I try to follow its path, but its steel-gray body disappears against the backdrop of water and sky.

My dad points the nose of the boat west as we follow the shoreline counterclockwise around the lake, the sun an orange glow at our backs, hanging just below the horizon of poplar and maple and

94

sassafras. I cut quick zigzags behind the boat, my body hurtling through that August air, throwing up a wall of spray at the arc of each turn, every muscle in my shoulders and neck yanking in unison to a rhythm of pull and release. Like a Foucault pendulum, this ritual of dad and daughter seems as perpetual as the earth's rotation.

On the straightaway before heading back into our dock, my dad knows to look back at me for a sign. I watch him and wait for him to look, then make the "around again" symbol with my right hand, tracing an imaginary circle with my pointer finger pointing toward the sky. I see him smile in recognition and pass by our dock, making another loop around that mirror of a lake while the rest of the world sleeps.

I am hardly aware of the water beneath me; I know only of its ability to hold me, this trick of momentum and tension—*the pulling force exerted by a string*—a physics lesson I learned at age four, my dad up to his waist in water, holding me in the crook of his body, my small hands wrapped around the rope's handle, my feet barely big enough to stay in the bindings of my tiny wooden skis. *Hit it*, he yelled to my mom driving the boat, and quieter, to me, *Hold on tight.* The rope's gentle tug, hoisting me from water to air.

As we complete the circle of the lake a second time, my dad looks up again, and I point and mouth, *Home*. He swings the boat in close to our dock, and I pull out of the wake, using the momentum of his spin to slingshot into shore. I wait until the last possible second to let go, and skim the water's surface, coming to rest where the water is ankle deep. He completes a full circle then slows the boat to a stop and stands to reel in the rope, making neat coils, each the width of his wingspan, the rope in his hands as familiar as breathing. At my ankles, the waves we created heave onto shore like four evenly spaced sighs, tumbling over themselves in a push to unfurl.

* * *

It was winter break and snowing. Out the dining room window, the lake looked like a vast open field, a blanket of white pulled taut, staked down by a rim of houses. Ryan and I were at the counter eating Rice Krispies. *Mom, can we skate today?* Ryan asked. During the past week, my dad had made a habit of checking the temperature out on the deck each morning to gauge how long the lake had had to freeze solid. *Three inches of rail freshy,* my dad reported, returning from the dining room, a smirk in his voice.

For Christmas, my mom bought my dad an ice auger. The contraption was bright purple and looked like a giant drill bit, as thick as his leg. *It has to be six inches,* she said, firm on this rule despite the ice fishermen who had been out on the ice for days. My dad was wearing his long underwear and a light purple Steamboat sweatshirt fraying at the cuffs. Ryan and I watched him move around the kitchen like a dancer, pinching my mom's behind while she stood at the sink, teasing her for being such a worrier. We watched as he slipped his feet into his bright blue Kombi boots and headed down to the basement then out the back door, the giant auger over one shoulder.

Mom, where are my snowpants, I whined. I had spilled the contents of a drawer full of mittens on the floor and picked through the piles of fleece, selecting purple knit gloves, a black neck gaiter, my American flag knit hat. Outside, my dad had his skates on already and was shoveling neat stripes up and back, making a rectangular rink. Ryan and I pulled on ski socks and boots and carried the hockey nets out of the garage and down to the beach. The nets were PVC pipe skeletons we used for street hockey in the summer and pond hockey in the winter. The plastic was prone to shattering in the cold, and my dad had patched them in a few places. One of the nets had a yellow tarp stretched across it, decaled with the image of a goalie, the four corners and the five-hole between the goalie's legs the only places to score. Ryan named the goalie Dave, and we cheered him on like a teammate whenever someone hit the puck straight into the yellow plastic. *Great save by Dave,* we said.

Down at the beach, Ryan and I brushed the snow off one corner of the dock and sat to put on our skates. Our dad had taken the dock out at the end of October and stacked the wooden sections on shore in preparation for this winter, just at the lake's edge, so we wouldn't have to walk through sand with our skates on. The dock's metal frame was just behind the stacked wooden sections, and each giant stake, rusted to the waterline, leaned against the others, like some kind of marina junkyard, detritus of summer, the color gone out of every inch of this place.

Our dad skated toward us, leaned the shovel against the neighbor's poplar tree, and crouched to tie our skates. *Dad, can I help shovel the rest?* I asked.

Sure, he said, *like this*, and held the shovel at an angle so all the snow dumped off to the unshoveled part of the rink. I followed the pattern he'd started, careful to keep the shovel at an angle, watching as the sheet of snow accumulated in the curve of the blade, curled in on itself, then fell off to one side, the same motion as a wave. With each of my passes, the rink grew bigger and bigger, and soon the job was finished. I traded the shovel for my red wooden stick my dad had cut down to size on his table saw Christmas morning, and we played for hours on that frozen solid lake.

Later that night, we returned to the rink. *Night hockey*, my dad called it. Ryan and I had the idea to light tiki torches on each corner of the rink, and we found them in the back room next to where my dad had propped up his slalom ski and our mom's slalom ski and the set of combo skis I still used. The torches were made of bamboo with a basket at the top that held a citronella canister. They were as tall as I was and smelled of bug spray and summer. Ryan and I each carried two out to the four corners of the rink, still in our snow boots. *Make sure you carry them upright*, my mom said, warning us not to spill oil down the fronts of our ski jackets. She had agreed to play, too, and was tying her skates on the stacked sections of dock.

The night was moonless: the sky, a dim gray glow of cumulus clouds. The only sounds were the scissor scrape of our skates against ice and the slow rhythm of so many breaths, each made important by its condensation into fog. Our four shadows intersecting in the glare of floodlights, the puck stitching a thousand dotted lines between us.

That spring, the ice grew weak in the span of a day. Twelve hours of rain, and our mom declared it no longer safe to walk on anymore. We forgot to bring in the tiki torches from the corners, and we watched as they sank shorter and shorter into the slush crust that was left until one day in March, while Ryan and I were at school, when they disappeared entirely.

A month later, once the water had warmed enough to swim in, I put on my snorkel mask and flippers and went searching in the muck and weeds past the dock. I guessed at the locations of the rink corners in proximity to where our dock was now, and I scanned the bottom of the lake for some glint of bamboo, but I never found anything. I knew in that moment that it didn't matter how hard I searched or how far down I dove, whatever the lake swallowed was gone forever.

* * *

I learned to slalom on one ski the spring after the tiki torches sank. I was nine years old, and my dad taught me to jump start like him, standing in knee-deep water while my mom drove the boat and Ryan, age seven, sat in his jeans and sweatshirt in the spotter's seat.

You ready? my dad whispered.

Yeah. I wobbled, floating the hollow plastic ski on my left foot to the surface, digging into the muck with my right. I was small-boned and tentative, and he held my hand, helping me keep my balance.

Hit it, he shouted to my mom. Then quietly, to me, *Count with me. One Mississippi, two Mississippi, then jump.*

It took only two tries.

This is how we became legends on that lake, a dad and his daughter and the roar of a 300-horsepower engine accelerating, as regular as the sun rising.

When I was six, on a weekend when my mom had to work at

98

the hospital lab downtown, I watched my dad ski a slalom course for the first time. The weekend had been rainy, and then not, and I'd just learned to ride my bike without training wheels. Across the street from our house, builders were digging a hole for a new house, and sand smeared the asphalt, etching it with small rivulets of rain running downhill. Another house on the cul-de-sac had a long, steep driveway that I'd been riding down at top speed to feel the thrill of wind on my face, a thrill not unlike holding onto a ski rope with two clenched hands. My dad, inside the house with my toddler brother, never heard my scream, but a neighbor did. I'd skinned my knee, blood dripping down my left leg, and the neighbor, a friend of my parents', carried me in through the garage, where my dad had pulled out his car to wash it in the driveway, and through the screen door into the kitchen.

My dad hated blood, didn't know what to do about skinned knees and whatever else he sensed in me: something akin to home-sickness, to wanting my mom. Typically, we were stoic children. He thanked the neighbor, carried me upstairs to the bathroom where my mom kept Band-Aids in the medicine cabinet, washed the sand and gravel out of my purple flap of skin, covered my knee with a small piece of folded gauze, and secured the bandage with a Snoopy Band-Aid. I asked him why blood looked blue inside our veins but red on the outside. He said he didn't know, that I should ask my mom.

Later that day, he took me with him to his friend Marv's house on a different lake twenty miles north from where we lived. Marv and his wife had no kids of their own, and I liked how Marv talked to me like an adult. While my dad packed up the cooler in Marv's kitchen, Marv pulled his set of kid's skis out from under his deck, three-foot wooden skis tied together at the tips and the tails, and asked me if I wanted to go first. Pouting, I pointed to my bandaged knee, gloating a little over my injury. My dad said a little scrape was no reason to forgo skiing, and so, reluctantly, I squirmed into my life jacket, letting my dad help me into the skis in the shal-lows before he hopped in the boat with Marv. And the whole loop around the lake, I tried not to smile, but I couldn't help forgetting myself, my blonde hair whipping through all that air.

After, I sat in the passenger's seat, fingering my Band-Aid, now a flap, the adhesive worn off on one side, while Marv and my dad took turns skiing the slalom course. Skiing is 90 percent timing and 10 percent balance, born in the inner ear. We spent the entire afternoon at the sheltered end of the lake where the slalom course loomed, those red and yellow buoys bobbing eerie and menacing like the lights lining an airport's taxiway. I watched in awe as they weaved in and out of the buoys, their lines like a mathematical function, every muscle in their arms taut. I was their spotter, shouting *Down!* to the driver, like I'd been trained to do, when either my dad or Marv would crash headfirst over the tip of his ski. My dad hated falling, hated how his head would fill with water and how he'd spend days sneezing, nursing a sunburn or a sinus infection, or something else I didn't quite understand about pride.

My dad grew up waterskiing with his Uncle Bob on the Shiawassee River that drained out of Saginaw Bay of Lake Huron. He told me river skiing was nothing like lake skiing. That sometimes the boat would hit an invisible underwater snag, throwing everyone in the boat out of their seats. That their 70-horsepower engines would strain against the current going upriver, but you could max out the boat's RPMs going downriver and almost double the boat's top speed. In the winter, the river would freeze over, and they played pond hockey on the rough and pocked surface, the river still very much alive just inches below their skates. One winter, my dad's mom told him he wasn't allowed to play hockey on the river, that the ice was too thin, but he went anyway, and one of the other kids fell through. He didn't drown, but my dad remembers it as a near miss. In his version, the story is less a warning about waiting for the ice to freeze thick than it is a parable about how mothers have intuition, and how Ryan and I should listen to our own mother when she tells us not to do something.

* * *

One winter, when I was ten, on a visit to my mom's parents in Florida, my dad signed us both up for a half-day ski lesson on a gravel pit with a slalom course, those six red buoys thirty-eight feet from the yellow boat balls, forming a corridor. It was my official introduction to the competitive world of slalom skiing, a world I'd been studying avidly for two years, cutting out centerfolds from my dad's cast-off issues of *Waterski Magazine* and taping them to the insides of my locker at school. I knew I'd have to cut hard and fast to make it through the gate buoys out to the first ball, then back across the wake to the second, and that after the third ball, if I kept the same rhythm, I'd be able to finish the set off momentum alone. My dad coached me the whole drive to the gravel pit. He said I should make up a shadow buoy before the gate balls and always *always* remember to turn early, before the buoy. But when I got behind that competition ski boat and shoved my foot in someone else's ski, something heavy and made for a full-grown person, this ride, which had once been as natural as mounting a bike, felt suddenly foreign and important, and the surface of the gravel pit lake—as flat and glassy as any cool, foggy morning on our lake—seemed suddenly as solid and unforgiving as asphalt.

My dad sat in the back seat and yanked the rope, shouting *Now!* to help me get the feel for the timing. I pulled hard against the rope, but that day I only made it through the gates and around the first buoy. On the drive back to my grandparents', I hung my head, tracing the outline of the van's automatic window button. *You'll get it, Carly,* my dad said. *It just takes some getting used to.*

Back at my grandparents', I overheard my mom tell my dad *I told you so*, that she thought it was a bad idea from the beginning. She wanted my brother and me to experience failures, but she worried this particular failure was not the result of my own self-sought pursuits but rather a classic case of a child forced to carry out the dreams of a parent. What she did not know, and I didn't know how to explain to her, was that waterskiing had become a shorthand for reciprocal love between a daughter and her dad. Sure, I loved the sport for its relegation to the quiet of early mornings, what felt like our own secret wormhole in time, the lake a mirror of sky. But I wanted to excel at for its own sake, which had come to be less about skill and athleticism and more about belonging.

Our first winter together, I took Lucia to a Girls Try Hockey Free event at the ice rink in our neighborhood. *It's like soccer*, I said, *but with ice*. Afterward, she began salvaging my *USA Hockey* magazines from the recycling bin, taking them to school with her, then spending all two and half hours at her after-school program teaching herself how to draw the angle of a goalie's kneepads in the butterfly position. With the fervor she reserved only for the Brazilian Football Confederation, she began following the NHL. Her favorite team: the Detroit Red Wings. In the span of one season, she knew more about the history of the sport and the rivalries between teams than I did. When I watch Lucia practicing slap shots on our back porch, I think about all the hours I spent rollerblading alone in our cul-de-sac. I'd set up cones and create elaborate drills for myself, shooting on the plastic goalie Dave. I'd tell myself that I had to score in all four corners and the five-hole before I could call it a day. I think that maybe time is a Mobius strip, Lucia's childhood a distorted photocopy of mine, mine a repetition of my dad's, all three distinct times overlaid like carbon copies of each other. I wonder if at the heart of every parent's passed-down hobby is a desire for immortality, a snake swallowing its own tail.

* * *

The following summer, the four of us took a camping trip for a long weekend to Glen Arbor in northern Michigan, near the Sleeping Bear Dunes. We towed our boat up for the trip and dumped it in at the boat launch each morning, taking it back out at the end of the day and parking next to our tent at the campsite. Glen Lake was famous to us for its teal clear water and for the permanent slalom course set off of Inspiration Point on a part of the lake that was always calm. We spent ten hours a day on the boat, from sunup to sundown, Ryan and I snorkeling off the back, eating Reese's Peanut Butter Cups in foil wrappers straight from the cooler, our parents

102

working on their suntans, all of us absorbed in our own books, their pages turning wavy and warped from water damage.

Six months after my dad died, my mom mailed me a photo she'd found from that trip of Ryan and me standing barefoot at the base of the dunes. The photo was her way of saying, *Look at how happy we were.* My dad announced on that trip that Glen Arbor was his favorite place in the world, and Ryan and I decided that if it was his favorite then it would be our favorite too. In the photo, Ryan is wearing an oversized T-shirt that says Hockey Is Life. He is making a ninja move for the camera, his hair hovering in mid-jump. I'm wearing acid-washed jeans and a Save the Manatees T-shirt, giving my mom a jaded smirk. *I am too old to be photographed,* my face says.

That summer I learned to ski the course on the inside buoys, a set of green balls set halfway out to the competition-distance red ones. My dad was driving, my mom holding her breath. I remember the sun like a glare on the water, and the wanting—wanting more than I'd wanted at any sport ever—to ski around those six buoys successfully, for him or for myself, it didn't matter, they were synonymous. He was watching in the boat's rearview mirror, and when I made it around that last buoy and through the exit gates, he flicked the boat's horn over and over, his right fist pumping the air. I tossed up the rope handle, grinning.

* * *

The summer I turned sixteen, my dad bought a portable slalom course kit. The 250-acre lake was too small to accommodate a permanent slalom course and too busy with boat traffic in the height of summer, so this was our compromise. Looking at the kit itself, it was hard to imagine it all fitting together to make a slalom course: two piles of twenty or so six-foot-long PVC pipes, a spool of bright yellow one-eighth-inch polypropylene rope with big fishing weights on it, and a mesh bag of sixteen yellow boat buoys and six red ones.

My dad explained that the whole course was held together by

the polypropylene rope that we would unspool out the back of the boat and, at intervals of forty meters, we'd attach the telescoping PVC pipes to the rope, let them fill with water and sink, and then attach the buoys with a bungee, the whole hundred-pound mess held afloat by the twenty-two buoys. If the lake water had been clearer, the course would have appeared from above like a bright yellow cat's cradle held taut by eight bone-white PVC pipe fingers. The entire course, when unloaded from our boat, was 260 meters long and 23 meters wide, or roughly the equivalent of two football fields set end to end.

On the morning of my sixteenth birthday, I got up at five, put on a two-piece bathing suit under my jeans and hoodie, and carried the spool of yellow polypropylene rope and set it at the back of the boat. Then, I walked barefoot across the dewy lawn and up to the house for a second trip, grabbing the mesh bag of buoys and my life jacket. My dad was wearing jean shorts and his neon-teal-and-hot-pink Connelly windbreaker, the one my mom tried to throw away because it was faded and mildewed, but he rescued it from the bin on the curb before the garbage truck arrived to take it away. He carried the two bundles of PVC pipes down and set each on one side of the inboard motor cover. Neither of us said anything to each other for fear our voices would wake up the neighbors. Silently, we pushed off from the dock.

On mornings like this, the sun not even cresting the horizon and already the air was seventy-five degrees, heavy with humidity, the lake a sheen of black glass, disturbed only by the cleaving of the bow of our boat, transforming what was mirror into a polished sheet of corrugated tin, the only thing quivering in the morning stillness.

Once away from shore, we began to whisper to each other. *The strategy behind assembly*, my dad said, *is to try to set the boat corridor*, marked by the yellow buoys, *perfectly straight*. We started by tossing out an anchor tied to the end of the yellow polypropylene rope, securing this end of the course deep into the muck, and then slowly put the boat in gear, the yellow rope uncoiling off the spool out the back of the boat like a spider's silk. When we reached a Y in the rope, I would hit reverse once to slow the boat from drifting and then kill the engine. My dad would pull one of the PVC pipes off the top of the stack and I'd join him, both of us scrambling to telescope the pipe out to its full length and then fasten it to the rope before the boat drifted too far off course. Our hands were cold and rough from so many wet-dry cycles, and we'd curse at the pins in each PVC pipe, coaxing them to pop into place. At the end of each PVC pipe was a rope and then a bungee with a clasping hook to secure the buoy. *If you hit the buoy with your ski tip*, my dad said, *don't worry. It's designed to pop underwater and then right back up.*

That morning, like so many mornings, we fought. He'd given me the easier job—driving—and for that I felt an enlarged duty to make his job—telescoping the PVC pipes—easier. The PVC pipes were full of holes and designed to fill with water and sink down seven or so feet, low enough to be out of reach of the engine's propeller. Already he was frustrated because he'd messed up the entrance gates, failed to telescope out one of the pipes all the way, and we had to backtrack, hand over hand on the yellow line with the engine off, and pull it up, lake water spilling out of the PVC pipe all over the boat, all over my jeans. The polypropylene web took several minutes to settle deep enough to be able to drive over, and neither of us had the patience to wait. After we fixed the entrance gates and had two out of the six turn buoys in, I reversed the boat overtop the section my dad had just finished assembling, running over the line while the prop was still spinning. The yellow cord holding the whole system together wrapped around the prop, coiling tightly. My dad shouted at me to kill the engine. But before I could even ask him what had happened, he'd flung off his shirt and jumped overboard, making a show of this thing I'd done to ruin the morning. Our time that was supposed to be sacred.

He tried to hold his breath long enough to untangle the mess one strand at a time, but the prop was under the center of the boat, not at the back like on outboard boats. And he had never really learned to swim. Had a fear of drowning.

I hated seeing him this way, gasping for air, one hand clinging to the boat, as if he might not be able to find his way back to the surface, back to air, without this hand on the wooden platform at the back of the boat.

It's my fault, I said. *Let me try.* I stripped off my jeans and hoodie, my skin goose bumped at the sudden temperature change. The lake water in late July felt warmer than the air. Under the boat, I braced myself on the rudder, opening my eyes in the murky, green-brown underworld to try to understand the mess I'd made. I was the go-to knot detangler in the family, constantly fixing my mom's necklace chains and my brother's shoelaces. I'd been on the swim team. I'd learned how to hold my breath.

It took me five minutes, three breaths, to loosen the knots enough to uncoil the rope. *At least I didn't slice it,* I said, relieved, trying to dissolve the tension into humor. *Just forget it,* he said, still seething. *I don't know why we're even going through all this rigmarole.* I felt inside me the hot flare of impulsivity to match his sarcasm with my own, tit for tat, say something like, *Fuck it. Let's just throw the rest of this thing overboard and go home.* But another larger part of me turned timid, turned into pleading with him. *C'mon, Dad. Let's just finish this and ski, okay?* Really, we had no choice. We were out in the middle of the lake, the course anchored on one end a quarter mile away, the other half still coiled inside our boat. I felt shame at my lack of spatial awareness, knowing if he'd have been driving, none of this would have happened. I wanted the morning to go back to being unsullied, two diehard waterskiers, a father and daughter, up at dawn with the blue herons, working together on some intricate puzzle, their shared love for this time of morning, the lake, each other, as palpable as the fog that hung at the water's surface. We finished assembling the course in silence and went home to pick up our skis and a spotter.

Later, we took turns skiing the course, and I'd make all six balls at twenty-two-off and twenty-nine miles per hour, a new record, and we'd forget about our fight, about all the clumsy ways our temperaments overlapped.

* * *

A year and a half after we bought the portable slalom course, my dad would have brain surgery. They'd taken out part of the right temporal lobe, taken his ability to balance on one ski with it. That June, the neighbors watched from their deck as he limped down to the lake, struggled with the rubber binding, then waded out into the water until it was knee-deep as he had so many times before. My mom drove the boat, and I sat next to her, recoiling the rope with each of his failed starts, casting it out to him over and over, all of us refusing to let this be the end.

9

The summer after my senior year of high school, I went on my first backpacking trip to Pictured Rocks in the UP, Michigan's Upper Peninsula. The trip was with my youth group, intended to be a rite of passage marking our transition from high school to college.

The UP is surrounded on three sides by water, Lake Superior to the north, and Lakes Michigan and Huron to the south. It's connected by land not to the Lower Peninsula but to Wisconsin, the state boundary tracing the Montreal, Brule, and Menominee Rivers. The UP has some of the snowiest weather and most wild, still-forested land in the eastern half of the United States. It contains nearly 30 percent of the state's land and less than 3 percent of the state's population. My family took a weeklong camping trip in the UP the summer I turned ten, and the place, the trip, became yoked in my mind with a fondness for being "in the woods."

There were a dozen of us on the trip: ten seniors, our youth group director and assistant director. The four-hour drive from Grand Rapids to the Mackinac Bridge was mostly unremarkable interstate through maple, beech, and birch deciduous forest. But after the five-mile steel suspension bridge, what was freshly paved and painted interstate in the Lower Peninsula, turned abruptly into a cracked and potholed two-lane with fifty-some-mile stretches between towns. "Town" in the UP is just a bait and tackle shop, a liquor store, and a convenience mart selling venison jerky and Cornish meat pies. The forests lining the highway in the UP turn predominantly coniferous: white pine, balsam fir, northern white cedar, eastern larch, and—in the sandy, logged-off places—savannas of jack pine.

Returning to the UP when I was seventeen for what was only the second time reawakened something inside me—a craving for the solitude and quiet of a shady spot, the wind stirring in the branches overhead, a romanticization of a life lived in an off-the-grid

A-frame—and something else I couldn't quite put my finger on then—an aesthetic for a four-wheel-drive pickup, a greased and sun-faded baseball hat turned perennially backward, for the corduroy collar of a Carhartt jacket against my neck—something I know now as wanting to hide out, to live a private life away from the prying eyes of neighbors. That trip, I learned how to tie a bowline, how to start a fire from duff and downed twigs, how to roll a bandanna into a sweatband. Church on Sundays had never felt like a comfortable place. But on this trip—the mandated casual dress, the six hours each way of country radio, the rain tap-tapping on the nylon roof of our tent—the woods became calcified in my mind as the only place where I could be my whole self.

I had packed everything for the three-day trip into my school bag—clean underwear, water bottle, jeans, hoodie, swimsuit, toothbrush—and tied my dad's cotton sleeping bag to the outside with twine I'd found in the garage.

That day we walked maybe four miles through open forest, trilliums and yellow trout lilies lining the sandy trails. My sleeping bag kept coming unraveled and falling out of the twine sling I'd made for it on my backpack, so eventually I just carried it folded in half on my head. That night we ate peanut butter and jelly sandwiches, the peanut butter spread with our youth group leader's college ID card, and watched the sunset on a cliff overlooking Lake Superior. Another kid had brought his guitar, and he plucked absentmindedly while the sun drooped lower and lower until it slipped behind the clouds at the horizon.

That night I helped build the fire, and we all stayed up late singing and French braiding each other's hair. The trip leaders had had us set up the boys' tents south of the fire ring and the girls' tents on the north side while they'd sleep out next to the fire to keep watch in case any of us had any ideas about sneaking out.

The night was sleepless and long. I slept in all my layers, the hood of my hoodie pulled up over my head. At one point, I felt the girl beside me inch her bag closer to mine. I rolled over to face her and whispered, *Hey, Lisa, you awake?*

Yeah, she said. She was sleeping on the wall side of the tent, the lake side.

You cold? I whispered.

Yeah.

You want to get in my bag with me? My sleeping bag was my dad's 1970s flannel-lined hunting bag, the lining patterned with mallards set against a mustard yellow backdrop. Her hair was blonde and in two French braids like mine.

She said nothing but began unzipping her sleeping bag, slowly, so as to not wake the other two girls in our tent with us. I held the cuff of my sweatshirt to the back of my sleeping bag's zipper to dampen its sound, and she climbed in with me.

The bag was too small to zip up with both of us in it, but she draped her empty bag over us, and we spent the rest of the night in the same position, spooning, her body softening against mine. Eventually, she slept, her bare feet grazing my bare feet, one arm under my arm, her steady breathing at the back of my neck.

* * *

When my brother and I were in grade school, my grandma would take us for walks in the seven-acre forest behind their barn. The property was half swamp, half deciduous forest—home to rabbits and deer and robins—the same house my mom had grown up in. My brother and I played often in the woods at the end of our street, but it is the woods at my grandparents' house that has become fused with my mental definition of "nature," a place that offered comfort and solitude.

Each summer, my parents would go to a NASCAR race at Michigan International Speedway, and my brother and I would spend a few days with our grandparents. My grandma had red plastic hummingbird feeders outside her dining room window; had a rain gauge in the shape of a graduated cylinder that she'd empty every time it rained, writing down the rainfall in inches in her diary; knew the names and calls of all the birds. We'd catch frogs and garter snakes, and she'd let us bring them inside, cupped in our hands, to watch cartoons in the den, after the stock markets closed for the day and my grandpa would give up his TV.

My grandma made us bacon, lettuce, and tomato sandwiches for dinner, or meat loaf with ketchup and mashed potatoes, or sometimes we'd just have popcorn and Klondike bars. After dinner, she'd teach me how to oil paint, or she'd read to us from Ruth Stiles Gannett's *My Father's Dragon*, or we'd play Rummikub on the dining room table.

At night, I would lie awake for hours beneath the 1950s chenille bedspread that had been my mom's, too hot to sleep, and listen to the katydids singing. Outside the screened-in windows, the yellow light in the orchard buzzed, its sound hypnotizing.

* * *

Just north of the Mackinac Bridge is a giant statue of Paul Bunyan and his Blue Ox, some kind of inside joke between my parents, a tourist trap they both visited as children, one they insisted Ryan and I must see. We were not impressed. *What's a tourist trap?* I wanted to know. *Why is his ox blue?* Ryan asked.

In the photograph that conjured this memory, both Ryan and I are leaning against the tall chain-link fence separating us from the famous lumberjack and his ox, my fingers laced in the wire, neither of us smiling.

This photo was from a stack my mom brought up from the basement of the family vacation we'd taken camping in the UP the summer I turned ten. We brought the canvas tent my parents had bought from Sears the first year they were married, some fifteen years earlier, the same day they sold their mobile home and put a down payment on their first house. It had been a joke they liked telling, that if their house didn't work out, at least they could stay in their new tent. But the week before our vacation, they had loaned the tent to some family friend's kids, teenagers, and when we went to set it up that first night at the Mouth of the Two Hearted River campground, the zipper to the door was completely shot, off its track. *No big deal*, my mom said, and safety pinned it shut. This vacation had been months in the making, an attempt to retrace the places my parents had visited as kids, before they met. My dad usually took a week off every summer, when we'd tow our boat up to Traverse City and stay in a hotel on the beach that would let us anchor our boat on their waterfront. But this trip was the first we'd taken without our boat, our first time camping somewhere other than our backyard.

The campground is situated where the mouth of the Two Hearted River dumps into Lake Superior, a place popularized by Hemingway's Nick Adams stories. My parents had both read *The Old Man and the Sea* in high school, but my dad was never really taken by war stories—he had been relieved to be too young to sign up for Vietnam—and my mom preferred Steinbeck to Hemingway. Neither of them had ever read any Nick Adams stories. They took us to the Big Two Hearted River for its obscurity, thirty miles down a dirt road, and its proximity to the water.

Neuroscientists who study memory suggest that the more times you replay a memory, the more you change it—that the act of recall itself changes some small detail or taints it with the present-day emotional milieu—so that the next time we replay it, it is the facsimile we are remembering, and inevitably altering again, not the original. In this way, memory is like generational data loss, a photocopy of a photocopy, and our most well-preserved memories are the ones we don't remember at all, so we are never tempted to recall them.

Even the protagonist in Henry Wadsworth Longfellow's epic poem "The Song of Hiawatha," for which the Hiawatha National Forest of the UP is named, is the product of this game of telephone, a chain of distortions and mistranslations. Longfellow's narrative content, a basic rehashing of the inevitability of post-contact submission, came from Henry Rowe Schoolcraft's retelling of his Chippewa wife's culture, itself a revisionist history: the reports of the conquered as told by the conqueror. Longfellow not only mistook Schoolcraft's ethnography as credible but also mistook the Ojibwa spirit Nanabozho as synonymous with the Iroquois leader

Hiawatha, arguing Hiawatha was more a manageable name in an English-language poem.

Susan Sontag, in her 1977 book *On Photography*, argues that individual photographs all too often offer up a similar opportunity for misrepresentation as single slices in time, moments disjointed from their surrounding contexts: "because each photograph is only a fragment, its moral and emotional weight depends on where it is inserted. A photograph changes according to the context in which it is seen." I thumb through the stack of ten or so photos my mom brought me from our vacation to the UP—here, a photo of me hunting for rocks with my mom on the beach, Ryan filling his green bucket, me filling my pink one; here, we are fishing in the Two Hearted River, Ryan wearing his water shoes and an oversized sweatshirt, and I'm in a white skirt I never remember owning—and I trace over them with a yearning to go back in time. The photos spark the memory of a story, one told and retold so many times it had become familial myth: the story of a flood and of my dad as the cement holding us all together.

After the Two Hearted River, we followed the back roads along the Lake Superior coast to Copper Harbor, a town at the tip of the Keweenaw Peninsula. Our mom kept us entertained on the drive by telling us to look for bald eagles. In the back seat, I held my head upside down, trying to see the tops of trees, not really believing that we'd see any eagles, until we did see one, and then another, and then more than ten in the span of the day. I remember thinking we must be in some wild and remote place for there to be eagles here. In Houghton, we were allowed Taco Bell for dinner, my mom ordering the cinnamon twists Ryan and I favored, and told not to make a mess in the new van.

We pulled into Fort Wilkins Historic State Park late in the evening. *Only one rustic campsite left*, the ranger told us. *We'll take it*, my dad said, and we pitched our canvas tent on the flattest ground we could find. While my dad pounded in each plastic yellow stake with his blue-handled hammer, my mom inflated the air mattress she and my dad shared, pumping the foot pump with her right foot and then her left, taking turns until it was full. Then she zipped her sleeping bag to my dad's sleeping bag and laid them on top of the air mattress. This was all I knew of married couples: both of them tag-teaming the chores, both of them wanting to be physically close to each other, their connection to each other the source from which their connections to my brother and me flowed. In the mornings, Ryan and I would crawl in there with them, a whole family held by those two cotton sleeping bags.

Earlier in the trip, we had camped at Tahquamenon Falls, had seen the yellow water raging over rocks, had learned about hemlock trees, that the same tannins that turn cola brown rage through the rivers in the UP. We camped at Whitefish Point near the Great Lakes Shipwreck Museum, my dad fascinated by its one-room exhibit on the wreck of the *Edmund Fitzgerald*. We had camped at Twelvemile Beach, where my mom taught me that the scat I found on a trail adjacent to our tent was bear scat, *Like a no-bake cookie*, she said. By the time my parents drove into Fort Wilkins State Park, just a few minutes outside of Copper Harbor, we were good at camping, good at cooking sausages on the tripod grill my dad hung over the fire, used to sand in everything, our fingernails caked with dirt.

That night it rained, and our campsite was on the lowest ground in the campground, in the path of all that water carving a new drainage to the creek. I woke up soaked, the tent pitch-black, and whispered, *Dad, I'm wet.* He said, *Yeah, I know. It's raining. Go back to sleep.* I said, *No, Dad, I'm really wet.* As the story goes, he clicked on his flashlight. We had a small plastic basin leftover from the hospital—some mass-produced bedpan, standard in every hospital room—and we used it on that trip to store all our games: Uno and Catch Phrase and a deck of cards. In the beam of the flashlight, he saw the plastic tub floating around the tent and said, *Jeanne, the kids are sleeping in puddles.* Ryan and I had two foam pads, water toys for the lake. Our parents' sleeping bags were dry, their air mattress higher than the waterline.

My mom carried Ryan, still asleep, out to the van. Outside the

114

tent, it was pouring; lightning and thunder continued in the distance. All I remember is darkness and my parents frantically tearing down camp, throwing everything into a sopping heap in the back of the van. Our clothes, our sleeping bags, everything was stained brown from the tannins in the water.

Copper Harbor is an hour from the nearest town, like everything in the UP, proud of its rural, backwoodsy appeal. My dad cranked up the heat, and we drove, headlights reflecting off wet pavement. Somewhere along that dark, rain-slicked, deserted highway, my mom spotted a black bear sniffing around on the side of the road and my dad stopped, headlights poised on the bear. Wide awake in the back seat, taking cues from my parents, I saw the bear as an omen, one we had the good fortune of seeing, something to revere.

In Houghton, as the sun came up over the horizon, the sky still heavy with clouds, my mom insisted on a laundromat, converting quarters into clean, dry clothes, sleeping bags, everything as good as new. She said, *Let's take a vote.* This was how we made decisions then, ensuring everyone's voice was heard. *Everyone in favor of checking into a hotel for the night, then heading home tomorrow, raise their hand.* No one moved. *Okay*, she said, unveiling the next option, *everyone in favor of Dad getting a new tent in Walmart and then finishing the trip as planned, raise their hand.* Three hands shot into the air. This is the way votes usually went in our family, 3–1, my mom joking that our dad was just an oversized kid masquerading as an adult.

We waited in the van while our dad ran into Walmart, came out smirking, a boxed tent under one arm. He drove the van over to the edge of the lot, hopped out and opened the trunk, threw the old tent in the dumpster. *I'm pitching the tent*, he joked, Amelia Bedelia come to life, our mom not even bothering to hide the smile tugging at the corners of her mouth.

We drove that day to the Porcupine Mountains, set up our new tent at Presque Isle Campground, Ryan and I zipping and unzipping the tent door a hundred times, elated with the turn of events and with the love we had for everything just-out-of-the-box new.

Fifteen years later, my mom and I would return to this campground after leaving the Two Hearted River, retracing the steps of that trip, trying to reconjure a time when our family had been whole.

I'd been working out some theory about how places, like bodies, have a kind of metadata encrypted within them—like a meticulous minute-by-minute account of everything that has transpired there, with increasing digressive references and interlaced annotations on emotional context—that could be unlocked only by being physically present and moving through them kinesthetically. Especially in hallowed places and places of personal significance, that they contained within them a trace of our previous selves, and that going through the motions in the exact place would yield a kind of affirmation from the physical world, a more detailed remembering.

It had been two years since my dad died, and I wanted to re-remember our vacation there, to see the tannins in the river, to go back to the Great Lakes Shipwreck Museum, to stand on the shore of Lake Superior, feel the wind whipping across my face, and remember what it meant to be alive.

In the two years since my dad's death, I'd been expecting its repetition. Things I'd never been afraid of before became indomitable: I refused to drive anywhere when it had been snowing, hunkered down in the ditch with my dog every time a car passed us while we were running. I kept imagining that something would happen to my mom, that no one would find her for days, kept running scenario after horrible scenario of her and my brother through my head, feeling as if it would be easy to lose them, too.

On the drive to the Two Hearted River Campground, my mom remembered the washboard road. She said the van had been new when we took that trip fifteen years prior—new to them anyway—and that she worried the road would ruin her struts. A recent forest fire had swept through the area, changing the landscape, and I worried about the slippage of memory. We passed more than twenty logging trucks hauling out all the half-burned wood, making the most of the destruction.

At each fork in the road, we argued about which road to take, if we had made a wrong turn, if we should backtrack. I was going off the Google directions I'd printed; my mom was going off intuition, a fifteen-year-old memory of a road she'd traveled once, when she hadn't even been driving, and we both wondered for a while if we'd ever find the campground, if we'd even stayed in such a place all those years ago, if it even existed. This was a feeling I had often after my dad died, wondering what was real and what was imagined, what was a part of the idyllic childhood I'd constructed to preserve him and what was truth.

My mom and I eventually did find the campground, and I parked the car next to the river, the view of it dumping into Lake Superior one that I instantly recognized. All I'd remembered from this part of our trip was the safety-pinned tent door and a swinging bridge Ryan liked to jump on to scare me. The bridge was still there, but remade, sturdier, with less give. I let my dog, Scout, out of the back of my car and leashed her to walk across the bridge. It was overcast and windy, and the waves were crashing hard against the shore. My mom wanted to find a rock, a memento she'd been in the habit of collecting, a way to keep track of all the places she'd been. I let Scout off leash and watched her run, biting at the waves for drink.

The previous summer, my mom and I had taken a camping trip together in Glacier National Park and Banff, and we had our routine down pat. I set up the tent while my mom made us gin and tonics. We'd brought my two-person backpacking tent and the same air mattress she'd shared with my dad years ago. The air mattress, fully inflated, didn't fit through the tent door, so I'd set it inside the tent first and pump it up with the foot pump dangling out the door. Before we left home, I'd found two holes in it, patched them with super glue, and the mattress was holding air again through the night.

After our night at the Two Hearted River, my mom and I drove to the Great Lakes Shipwreck Museum at Whitefish Point. When we arrived, the museum was closed, but the lighthouse was open. We wound our way up the metal spiral staircase, and I remembered, or I imagined I remembered, my dad holding my hand to keep me from tripping, urging me to pick up my feet. At the top, the house was an eight-sided turret of glass, like an old-fashioned lantern with metal seams welding each pane together.

I had looked through photo albums for pictures from that day but couldn't find any. I thought I had been wearing my red sweatshirt with GAP across the chest and white Keds, but I knew I'd just time-capsuled that sweatshirt because I liked to suck on the fleece collar, and the shoes because I picked constantly at the blue rectangle on the heel. More than confirmation of the red sweatshirt and sneakers, I wanted to remember what my dad was wearing. Jean shorts probably. A windbreaker? Maybe my memory of that day was more accurate because there weren't any photos.

At the top of the tower, my dad and I pushed through a trap door onto the narrow platform surrounding the glassed-in house. I gripped the metal railing with both hands, and my dad pointed out across Lake Superior and said, *See that land there? That's Canada.* The wind whipped in off the water, and I imagined without the whitecaps there would be hardly a distinction between the gray of the water, the gray of Canada, and the gray of the sky.

That night my mom and I stayed at a walk-in campsite in the Porcupine Mountains. She said she remembered there were rocks at this campground that Ryan and I climbed on for hours. Signs everywhere on our way down to the beach warned us not to walk on the rocks. After dinner, we followed the trail leading west out of our campground, and sure enough, we saw a river and a few sections of rapids, small waterfalls, and people all over the rocks. The rocks were like stacks of plates, ledges with smoothed corners, where water rushed in early spring. A family with a toddler stood close to the water's edge, the child toddling around on the rocks. I kept Scout on leash, worried she would slip and fall in. My mom smiled in recognition, this small corner of the world familiar to her.

Suddenly, I saw her differently. She was thirty-five again, the mom of two, letting them explore. When I asked, *Weren't you worried we'd slip?* she said, *No. We'd just been through the worst with you, were just happy to be together, that everyone was healthy.* Her answer surprised me. She seemed to hold both truths at the same time: the cherished irreplaceability and the inevitable ephemerality, that to love her husband and kids as she did, she had to make her peace with holding them lightly.

That night, it stormed. Huge thunderclouds rolled in from the north off Lake Superior, the rain coming down in sheets. Outside the tent, the wind howled and the branches above us creaked. My mom made a joke about widow makers, and then we laid awake side by side, both silent with our fears, listening to the storm. In the morning, I toasted English muffins over the two-burner stove while my mom loaded up the car with all our soggy camping gear, a reprise.

My mom asked, *Do you want to drive?* and I said, *Sure*, and queued up Sufjan Stevens's banjo and brass on the car CD player, "Like a father to impress / like a mother's mourning dress / if we ever make a mess / I'll do anything for you."

Looking back now on that trip, I think our retracing our own steps evoked a kind of flip-book gestalt, that illusion of wholeness, and that no amount of conjuring his ghost would ever bring him back.

10

In February 2003, when I was a junior in high school, I watched coverage of the space shuttle *Columbia* burning up upon reentry on the TV monitor at my work. With my teenage acute antennae for tragedy, I felt a pang of grief for the families of the seven crew members. Something about the catastrophe seemed familiar to me, like a glimpse of déjà vu.

It had been nearly a decade since my diagnosis, my dad nine months away from having his first seizure, and I had begun to believe in the myth of my cancer as a fluke.

After the *Columbia* disaster, NASA would invest in a decade-long investigation and, for the first time, release the accident report to the public. For this reason, the disintegration of the *Columbia* became codified as proof to many that NASA's shuttle program never moved out of its experimental stage into being a fully reliable, operational mode of space exploration. The capacity for malfunction embedded inherently in each mission, people argued, was too much of a risk.

* * *

When I was in fifth grade, my parents signed me up for Space Camp in Cape Canaveral, Florida, with a friend, Danielle. They wanted desperately for me to have a normal childhood, to replace all the attention I'd received as the sick kid with a different kind of attention. But everything was tainted now. Soccer had mutated from just being compulsory—another teal-shirted kid on defense—to being an act of defiance—the kid who was athletic *despite* her fragile health. In second grade, I'd been kicked out of a game by a ref for wearing a baseball hat and refusing to take it off, waited in the car with my Nutty Bar and orange pop, in the vast silence of childhood unknowing while my dad screamed at the ref in front of everyone. I felt responsible for proving to my parents that I was a normal kid,

120

that we were fine now, that we would stay fine, that there wasn't any more unexpected bad news lurking inside me. I was hyper-attuned to my parents' unspoken desires: that I would learn how to have fun and be less serious, that I would blend in among my peers, that I would make friends easily and none of my experiences of having been gravely ill and hospitalized for the better part of a year would contribute to any perceived or real sense of otherness. Like all well-loved kids, I suppose, their doting made me feel conspicuous.

That year, the year I was in fifth grade, every kid in school wanted to be an astronaut. It was the year *Toy Story* was released, the year of quoting Buzz Lightyear, *to infinity and beyond.* Something about the cowboy allure of bravery and risk and adventure, the final final frontier, the beauty of stars, zero gravity, outsmarting death with human ingenuity. For Halloween my mom made an astronaut costume for Ryan, white duct hose for leggings, a milk jug helmet. I was the Statue of Liberty, wrapped in a green toga, green face paint, happily grounded, surrounded by water.

As a child of the 1980s, I grew up with commercials for Mattel toys, *batteries not included*, grew up believing high-tech meant better quality. My favorite sneakers as a kid had hot pink curly elastic laces, my favorite outfit: a matching black tank and shorts with neon lightning bolts in green and teal and yellow. But the uptick in reliance on all this innovative technology inevitably held greater capacity for glitches. I was born in the shadow of Chernobyl, the investigation of the 1986 *Challenger* explosion still underway.

My first-grade teacher had taught us about outer space. We sat cross-legged on the carpet and listened to Ms. Frizzle's class trip. She told us that our Very Excellent Mothers Just Sent Us Nine Pizzas, that Jupiter had a moon called Io, and that everything was meant to orbit a Styrofoam sun. She took us outside one Tuesday for a solar eclipse, our heads stuck inside shoe boxes lined with aluminum foil, told us not to look at the sun directly.

Before Space Camp, I'd had sleepovers at the house of a friend who lived two houses down from mine, whose parents were like surrogate parents to me, but otherwise, I had never spent a night away from home without my parents or grandparents. On the American Airlines flight to Florida with Danielle's parents, I won at solitaire for the first time on her dad's laptop, watching the cards zoom in parabolic arcs across the screen. I thought this boded well for my week of independence.

The next morning, Danielle's mom made me shower in the hotel room shower, but she didn't know how to French braid. I tried to blow-dry my hair by myself, replicating what I had seen my mom do, head upside down, shaking like a dog. This was what I was most unprepared for: the sudden ache for my family in moments that were usually a part of our daily routine.

The dorms at Space Camp were windowless cinder-block cells of alternating blue and red metal-frame bunk beds with a locker room attached, six metal stalls with toilets, an open bay for showering, all the shower heads facing each other. I was shy with my body, hiding in the bathroom stalls for all of my changing, avoiding the showers for the whole week.

I had a suitcase full of clothes I didn't pack: jean shorts and baggy sleeveless T-shirts and socks with ruffles when I folded them over. I had my stuffed animal, a black-and-white milk cow with a red bow, salvaged from the stack of brand-new stuffed animals destined for the community center after my last inpatient treatment. In the top of my suitcase, my mom had left a note, something to remind me to have fun, use this cash at the camp store, that they will see me at graduation on Friday. Reading it on my first night, my missing them welled up like electricity behind a switch, invisible and quiet. I knew that Space Camp was expensive, something most kids my age were begging their parents to send them to, and I felt a weight I couldn't shake for the entire week.

* * *

The first day was all sun. We were building model rockets outside on a patch of hot cement, squinting at the supplies laid out on the white plastic folding table. I sat with my shoulders hunched, bare and prone, supergluing fins onto my skinny cardboard tube, spots of wet glue glinting in the sunlight.

Migraines came easily to me then, hereditary, from my mom's side. I'd come home from the bus stop, not having eaten anything since lunch, tired from too much overconcentrating, and my mom would recognize in me the same nausea and sensitivity to light she had and tell me to go lie down in Ryan's room, the darkest room in the house. *What side is it on?* she always asked, looking for a pattern, her eyes on the horizon, expecting the worst.

The nurses' office was dark, and she was suspicious of homesickness but gave me Tylenol anyway, making a big show out of my ability to swallow the pills. She gave me a wet cloth for my forehead and went back to her bookkeeping. My group was made up of the youngest kids at Space Camp, but I was the first one to cave, sleeping off the afternoon.

When I woke, my group was shooting off their rockets on the lawn in front of the auditorium. It was shady there, and Danielle had finished my rocket for me. The counselor was making it fun, doing the voices of Mission Control for each rocket, *Houston, all systems go, ready for liftoff,* and for a minute, I forgot myself, forgot my burden of melancholy. Together we chanted a countdown from ten, then the thing, paper and plastic and powered by hydrogen peroxide, burst from the ground in a moment of inspiration, our fourteen pairs of eyes tracing its arc against sky so blue it was white, until the counselor broke our open-mouthed silence, shouted *Clear,* and we sprinted, all of us, ten years old and wearing our closed-toe sneakers, racing to retrieve a fallen rocket.

* * *

I spent that whole week living in a wing of the dormitory named after Sally Ride, staring at the framed photograph of her in a flight suit, recognizing something I wanted for myself in the casual way she carried her body, her pockets loaded with gear and equipment. This was 1995, twelve years after she became the first American woman astronaut. It wasn't until her obituary in 2012 that she came out publicly as a lesbian. She and her partner of twenty-seven years, Tam O'Shaughnessy, cowrote her obituary, which was published on her website on the day she died. I wonder now, how much of our history, our heroes, have been silenced, vacuum-packaged for ease of consumption?

My mom was an advocate for girls in the sciences. She was on the PTA at our school, actively involved in recruiting speakers for science-enrichment assemblies. Once she invited a traveling tide-pool exhibit, another time a live birds of prey troupe. At the university where she taught, she ran a summer science camp for middle school girls of color, handpicked by their teachers for demonstrating promise in math and science. I knew that my parents didn't care what profession I would pursue as an adult. They just wanted me to know that girls could do anything boys could do. Danielle and I were two of four girls in our cohort of fourteen.

Inside the auditorium, my group was on station rotation, trying out all the simulators. The counselors had split up Danielle and me on day two, a small traumatic moment, and I was strapped into the 5DF chair. Five degrees of freedom. The simulator had a series of hinges, designed to pitch forward and back, rotate around a vertical axis, spin sideways like a fortune wheel at an expo. Any sudden displacement of our centers of gravity, raising an arm, turning our head, and we were sent spinning. All the while we were supposed to complete a puzzle on the wall: *Stick that green peg in the green slot. Find your center, that's right, now hold still and I'll bring you down.* I wasn't afraid of heights, not prone to motion sickness, but when my sneakers were back on the rubber gym floor, it felt like the earth was rocking, that we were somewhere at sea, lolling, the floor rising to meet me midstep.

Most of the simulators were meant to disorient us. Practice for our futures, our counselors said; practice for zero gravity. I volunteered to be first on a simulator called the MAT, a human gyroscope. The three giant concentric steel rings, momentarily static and orderly, did not intimidate me. I was antsy, like I was waiting in line for the Zipper at the county fair. Our counselor was a clean-shaven carnie in khaki shorts and a polo shirt, ready to give us the ride of our lives. He handed me a helmet—I thought, *Maybe people fall out sometimes?*—then he buckled me in, a belt over my shoulders in the shape of a Y. I was da Vinci's *Vitruvian Man*, my body geometrically proportionate, cartwheeling through three dimensions.

Later that day we took a bus out to the Cape Canaveral Air Force Station, home to the Vehicle Assembly Building (VAB), one of the largest buildings in the world by volume, the womb where shuttles are forged.

On the bus, Danielle's counselor took me aside. She was gentle in her teenage body, soft brown hair and freckles. She crouched in the aisle to meet me at eye level, asked why I'd come to camp, fishing for an answer about the value of this kind of social experience that I couldn't conjure, said I should try making new friends, try sitting with other kids at meals besides Danielle. I interpreted her pulling me aside as getting in trouble and spent the rest of the ride stunned and red-faced, trying not to cry. I remember nothing from the VAB, this moment on the bus, the single most memorable incident from the whole week, one I continued to conjure for years.

I imagine we stood inside the main atrium of the VAB, heads tilted toward the ceiling, feeling small and out of place in a room intended for rockets.

After dinner that night, I bought Neapolitan space ice cream at the camp store, and it crunched like chewing on Styrofoam, a giant Lucky Charms marshmallow. We watched *Apollo 13* with our brother cabin, holding our breath as everything that could possibly go wrong did. We were young and still believed in the inevitability of survival. We knew they wouldn't show us this movie if the astronauts died. We were sprawled out in our pj's, our chins in our hands, all fourteen sets of eyes fixated on the twenty-inch screen, Tom Hanks in a flight suit, our hero.

No one told us about the *Challenger* disaster, that plume of smoke broadcast on live TV nearly ten years earlier, the year most of us were born. Seven bodies inside an aluminum cabin, dropping

48,000 feet into the Atlantic, *Obviously a major malfunction.* Two minutes and forty-five seconds spent in free fall, enough time for three astronauts to detonate their emergency air packs, slapping down onto this cold blue planet just offshore from where we were learning the science of combustion, the innovation of space travel, the technology propelling us into the future. To infinity and beyond. A cold January morning, too cold, a faulty O-ring, a liquid hydrogen leak, and seventy-two seconds pushing against sky. I was an embryo, two months in the making, growing an umbilical cord, growing cells that would eventually differentiate, growing a damaged ovary, mitosis gone haywire already pre-encoded in my germ cells at eight weeks.

* * *

In order to graduate from Space Camp, we had to successfully complete a simulated launch and landing. Half of the cohort was assigned to Mission Control, half to the cockpit of the shuttle, astronauts. The counselors made this simulation out to be a comprehensive exam: the final test of our aptitudes, our characters. They said they were watching us all week, observing how we interacted with others, determining which roles we were best suited for. We all wanted to be assigned to the cockpit, to get to be astronauts.

The shuttle was a model, cut in half as a display in the center of the auditorium, a dissection. The cockpit was dark, and the walls and ceiling were lined with buttons, gauges, miniature TVs gone black. On the day of our simulation, we each got a headset with a microphone. Danielle was picked early, an astronaut. I was picked last, flight director, Mission Control. Every command for our simulation went through me, my voice carrying through the wiring from bunker to cockpit, ringing in the ears of my teammates.

That afternoon, there was a routine rocket slated to launch, an uncrewed mission, seemingly commonplace for Cape Canaveral and for the camp's staff. Hours before the launch, we were chaperoned onto the white roof of our dormitories, the ocean only minutes away. Up there, we could see the launch pad on the horizon, the rocket, like some absurd white needle waiting to prick the sky. Waiting, to me, seemed infinite. I was bored and fidgety. I used up all the remaining photos on my disposable camera trying to capture dolphins, thumbing the camera's winding wheel and waiting with my eye at the scope for their fins to reappear, squinting into the sunlight. When the launch became imminent, we counted down from ten and watched the silent rocket rise from smoke, a missile arcing through our atmosphere.

Later, when my mom developed the film, I never mentioned the rocket launch. There were photos of Danielle in her camp-issued red polo and a snapshot from inside the shuttle simulator and, at the bottom of the stack, a series of twenty gray photos. The dolphins existed only in my memory, indistinct against the vastness of space and sky and open ocean.

The night after the launch, we were shuttled into the auditorium bleachers with the rest of Space Camp for our final assembly. A scientist was demonstrating the magic of oxygen as oxidizer, using a lit match to suck a boiled egg inside a bottle. Somehow this was related to the way shuttles were ignited, catapulted into outer space, but I missed the rest of his talk because my counselor shook my shoulder, told me I had a phone call.

Out in the lobby there was a receptionist and a phone with a long curly cord, and, on the other end, was my mom's voice telling me they weren't going to make it to my graduation the following day. *There's been a problem with our flight. The plane is broken.* Maybe I didn't understand what this meant at age nine, that hiccups in commercial airlines happen every day, and the malfunction occurred on the runway in Grand Rapids while they were firmly grounded, could walk back to their car in the parking lot, drive home and sleep in their own beds, then hop a flight to Orlando the next day, get some comp tickets from American Airlines for all their trouble. Maybe I associated *The plane is broken* with *Houston, we have a problem*, too much time spent wearing my helmet, on the fringe of understanding imminent danger, immersed in a program all too familiar with worst-case scenarios. I was wrapping myself in phone cord, completely undone by the sound of my mom's voice, her inability to comfort me from so far away. *Grandma and Grandpa are coming,* she said—they spent half the year in their mobile home two hours inland from Cape Canaveral, and my parents had planned my week at Space Camp to abut a family vacation to visit them—but despite my fondness for her parents, I was inconsolable.

The next day, my grandparents sat with Danielle's parents in the auditorium bleachers while the camp director called each of our names, and we walked across stage to receive our diplomas. After, Danielle and I gave my grandparents and her parents a tour of the cockpit of the half shuttle. My parents arrived sometime that afternoon, and, once reunited, we visited the memorial for the seven astronauts who died in the *Challenger* accident. My grandma had been a schoolteacher at the time of its launch, and my parents had closely followed the highly publicized life story of Christa McAuliffe, the civilian chosen as a part of Reagan's campaign to send a teacher into space in hopes of reinvigorating America's love of the space program.

The year I was born was supposed to be the International Year of Peace, according to a UN declaration, in honor of the agreement by both the Soviet Union and the United States to decrease their nuclear arsenals by 50 percent. But in 1986, "disappearances" were happening across Central America at the hands of US-backed coups; the Iran–Iraq War raged on; and South Africa declared a state of emergency. The US Army bombed Libya in retaliation for their attack on a discothèque in Berlin, a hangout for US soldiers stationed there. AIDS had become a pandemic, while the National Institute of Allergy and Infectious Diseases looked on idly, calling it natural selection. Reagan continued to wage state-sanctioned racism, what he'd dubbed his "war on drugs," and the Statue of Liberty was reopened after a two-year renovation.

It wasn't until after my dad's death that I learned chemotherapy was developed as a byproduct of war. During World War II, hundreds of tons of mustard gas were released off the coast of Italy. Physicians found the locals to have significantly reduced white blood

128

cell counts, so pharmacologists developed an intravenous version, pumped it into the arms of terminal lymphoma patients just to see what would happen. Now, it's a multibillion-dollar industry. Had I been born a decade earlier or even a year earlier, I may not have lived. One of the chemotherapy drugs I was given didn't gain FDA approval until nine months before I was diagnosed.

At age sixteen, the year of the *Columbia* disaster, I had opened and reopened the door of wanting to know where my cancer had come from so many times that it had begun to feel banal. Always, behind that door was a dark, limitless expanse of no answer. Maybe exposure to chemical toxins, maybe eating too many processed foods, growing up on milk from cows treated with synthetic hormones, maybe just bad genes. None of this wondering had turned me into a hippie, vegetarian kid or made me outspoken about the overuse of pesticides and insecticides. I was secretive still about my having had cancer, secretive, it seemed, even from myself. However, I had a vague inkling that my cancer was tangled up somehow in the extolling of scientific advancements and the wholesale transformation of American life to processed foods, industrialized agriculture, and a cavalier attitude about warning labels for asbestos and DDT and lead-based paint. Even though my treatment had been on the cutting edge of medicine at the time, I was skeptical and jaded about newfangled technological "solutions" to human-invented problems—how to store nuclear waste, how to preserve and later clone the DNA of endangered species, how to regrow tissues and full organs from embryonic stem cells. I kept quiet about my opinions, preemptively avoiding having to explain my reasoning. One time, I walked out of my tenth-grade biology class during a documentary on prenatal genetic screenings, overwhelmed, I think, by the what-ifs of my personal existential reality, but I never said anything to my friends about it later.

The heroism of the NASA program, as sold to us at Space Camp, was that it combined human's capacity for bravery with human-made technology. Even at age nine, though, I had a seed of skepticism for overexuberant lauding of gallantry. How else was I to perceive the glorified notion of being an astronaut other than through the lens of my lived experiences, to recognize the similarities between the ambitions of the space program and the optimism of my own team of doctors? *Here, let's try this and hope it works.* Strap me in, then later call it something like bravery.

11

On a midsummer weekday, Ryan stood on the end of the dock in his teal board shorts with white stripes running from hip bone to the outsides of his knees, preparing to jump. He was bare-chested, his skin as pale as it was in winter, save for his forearms and back of his neck and from his knees down, where his skin was farmer's tanned. His hair was light brown, like our dad's, and stick-straight, kept in a bowl cut with the back of his head shaved short. Around his neck, he wore a hemp necklace I'd made him with a clay bead in the middle—a peace sign with Rastafarian colors. I could see his ribs even though he was just standing there, not even trying to suck in like he sometimes did to show me the cliff his chest cavity made, how concave he could make his stomach if he vacuumed out all the air.

I was nearly thirteen, and my body had taken on a new permanent posture; I arched my upper back, pushing my shoulders forward in an effort to make my shirts hang flat over my chest. But if Ryan was at all aware of the changes happening in my body, he graciously kept quiet. We still shared a bathroom, still peed with the door open, still walked in on each other and sat on the bathroom counter, carrying on whatever conversation we were in the middle of. Only when I was on my period did I shut the door in his face, hollering, *Can't anyone have any privacy around here?* and he would keep on talking to me through the door.

Our mom was reading in her bikini on one of the lawn chairs in the sand, and I alternated among lying next to her, reading or weaving hemp into another necklace, and swimming with Ryan. We begged her to take us out in the boat so we could practice our diving in the middle of the lake, where it is deepest, but she said the boat's battery was dead and we'd have to wait for our dad to come home from work. Ryan and I decided we could swim off the dock, and we dragged our boogie boards and foam noodles out from the back room. I watched from shore as he dipped in his right foot, testing the temperature, then as he flung his boogie board onto the surface of the water just in front of the dock. His body wound taut; his movements seemed to come from some axis inside his chest, stretching from the dip in his collarbone to the backside of his belly button. When he jumped, everything hinging on that axis swung outward, like the Flying Trapeze ride. His hair hovered for a moment as if he'd touched his hand to a static ball, but then he fell, knees onto boogie board, careful to not let his feet dip too far beneath the surface where the weeds would brush against his leg and imagined snapping turtles loomed in waiting, starving themselves in preference for the pale pinkie toes of swimming children. I ran and jumped off the end of the dock, belly to boogie board, and we swam in tandem out to the center of the cove, where the weeds didn't grow close enough to the water's surface to disturb our swimming.

Everything was a competition. We invented a game to see who could stand on their boogie boards the longest before losing their balance. Ryan was better at balancing because his boogie board was warped concave, its edges pulled ever so slightly upward, and mine was warped convex, like a dolphin, better for diving, we both decided, but not for balancing.

I envied his flat chest, his surfer hair and board shorts. Dressing up was straightforward for him—khakis, a belt, and button-down shirt—a hardly perceptible difference from how he usually dressed, no one commenting on how he "cleaned up nice." Things that were difficult for me came easily to him: chess, moguls, beating the boss at the top of Ganon's Castle in *The Legend of Zelda: Ocarina of Time*. Ryan was a prankster, liked to swim under my boogie board and tip me into the water when I was trying to balance upright. I'm sure we fought sometimes out there, in the middle of the cove, the water carrying our voices to the neighbors in all directions, but what remains most salient is the passage of so many summers like this, our finger pads wrinkling, our ears full of water, learning companionship by the sound our names made in each other's voices.

Hey, Ry, I'd say, *check this out,* and I'd do a flip underwater with my arms hugging my boogie board. *Coooool,* he'd say, and try to repeat it, until our mom called us in for lunch.

* * *

When we were small, my mom read to us a picture book called *A Million Chameleons* by James Young. The book is a rhyming book. "A little chameleon all in vermilion danced alone in a garden pavilion." I remember rubbing the binding of my blanket across my upper lip while my mom read the story, my brother turning the pages, both of us not quite believing that such a color-changing creature could really exist.

* * *

The summer Ryan graduated from high school, he and I took a trip to Maine to backpack for four weeks on the Appalachian Trail. My mom and I had taken a trip together when I graduated from high school three years earlier, but my dad wasn't in good enough health to be doing much traveling, and my mom was taking him two days a week to Detroit for his treatment, both of them under semi–house arrest since he'd started the clinical trial. So, out of a self-appointed duty I'd assigned myself even before our dad was sick, I decided it was my job to be a surrogate parent to my brother, to fill in where our parents left gaps.

My mom was skeptical about the trip. She had read Bill Bryson's *A Walk in the Woods* and imagined worst-case scenarios awaited her eighteen-year-old son and twenty-year-old daughter in Maine: stranded, lost, molested, hypothermic, fallen off a cliff. She wanted to believe we were responsible, that we had our heads squarely on our shoulders, that we were mature beyond our years. I think she reasoned with herself that my tendency toward taking excess care in decision-making would counterbalance Ryan's impulsiveness, that his knack for problem-solving would make up for my inclination to get stuck. But she bought Ryan a North Face backpacking pack and a stuffable sleeping bag for his graduation, and she

134

bought me a couple books on thru-hiking the Appalachian Trail. I planned the trip from my college dorm room, typed up the mileage we would cover each day, which waypoints we would camp at each night, which roads we would cross where we could hitch into town for re-rations. I emailed my brother and mom the itinerary.

In one of the books I'd read, the author suggested mailing care packages to yourself General Delivery at post offices along your route if your trip was longer than a couple of weeks. This way, you could save money and time trying to find backpacking-appropriate food in tiny tourist towns along the way. Ryan and I bought peanuts and raisins and M&Ms and tuna packets and pitas and Nutella and pretzel sticks and Goldfish crackers and flavored oatmeal packets and armloads of Snickers bars. At a local outfitter we bought two number-ten cans, one labeled Mountain House Beef Stew and one labeled Mountain House Spaghetti and Meat Sauce. At home, we popped the seals on everything and placed evenly sized rations into Ziploc bags, then lined the counters with what we planned to eat each day. In a giant metal mixing bowl, we dumped the peanuts and raisins and pretzels and M&Ms and Goldfish crackers. Ryan was dancing around the kitchen in his red basketball shorts, mismatched tube socks pulled halfway up his shins, and an orange T-shirt with a baby blue triceratops on it. The shirt was from a ski trip he and I took together with our youth group three years prior. I had the same shirt in a size smaller, and we had labeled the tags with our names in case they got mixed up in the laundry.

We were giddy in anticipation of our trip, happy to be together again at home, surrounded by an infinite supply of snacks. Ryan looked at the overflowing bowl of trail mix and said, *How am I supposed to stir this?* laughing at the absurd quantity. I pulled the next-size bowl out from a cupboard below the counter and said, *Try this*, turning the bowl upside down and fitting it over the other one, then nodding for him to shake it. Pretzels and Goldfish and M&Ms flew out the sides of my metallic dome, and Maggie the dog came running into the kitchen, wagging her tail and cleaning up our mess.

Looking back, this anticipatory moment, making trail mix, was the best of the entire trip. We were full of expectation and a sense of adventure, elated at our own independence, at the opportunity to bring a pipe dream to fruition. We saw ourselves as young and invincible and going to Maine, a place neither of us had ever been, to hike a trail steeped in mystery and tradition.

Somewhere off stage, our dad sulked in a room with all the lights off, already angry for all the ways his illness had excluded him.

* * *

Ryan and I only overlapped one year of high school, when our dad had had his first surgery. He was in ninth grade, and I was in twelfth. At our school, freshmen were kept in a separate building on the same campus, a solution to overcrowding. School started at seven thirty and mornings were dark on the western reaches of the Eastern Time Zone, the lake covered in a blanket of fog that spread off the water and onto the roads between our house and school. Each morning, he'd climb in the passenger's seat of my truck, and we'd drive. He and I said little to each other those mornings, but it didn't matter. We had spent the last fourteen years together, had lived between the same walls of that house on the lake, had seen the same landscapes—all that green blurring outside the back seat windows of our mom's minivan—had been poised on the brink of adulthood with the same predicament: our dad in a rehab facility but with no diagnosis. Like when we'd been kids, playing chicken in the pool, his body an extension of my own.

When I'd pull into the drop-off lane in front of the freshmen building, he would unbuckle his seatbelt, swing his backpack over one shoulder. *Have a good day*, I'd say. *You too*, he'd say.

* * *

We made it four and a half days on the AT. It was early June and forty-some degrees—maybe fifty—during the day, dipping to almost freezing at night, raining nonstop. At all times, we could see our breath condensing into fog. The forest was dark and dense, tall loping cedars, ferns unfurling onto the trail, bog crossings every mile or so made out of logs sliced lengthwise down the middle. We alternated between looking up to make sure we were following the white blazes and watching our feet because the trail was littered with moose shit.

Our parents had driven us to the trailhead, a four-day drive round trip for them between treatments. Our first day on the trail, Ryan and I made it seven miles, as far as the first big creek crossing, and there was an obvious campsite with a corresponding name on our map, so we pitched our tent on the sodden black earth, peeled off our rain gear, and climbed inside. The tent was tiny, borrowed from the outdoors club at my college, meant for two people, I'm sure, but Ryan, laid flat, was longer than the tent's footprint, and our two mummy bags laid side by side rubbed against the tent's walls, encouraging the already soaked nylon to leak. We decided to lay head-to-toe, so we could sort of prop our legs on top of the other person's torso and not spend the whole night breathing down each other's necks.

By day two, my brother and I had run out of things to say to each other. We climbed and climbed in silence, gaining a thousand feet in elevation. The evergreen trees turned stubby and warped, orange and yellow lichen on every surface of rock. At the top of Spaulding Mountain, we were in a cloud. Ryan had stopped to eat every thirty minutes or so. He ate beef jerky and granola bars and trail mix and, on the descent off that cloud-covered mountain—soaked and shivering, wearing all the clothes he brought—he stopped to make oatmeal, using our small stove to boil water right there in the middle of the trail. We saw no other hikers the whole four days we were out. Everyone else was savvy enough to know June was a miserable time to be in the mountains in Maine.

Our second night, we holed up in a three-walled lean-to, rain blowing in. The floor was made of fifty or so baseball bat–width tree trunks fastened together, and neither of us brought sleeping pads, thinking they were a frivolous comfort, excess weight. To pass the time, Ryan boiled water for tea, boiled water for dinner, boiled water for oatmeal. He never stopped eating. At one point in the night the rain turned to snow, and my spirits lifted a little, loving the quiet dampening and the way the snow brightened an otherwise dark and muddy place. Ryan saved his M&Ms out of our trail mix, dumped them into my origami bowl, said, *Here. Eat something.*

There was a lot I didn't say to him on that trip. I was nursing the secret of a night I spent sharing a bed with Jessie, both of us braless and kissing, and the secret ate at me long after Ryan fell asleep each night. Jessie and I had been drunk on tequila, and in the morning she'd said it was a mistake, but I kept on playing the night over and over in my head. Even two months after, shivering in a sleeping bag in the soggiest of Maine's backcountry, I was thinking only of her, the way her arms folded around me, the way she whispered, *This feels more right than anything else*, and later, *You're going to be okay*, in reference to the conversation we were always halfway in the middle of about my dad's illness. I go back now to the journal I kept on that trip with Ryan, and I read each entry and hear the secret in every cryptic line, not even willing to let myself name it in the privacy of my own journal. I thought constantly of her those four days on the AT.

Cold and homesick inside my thin sleeping bag, I decided it was useless to complain. It had been my idea to come here, and whatever the miserable weather, we were in it together. I stuffed all of my layers into the bag with me, then stuffed my mummified feet inside my pack, cinching the mouth somewhere above my knees. I laid awake with insomnia, listening to the rain clicking against the corrugated tin roof.

On the third day there was fog over everything. We lost the trail somehow in a meadow. We had been following the white blazes marking the AT before being spat out into the blaze-less meadow, and the meadow had maybe ten trails spoking through it, none of which seemed to lead back to an opening in the forest with the obvious white blazes on every other tree. I thought then of wagon wheel tag we used to play in the snow at the bus stop. And about how we'd laughed at our mom's worry about us getting lost, told her that it would be impossible to lose the trail because it was so well marked.

Somewhere in the urgency of trying to get found, I let the idea of canceling the whole four-week ordeal take hold in my mind. For the entirety of the two days prior, I had been expending so much energy banning that thought from my mind, that when I let it seep in, it grew instantly intoxicating, too attractive. A year later, my therapist, in a facsimile of kindness, would explain my penchant for latching on hard to this kind of defeatist ideation as a byproduct of having an overactive imagination, of being an artist. As a cross-country runner in high school and college, I had cultivated an unarticulated theory about my mind as a feeble, bendable thing. Since I was a kid, I had been told I had a high pain threshold, was a fighter, full of grit, and in my burgeoning adulthood, I wanted those things to still be true. Instead, I saw myself as soft, full of self-doubt.

When Ryan and I eventually found the trail by skirting the perimeter of the meadow, we stopped so he could eat, and I worked up the courage to say, *Hey, Ry, I think I want to go home*. He looked at me from under the hood of his raincoat, rain dripping off the brim, and said, *Really?* And I said, *Yeah*. And he said, *Okay*.

He was a master negotiator. Under different circumstances, he might have tried to persuade me otherwise. But I think he sensed a deep sadness in me, one that was new to him and one he knew he couldn't console out of me, that I had made up my mind.

* * *

Once, when Ryan was nine, sleeping with his blanket and his cobra puppet, Pokémon cards spread on the floor, he woke up in the night and saw my empty bed. I was in middle school, at a sleepover, but in his grogginess, he didn't remember. He ran into our parents' room across the hall, screaming, *Where's Cara? Where's Cara?* Inconsolable. Refusing to believe I was at a friend's, coming back.

* * *

When the trail intersected with the nearest road a day and a half later, someone else's mom picked us up. She had been grocery shopping in the next town over for her son's graduation party. She looked into her rearview mirror at Ryan and then turned to me and asked, *What do you think you're doing out so early in the season?* I was riding shotgun, was supposed to be the explainer, but I said nothing.

We stayed that night in a hostel in Rangeley, used the landline to call home. My resolve broke the moment my dad's voice came on, and he handed the phone to my mom, his deference a new, permanent status quo following his first surgery.

In the morning we paid the host to drive us 130 miles to Portland to catch a Greyhound back to Michigan. It was sunny at the Greyhound station, and we sat outside on a picnic table and waited for our bus. The Greyhound route went south to New York City and then west through Pittsburgh and Cleveland and Toledo and Detroit and, finally, to Grand Rapids. The whole trip took us three days. We stared at each other, bleary-eyed and sullen, in the New York City bus depot while we waited for our next bus. It was almost midnight. I bought two Big Macs and Cokes from the McDonald's next to our gate, because I was sorry and full of chagrin and because to hold a warm paper bag from McDonald's and a cup with a straw was to feel almost human, enlivened by that pump of endorphins a Happy Meal gives, and because Ryan hadn't talked to me since we'd left Rangeley, and I thought buying him food might be a way of apologizing. When our bus finally came, he boarded behind me, sat with someone else.

There was a wreck on the interstate somewhere in Pennsylvania, and our bus was stopped for nearly ten hours. I thought about how Ryan had given up his summer job opportunity to go on this trip, that he'd told all his friends that he'd be gone for half the summer, and how he would have to say to his girlfriend, *I know I said I was going to be gone for a month, but here I am.* I wondered if he would tell her that it rained and rained, that we couldn't sleep because it was freezing, that we didn't bring the right gear, didn't research the area well enough to know not to go this early in June, or if he would say simply, *Cara got homesick.*

I thought about how we hadn't retrieved any of our care packages. Mostly, I thought about what it was that broke inside me. In those four days, Ryan and I never once talked about what was happening to our dad, though I know it weighed hugely on both of us as we tromped through the rain with nothing to do but think, both of us alone inside our own heads. In all reality, we had likely grown apart in the three years I'd been away at college, both of us learning to cope with the impending loss of our family as we knew it in isolation, independent from each other. A lot had changed about my identity since I'd last lived at home, which I am sure was true for my brother as well, but I felt sheepish revealing those changes to him. I was the one who had encouraged him to come to youth group with me, who had encouraged him to play keyboard in the worship band, and now I was ashamed of who I had been in high school, straightlaced and pious, but too embarrassed to acknowledge that openly. I knew he had always looked up to me, never took anything I said lightly. Most of all, I worried I had no idea who I was or what I stood for anymore, and that he would see me as a chameleon.

On that soggy dark stretch of trail in Maine and on that three-day Greyhound bus, it felt like, despite everything we had in common, we were left alone inside our own heads, inside our own skin, living separately, and there was nothing I could do to stop myself from hurting him. Only later, with Ada, would I come to understand that growing up with a brother taught me something essential about the contract of companionship: that our guaranteed alliance has little value unless it is in spite of, in fact only because of, each of our capacities to be miserable company sometimes.

12

The day my dad had his first seizure, I was babysitting. It was November 2003, a school night, too wet for the four kids to play soccer out on the front lawn as we had done every other Thursday, and so I put on *Lilo and Stitch* and promised popcorn to everyone. The microwave was on high when I got the call from my mom, and I let the popcorn burn, the smell hanging in that huge house for days.

My mom had received a call from an EMT, who had found her number in my dad's phone. He had had a seizure while driving, there had been an accident, he drove his car into the median of a four-lane expressway, tearing up grass in his wake. He was conscious. She told me they had asked him who Jeanne was, and he said, *Oh, she's my girlfriend.*

I didn't want to listen.

When I hung up the phone, I took the burned popcorn out to the garbage bin in the garage, put another one in the microwave, and settled in on the couch. The youngest of the children scooted down the L-shaped leather couch in her pink pajamas to sit on my lap.

The neurologist in Grand Rapids who took on my dad's case was someone we knew from hockey. His son had played with Ryan for a couple years, and in this, we all felt the process a bit more human, that behind those black-and-white brain scans that revealed something ghosting the right temporal lobe of my dad's brain was a man who had a son who played hockey, a man who ran the clock for all those games, who tied skates in the locker room for any kid who wanted them tighter, and none of us knew how this was happening, just that it was.

In December our dad had his first surgery in the neurosurgery center at Henry Ford Hospital in Detroit. When Ryan and I went to see him in the pre-op room, we saw a man who had been healthy and vital, a long-distance runner, now bare-chested and covered in electrodes, part of his hair shaven away, the pale scalp covered in blue pen marks, directions for the incision. Within seconds, Ryan's knees buckled and his head hit a metal examination table on his way to the floor. A nurse called down to the ER, said she was sending down a boy on a stretcher who had fainted up in neurosurgery. My mom sent me down with him. *He'll be okay*, she said. *Divide and conquer.* They took his blood pressure, gave him some ice, and sent us back upstairs.

A binary—try surgery or do nothing—had been our only options. My dad's doctors said something about wanting to biopsy the mass from multiple sides and that it needed to come out anyway. In the era of contemporary science, sometimes all our state-of-the-art medical interventions dead-end into simple causal conditionals—if *x*, then *y*. To be given the so-called choice between doing something—surgery—and doing nothing was to be given a false sense of autonomy. Doing nothing was never a real choice any of us even considered. From the day of his first seizure, we'd sprung into inaction, making no decisions, just nodding and signing papers. No one was saying anything to us, no hypotheses for discussion. It's not a tumor, technically, until biopsied; not epilepsy, because you can see the thing right there on the brain scan; not a fluke, onetime seizure that lots of young adults have, mostly males. We waited.

Looking back now, I think we were quick to assume cancer because of my illness, poised as we were on the brink of its return. A different family might have taken the doctors' words at face value—the *suspicious mass of cells* they saw on my dad's brain scan could be anything, really. But we were already accustomed to the purgatory of cancer, waiting for news, a routine rendered trite by its familiarity.

I think having gone through cancer once already made all of us more frightened. Alfred Hitchcock said, "There is no terror in the bang of a gun, only in the anticipation of it." We knew, or at least thought we did, what we were in for if the biopsy came back malignant.

During some operation of my dad's—I have since lost track of which one—I sat with my grandma, watching her knitting needles draw spirals backward and forward in the air, their quiet clicking a soothing sound. Hours spent like this, and I grew frustrated with the intermediate sudoku puzzles in my fifty-cent workbook from the gift shop, handed it to my brother, sitting silently with his headphones plugged into his MP3 player. He understood he would give me three more numbers, then hand it back. My grandpa paced the halls; my mom asked every nurse she could find if they knew anything. Eventually, my grandma put away her knitting and asked me to teach her that Japanese puzzle. I tore pages from the easy section, fished another mechanical pencil out of my backpack, and taught her that game of logical reasoning, an exercise in winnowing down all the possibilities to one sure truth.

* * *

Waiting for a diagnosis was worse for my mom because she was an insider. She understood the gravity of the situation not because of sensationalized media representations of terminal cancers, not because she'd Googled "brain tumor" in the past month and a half, thinking this was a part of her world now, that she might as well study up, but because she understood the behaviors of human cells at the molecular level and because she knew pathology. She'd made a career out of teaching college students to diagnose what they could see through a microscope.

The week of Ruth Bader Ginsberg's death, I read an interview she did with NPR nine years after her husband, Marty, died. She recounted that he'd watched over her like a hawk during her previous bouts with cancer, and once, he'd yanked a needle out of her arm when she was receiving a blood transfusion that had gone wrong—a mismatch of some antigen. I recognized something of my mom's vigilance in Marty in this story. I felt validated reading that mistakes were all too common and that quality medical care is a rarity, that medical personnel assume the family in the room won't know the difference. This was my mom's

144

second time around, and she'd had it with doctors' and nurses' sterile compassion, their practiced restraint in updating patients and caregivers, keeping her in the dark about their hunches and suspicions.

In an email exchange with my dad's neurosurgeon directly following his release from Henry Ford Hospital after his first surgery, she adopted a tone of nonchalance, a thin veil we all stood behind, as if this was our new state of normal, as if we were taking it all in stride. When he came out of surgery, he didn't recognize any of our faces, couldn't remember who was president, couldn't control the strength of his own grasp, holding our hands like vice grips, as if, perhaps, it might help him remember. We were all scared shitless.

From: Jeanne
Sent: Thursday, January 01, 2004 5:17 PM
To: abcd@neuro.hfh.edu
Subject: Rick

Dr. E—,

Just a quick message to let you know that Rick is doing well today and we are scheduled to check him into Mary Free Bed Hospital here in Grand Rapids tomorrow morning for rehabilitation. We had an uneventful night despite his lack of good mobility. Today he is camping out on the sofa watching football. We had a flurry of craziness checking out of HFH yesterday . . . mostly from the standpoint of Mary Free Bed being upset at us for taking Rick home and the ramifications of that to his admission to Mary Free Bed Hospital in not being direct from HFH. The insurance company seems ok with it at this point but it could become an issue or may be a problem in the future. We may need some type of information or statement from you to address this as far as why direct admission was not done and may know more about that after

145

arrival at Mary Free Bed tomorrow . . . just wanted you to
have the "heads up" so to speak on it.

I do have one question also on Rick's med schedule . . .
the discharge information said that he is to take 200mg of the
carbamazepine a day and that is lower by 400mg/day than what
he was taking upon admission and definitely less anti-seizure
medication that he was receiving in the hospital, so I wanted
to make sure we were ok with that dose. Thanks again for your
expertise and medical care. We hope that you had a Happy
New Year's and that you didn't have to work. Jeanne

I was seventeen at the time and embarrassed by my mom's insistence that the rules did not apply to our family. Looking back now, I realize that modern health care is the first-born golden child of senseless bureaucratic and corporate policies. Every hospital and clinic had lists upon lists of codes—you must transfer directly from inpatient to physical therapy rehab facility, you must stay inpatient forty-eight hours after brain surgery to be monitored, the patient must be awake and cognizant for the doctor to talk to you—and in my mom's eyes those rules existed to protect hospitals from lawsuits, not to actually provide humane, holistic care. Wherever my mom could monitor and administer treatment herself, she did, and whenever we could cut corners on the number of days in a hospital room, we did.

Five days passed before the doctor emailed her back. It was the holidays after all. And then this:

FROM: <abcd@neuro.hfh.edu>
SENT: Monday, January 05, 2004 7:29 AM
To: Jeanne
SUBJECT: Re: Rick

Hello, Jeanne. Thank you for the update. I'd have Rick taking
Tegretol XR 200 mg twice a day for the time being and have
Tim adjust it afterward in clinic if he feels he needs to. I'm

146

happy it turned out alright and hope the insurance issue doesn't turn out to be much of a hassle. We can certainly support you from the standpoint of the nonavailability of physical therapy in the hospital over the holiday and challenge them to see reason. I'll be in touch with you soon after the formal results are made known to me. I left Tim a second message regarding the preliminary path results. Happy New Year to you both.

My dad had been in the rehab hospital, Mary Free Bed, for four days at this point, my mom at his bedside, her laptop splayed open, working. It took her thirty-three minutes to read his email and respond with this:

FROM: Jeanne
SENT: Monday, January 05, 2004 8:02 AM
To: abcd@neuro.hfh.edu
SUBJECT: Re: Rick

Dr. E—,

Thanks for getting back to me about the tegretol, I will let Mary Free Bed staff know and have them increase his dosage. I also have a question about the post surgical MRI findings. I know that you assured us that we are fine without further surgery with what was already resectioned but I am nervous about the remaining seizure focus signal and also the remaining presence of some "tumor" tissue and want to know what that means if you can tell as far as prognosis and etc. He also has been at MFB for three days and still is not walking on his own without help and is very labored in this effort . . . is this what you expect to see after this surgery? He is still being evaluated and I have no formal reports from the staff there yet and I am very concerned about recovery. Thanks, Jeanne

147

The surgery had happened more than seven days prior, and still, we knew nothing. They had my dad's cells somewhere in a lab, and it was someone's job to look at them and place them in a category. Meanwhile, my dad still couldn't walk, not out of physical weakness, but because his brain couldn't tell his legs how to hold his body upright. Ten minutes after she sent that email, she got this reply:

FROM: <abcd@neuro.hfh.edu>
SENT: Monday, January 05, 2004 8:12 AM
To: Jeanne
SUBJECT: Re: Rick

The presence of seizure activity must be judged by EEG. The presence of a signal change on an MRI will not dictate this. Once a diagnosis is made, we can perhaps judge whether the signal itself will even remain.

I'd give Rick more time regarding his mobility. The postop MRI didn't indicate any unusual features that would prevent him from making a good recovery.

Later that week, Tim, the hockey dad neurologist, came to check on my dad and confirmed that my dad had had a stroke during surgery. *No shit*, my mom said. *And all this week, the staff here have been telling me to give him more time, like my expectations for recovery were unrealistic.* She had barely slept, had eaten little, refused to leave the rehab facility. The nurses asked my dad to squeeze his hand around a quarter, placing it in the center of his palm, but once he curled his fingers around it, he couldn't remember what a quarter was, couldn't remember what they'd asked him to hold, the worst possible scenario manifest.

Ryan and I made ourselves scarce, went to visit our parents at Mary Free Bed only twice. Our grandparents were staying with us while my dad relearned to walk, to write his name, to send an email. My grandpa helped me make a three-foot-tall trebuchet for a project for my physics class, teaching me the angles to cut each edge. My grandma sewed costumes for *Joseph and the Amazing Technicolor Dreamcoat*, the high school musical that year. Ryan was cast as Benjamin, the youngest of the brothers, blameless.

On opening night, moms in the greenroom outlined his eyes with a fat, black eye pencil. They smeared dark foundation on his face and chest where his costume gaped. He was fourteen, the furrow in his brow deepening as puberty took hold.

A week after Tim had told us it was obvious he'd had a stroke during surgery, the pathology came back. Benign.

* * *

In high school I learned that the brain is divided into hemispheres, separated by the corpus callosum, that whatever happens on the left side of the brain affects the right side of the body and vice versa. My dad's first surgery removed part of the hippocampus and amygdala from the right side, the parts of the brain that control facial recognition, emotional responses, spatial orientation, and the formation of new memories about experienced events. The theory is since your brain has two hippocampi and amygdalae, one in each hemisphere, the other side would compensate for what was lost or damaged—the same theory the doctors proposed would happen for my one remaining ovary. But in actuality, this compensation never happened. Not for him. He walked with a limp forever after that, weakest on his left side because of the inversion. And he could never again fully recognize faces, even of people he'd known for years, lost in the haze of knowing he should know, pretending to know. A man who had once coded his world based on who drove which boat on the lake, a man who knew what kind of engine was inside every car in the neighborhood, who kept track of his friends based on the cars they drove, could no longer place Dave Clark with red MasterCraft or Ed Hanson with Jeep Grand Cherokee. For six years, he thought California was east and New York was west, argued ceaselessly with my mom about directions, sitting in the passenger's seat of cars he was no longer allowed to drive.

Perhaps the biggest loss was his ability to register emotions

149

appropriately. Before the surgery, he had had high highs and low lows in accordance to the stimuli, but after, there was no differentiation. Every stimulus evoked the same response. He was flat, unmoved. With time, he learned to base his emotional responses on the responses of others, but to rid a person of his freedom to react is to scrape from him that which makes him alive, autonomous.

The changes were heartbreaking in their subtlety. For my first two years of college, he didn't even have a terminal diagnosis, just a suspicious shadow on a brain scan, seizure activity that wasn't epilepsy, and a personality altered by surgery and stroke. But the personality differences were inconsistent. In many ways he continued to be the same: same body, same likes and dislikes, same daily routines, same positional identity within our family as Dad. By age forty-six, it seems that so much of how we move through the world and interact with those we are closest to has become rote. It was hard for me to categorize him in my mind as a wholly different person when the visible shell of who he was remained the same. It was hard for me to empathize with what he must have been going through himself, internally. Even now I have no idea to what extent he was aware that who he was had fundamentally shifted. Did he have any concept of before surgery versus after? Did he recognize his own mind as murky, his own flattened affect, his mental fumbling through the Rolodex of contacts trying to place people's faces, even the faces of his own family? Was he afraid?

* * *

On a road trip with Ada and Lucia across the shrub-steppe of eastern Washington, driving through Grand Coulee, a sixty-mile-long, one-thousand-foot-deep ancient riverbed that formed when the ice dam on a glaciated Missoula Lake broke some thirteen thousand years ago. We stopped off at the Dry Falls overlook where Lucia read all the signs. She stood next to me on the rim, holding my hand, staring below us at the monochrome of basalt and rabbitbrush, an aqua-teal lake tucked into that horseshoe bend. She said, *Where's the waterfall?* I explained the flood to her as a dynamic event, a wall of water moving at sixty miles an hour, a lake the size of Lake Erie in western Montana draining across the state of Washington in the span of a day, carving its own path as it flowed.

Later that day, I wondered aloud to no one in particular, *What's the difference between a canyon and a coulee?* Lucia, from the back seat, chimed in, *A coulee is a giant valley made from the erosion of a flood.* Like a sudden, surprise loss, I thought then, a lifetime's worth of debris breaking behind a dam, razing everything in its path in its search of that sea of grief. Then, a slow loss must be like a canyon. The water still flows there, still scoring away at bedrock, that continuous ribbon of light hidden beneath reeds and willows, nearly invisible inside an amphitheater of air, the emptiness between rock walls, a quiet, incessant grief.

It wasn't until ten years after my dad's death that I first heard of the concept of "ambiguous loss." Pauline Boss coined the term in the 1970s while interviewing the wives of pilots who went missing in action in Vietnam. She went on to apply the concept to include "anticipatory grief"—the grieving for loved ones who are physically present but effectively gone. Boss is critical of our culture for teaching us to be so uncomfortable with people who are suffering, people who don't have a solution or ability to "move on," through no fault of their own. Our culture teaches us that it is undesirable to "dwell" in the negative and instead encourages us to "get over it," to focus on the positive, "good vibes only."

Learning this concept of "ambiguous loss" was validating. I had a student in a composition course I was teaching who, after failing the first two weeks of reading quizzes, came to my office hours. He described a lifelong struggle with reading and writing, and I began to suspect he might have some type of dyslexia. I asked if he had ever been tested, and he said he'd never heard of the condition. I referred him to someone at the Center for Students with Disabilities. Two weeks went by, and he wasn't in class, didn't respond to any of my emails. Then, halfway through the quarter, he came by my office hours again, dressed impeccably as a jock, the brim of his black baseball cap perfectly rounded in the shape of his hand.

He said he was dropping out for the quarter but that he wanted to thank me for giving him a word to name what his father had told him was just his own stupidity. That he didn't know there were other people like him who struggled with reading and writing. I thought then about how language is a kind of salve that rescues us from our propensity for feeling singular and alone in the same way that having a diagnosis, even when it's not good news, is a kind of mercy.

In those first two years, before my dad's diagnosis, I don't think I ever let myself call what I felt about my dad's illness "mourning." I doubt I even called it "illness." Most of all I felt ashamed for preferring the "before" to the "after." How could a child tell their parent that they liked them better before they had a stroke? I felt I should not be grieving for someone who was still very much alive, that, for his dignity's sake, I needed to pretend as if nothing had shifted. I didn't want my dad to be able to tell I had an ambient sense of loss and impending dread that was related existentially to him.

He must have known we were all worried. We were a family well versed in the rhetoric of worry. But some familial code, years ago, had decreed that naming our worries aloud to each other would be a bad omen. Of course we were worried. But what good would it do any of us to talk about it? The only way any of us knew how to quell worry was to try to resolve the underlying cause, and we couldn't do that now. I would spend the last six years of his life worrying, let that worry stand between me and the dad he might have been to me in my early twenties. Whatever knowledge my dad had of my fears, he kept to himself.

* * *

In a home video labeled "Cara's 2nd Birthday," my dad comes back from the dead wearing an alligator puppet on his right hand. He is talking to me through the alligator hand about my cake. The cake is a white bunny, in honor of my favorite stuffed animal, and is mounted on a piece of plywood covered in tinfoil, frosted with

152

coconut. My mom is holding the camcorder and snipping black licorice for whiskers. She hands me a piece of the candy. My dad sets me on the counter next to the bunny cake and asks me what the cake is for, and I keep telling him, *Bunny*, and pointing to the cake. Eventually he tries a different angle: *Where's the bunny's ears?* and I point. *Where's Cara's ears?* and I point.

It seems that my whole life can be arranged in order of what came before and what came after his first surgery, like a curtain that fell between Act I and Act II.

For two and a half years after his first surgery, we told ourselves, unconvincingly, it wasn't cancer. Then, the week I came home from my second year of college, an ambulance came to our house in the middle of the night. Ryan sprinted down the stairs, stood in my doorway, and said, *Cara, something's happening with Dad.* The paramedics were already there, shouting at me in my pj's, *Put that dog somewhere.* How did I sleep through their arrival? My dad was in bed in only his boxers, smacking his lips, opening and closing his left hand like a claw.

Ryan and I watched in horror, as if our dad had turned into a monster.

Two months later, he had another stroke suntanning out on the deck. Every phone in the house had a dead battery from spending too long out of its cradle. I was away, working at a summer camp, and Ryan was at a friend's house. My mom ran across the backyard to the neighbors, sitting in their bikinis and board shorts down by the water, and asked to use their phone. She dialed 911, but the neighbor had already loaded my dad into the back seat of his car, and they rushed to the emergency room, all of them wearing bathing suits and smelling of suntan oil.

I don't know now if any of us, between November 2003 and July 2006, ever fully believed in the word "benign" or the word "cyst" or the word "lesion." All I know is that brain tumors are notorious for having heterogeneous cells, that you can take a biopsy from one part of the tumor and see nothing but normal healthy cells, dividing at their normal rate, innocuous; and you can biopsy it again and

153

see aggressive cell division, stage 4, terminal. In 2006, this was the surgeon's explanation.

In the six years my dad was sick, I often felt that I was playing an infinite game of Concentration, flipping over card after card in my mind, searching for rhyming action, for completion. I think I reasoned then that our expecting the worst was a kind of superstitious way to ward off a diagnosis, that I still believed cancer only happened when you least expected it. But looking back now, I think our wanting to be right went beyond just trying to preempt bad news. A part of us still believed that even though we were not fully in control, there was still some logical string of cause and effect that we might be able to grab ahold of and, hand over hand, feel our way back to safety.

* * *

After the second stroke in July 2006, my dad would have a second brain surgery in Detroit, and Ryan and I would stay a week in the apartments attached to the hospital, each of us with only one change of clothes, trading back and forth. When he was eventually—finally—diagnosed, he would qualify for a clinical trial, which required that he travel twice a week to Detroit for treatment, a three-hour drive each way from our house on the lake, and my mom would rearrange her teaching schedule to be able to take him. I would return to college in Ohio, taking electives with names like Anthropology and Activism and History of Contemporary Africa. Ryan would graduate from high school that year, salutatorian of his class.

For the duration of my dad's illness, my mom juggled medications and their side effects. The anti-seizure meds made him moody, depressed, and so she tried to keep him on the lowest possible dosage while still controlling the seizures. My mom kept meticulous records of all the seizures he had, hypothesizing their cause—a missed med, fatigue from lack of sleep, too much stress at work—pointing at anything she could that wouldn't mean the tumor had returned. He'd had a grand mal the day he drove his

154

Corvette into the median and another the night when the EMTs showed up, but he also had smaller seizures, often when his mind was most idle, in the night or while on the couch, watching TV.

We often knew when a seizure was coming. Sometimes he'd say something that didn't make sense, start smacking his lips, and then his left hand would turn into a claw, opening and closing involuntarily, like a puppet, trying to remember what it had to say. The seizures stripped him of his dignity, left him exhausted, confused, sitting in a puddle of his own piss.

Ryan used to race in sprint triathlons when he was in high school. My dad wasn't one to miss any of his kids' sporting events, so on the day of one of his triathlons, when my mom woke up with a migraine and said she couldn't go, I said I'd drive the hour and a half down to Three Rivers for the race. At seventeen, Ryan was six feet two and 110 pounds. He kept an electric razor next to his toothbrush in the bathroom now, though I rarely knew him to use it. I knew it had been my mom who taught him to shave, just as she had taught me, and that Ryan resented my dad for his absenteeism. Ryan had seen so many more of his changes since the surgery than I ever would, and on the day of the race, he opted to ride with his friend's parents, his bike strapped onto the rack on the back of their SUV. My dad had loved the race for its location, on the waterfront of another inland lake, ski boats resting in their Shore-Mate boat lifts at the end of nearly every dock, and because he'd handed down his 1980 silver Nishiki to my brother when he took up the sport.

The triathlon started with the half-mile swim—each swimmer released in heats on that sandy beach to swim out to a giant orange buoy and back. Ryan emerged from the water, waterlogged and dripping. His bare feet padded along the asphalt to the transition area, where he tossed us his swim cap and goggles, shoved his wet feet into mismatched cotton socks and then running shoes stained green from mowing the lawn, and hopped onto his bike. *Go catch Andrew*, my dad said, and Ryan smirked at us, peddling away.

After the race, we sat at the water's edge, eating bagels and cream cheese, then walked back to our cars parked in a field. Ryan said he wanted to ride home with his bike, save him a trip later, and so my dad and I drove the hour and a half home, the country music station on low.

Somewhere between Kalamazoo and Plainwell, my dad fell asleep. Commuting from college in Ohio a few times each semester, I had learned to love driving. This afternoon, I set the cruise to seventy-five, held my hands at ten and two on the steering wheel like my dad had taught me. The fields of soybeans and corn, high enough for picking, were a blur out the window. In the seat beside me, my dad looked frail. The anti-seizure meds had caused him to gain weight, but his cheeks were still hollow. His skin didn't hold much of a pigment anymore, despite it being summer, and the creases around his eyes were deeper than I'd ever seen them before—as if Eyes of Horus had been painted on his face in a last-ditch effort to bring him good fortune and good health.

Only minutes after he'd fallen asleep, he started smacking his lips, and, for a brief second, I didn't know what the sound was. I had been annoyed with him for months—the drugs had made him slovenly, a loud snorer, drool constantly on the left side of his chin. I was angry that so much had changed without my being there to witness it gradually, to get used to it. I had gone away to college six months after his first surgery, then returned home for Thanksgiving, and my dad looked like an old man, someone I didn't recognize. Now, in the car, it took me a moment to realize—he was having a seizure. I looked straight ahead, not wanting to witness, worrying I might get in a wreck. I considered for a brief second pulling off to the shoulder, but there were cars as far as I could see behind me, and the shoulder looked soft, a spray of gravel and then grass. *Dad*, I said, *Dad! You're having a seizure. Dad.* But he didn't respond. My mind was already warping itself around the event, normalizing it. I did nothing, kept the cruise control on, kept the car in the slow lane, blinking and checking my blind spot for every truck I passed. A few minutes later, he stopped seizing, wiped the drool from his face, and looked at me, bewildered. I said nothing. We had no change of clothes, and there was no use stopping. I just kept driving, pretending he was asleep. At home, I told my mom, sheepish, that he'd had a seizure on the way home, knowing this news would cause her to worry more, then I wiped down the seat in her car with bleach.

* * *

In the three months before he died, he seemed to exist in a perpetual seizure state, as if the line between lucid and seizing were a false dichotomy, as if we were all just marionettes strung up, flinching and jerking in accordance with firing neurons.

In the waiting room of the infusion center where he was still getting chemo up until a month before he died, there was a floor-to-ceiling water feature trickling over a slate-colored piece of granite, the water circulating through the system in an endless loop.

The nurse checking us in asked for my dad's birthdate, and I rattled it off as though they were the only numbers I'd ever memorized: May 11, 1957. While the chemo dripped, we played backgammon, and everything was the same, as if no time had passed, as if I were still seven, still the sick one, and we were going to go on forever like this, being dad and daughter, unstoppable.

13

On break from college, I worked for two seasons at a summer camp on a rural inland lake in West Michigan. Two weeks prior to starting my first summer at the camp, my dad had a grand mal seizure. It was his second grand mal, but the first I'd witnessed. Watching him that night felt like a bad omen. The paramedics stomped around the house in their work boots, filling out paperwork, monitoring his breathing, and then they left, and the house was suddenly quiet in their absence. I'd read and reread the passage about seizures in the American Red Cross handbook I'd been given a month earlier for my lifeguarding class, but those manuals were written for rescuers treating anonymous strangers. Nothing in that lifeguarding book gave any advice on how to be a teenage daughter watching her dad succumb to disease. I knew something terrible was taking hold inside his body, and I knew whatever it was, I didn't want to be there to watch.

Camp was a place designed to manufacture experience as metaphor. Jump off a wooden platform twenty feet in the air, strapped into a harness attached to a pulley, and you're bound to learn something about bravery, about expanding your comfort zone. Stand in a circle clasping the sweaty hands of two of your bunkmates you hardly even know—all twenty-four of your arms tangled in a knot—then figure out how to untangle yourselves—a task that takes patience and leadership and cooperation, all the skills teachers spend months trying to foster in classrooms. Friendships forged and then broken and then mended all in the span of a day.

The camp was vaguely Presbyterian in its affiliation, but to me, camp was a place run by bearded and breasted oversized white children dressed androgynously in overalls, worshipping John Denver. Situated on the precipice of my own dwindling childhood, camp appealed to my Midwestern beach bum aesthetic—holey jeans, tie-dye T-shirts, suntanned and makeup-less—all of it set against a *My*

158

Side of the Mountain–esque survival-in-nature backdrop. After a year of college, camp was refreshing to me for its utter lack of pretense.

On our campers' first night, after we'd tossed them all into the lake to test their swimming ability and then fed them piles of homemade pizza, they gathered in the field behind the arts and crafts building to play a game called Potato Round Up. Each member of staff wielded a halved potato carved like a woodblock stamp—a heart, a star, a tree—and a paper bowl full of tempera paint, chasing kids in their throwaway clothes, packed dutifully by parents who had read the packing list. Like a messier version of tag, the game was chaotic and loud. Here, stamp a kid shrieking with either joy or disgust at the orange paint in her pigtails; here, stamp another kid refusing to run, standing with his arms outstretched in the center of all that stained grass, *Get me, get me.*

I'd come straight from two semesters of reading Nabokov and Sartre and Derrida, nursing a perpetual state of gloom and self-pity about my dad's unstable health. Potato Round Up, to me, rewrote the rules of the world in which we lived, creating a place where adults behaved like children, and making a pointless mess was sanctioned. Afterward, I'd take a turn as lifeguard, standing in the center of the H-dock, looping the red guard tube strap over my head and shoulder, puffed up with importance and responsibility at wearing this sash, while the rest of staff bathed communally in the lake, wearing all their clothes. Long streaks of yellow and red and green paint skimmed to the surface of the swim area, roiling with the froth of all their wriggling bodies. Camp was a place wholly walled off from the outer world, a place where we, the staff, collectively created a community to be as we wished it were. I found comfort in the rituals, the mandatory attendance each morning at the flagpole, all of us bearing witness to the early morning light glinting off the lake.

* * *

Camp came back to me in a time capsule fifteen years later. Ada, Lucia, and I were on an after-dinner walk in Ada's dad's neighborhood. The neighbors had cemented a tetherball into the sidewalk, and Lucia wanted to play.

The idea of the game is to wrap the volleyball-on-a-string all the way around the pole in a series of one-handed serves. The two opponents face off, one trying to wrap clockwise, and the other trying to wrap counterclockwise. Truly, whoever is taller has an unfair advantage. At camp, I had gone easy on my campers. The tetherball pole was cemented into the dirt behind the dining hall, and we played to pass the time if we arrived early for meals. The game was mostly good for inducing bloody noses and hurt feelings and endless hours of negotiations about the rules. But with Lucia, there was never any need for me to level the playing field. At four feet six, she outcompetes her mom and me at all sports. *You're going down*, I teased. *Oh yeah?* she smirked back at me, untangling the ball from the pole.

For a year after my dad died, I had a recurring dream that I had a baby and that my dad was alive again, his body still yellow and rigid with death, his mouth hanging open. I had believed myself impotent for so long, the idea of having a kid seemed as impossible as his reincarnation. As is so common with dreams, we get what we desire but warped. In health class in ninth grade, during sex ed, we were supposed to write one anonymous question on a slip of paper, and then our teacher would answer it. My classmates asked things like *Can you still have sex when you're on your period?* and *Can you get pregnant if you have sex on your period?* I wrote: *Are you still able to get pregnant if they take out one ovary and one fallopian tube before you hit puberty?* The teacher never read my question aloud.

Lucia punched the ball with her fist to finish the game, and the string hugged tight around the pole. *Good game*, she said, smiling.

* * *

But fifteen years before Lucia came into my life, straddling my own childhood and whatever was to come after it, I wanted, desperately, for a reprise.

The camp was situated on the eastern shore of the lake, one that closely resembled Lake Bella Vista in size and shape, except that the 1950s and 1960s cottages outlining the camp's lake were dwarves compared to the huge homes that had been built on Lake Bella Vista in the late 1990s. The camp's property butted up against national forest land, and, in the off season, camp was home to deer and coyote and black bear. Here, the old-growth deciduous forest hadn't been thinned by suburban development, and maples and poplars and birch trees pressed up against the water's edge, their trunks bowing out over the water to get the most light.

The camp had more than forty acres of wetlands, an endangered habitat in Michigan because of agricultural development and suburban sprawl, and each summer at camp, hundreds of children's footsteps pattered down wooden boardwalks. Damselflies, in their armor of iridescent greens and blues and reds, flitted over rows of cattails, and red-winged blackbirds called to each other, their distinct *chak chak chaks* folding into glottal trills above our heads. At dusk, the sounds of bullfrogs, each like a single pluck on a dampened bass, echoed out across the water.

The six days of camp were designed to give campers the chance to try a little of everything—archery, horseback riding, canoeing, arts and crafts, high ropes—and at the end of the week, there was a ceremonial campfire honoring their transition from whoever they had been before camp to who they had become while at camp. Parents often reported to us that their kid was unrecognizable to them when they came to pick them up. That a kid who'd formerly been afraid of getting dirty was suntanned and bug bitten with dried face paint caked into her hair, a duffel full of folded underwear, unused. Or a kid who had, before camp, been unable to stuff her own sleeping bag or pack her own suitcase, was somehow magically transformed into a competent, self-sufficient toothbrushing, shirt-tucking preteen.

I spent most of that summer on or in the lake. The camp had two fifteen-year-old ski boats, Ski Nautiques, parked on either side of the H-dock, and I was in charge of keeping them running. They were lightweight inboards with closed bows, flat wakes, their vinyl upholstery faded from the sun. *Ski Nautiques are the Cadillacs of ski boats*, my dad told me when I reported what I'd been driving up at camp. I drove those boats from nine to noon every day, towing kids on an old set of combo skis my dad said I could donate, the same skis he taught me to ski on. The kids were skinny and overwhelmingly white, their pale skin stretched taut over their rib cages, their hair held back in neat blonde ponytails, bowl cuts. Any of them could have been my siblings. I taught them all the skiing commands. *Thumbs up for faster, thumbs down for slower, pat your head if you want to stop, wave when you fall to tell me you're okay.* They sat quiet in the spotter's seat, wearing their life jackets, squinting into the sun, the same concentrated look on their faces that I'd had for all my childhood, dutifully reporting *Down* when the kid behind the boat would fall. And when a kid got up on skis for the first time, we'd all cheer, and I'd honk the boat's horn, passing on that swell of pride, that tug of rope coursing through arms and shoulders into the chest, the thrill of moving through air and sky and water.

On one particularly hot day, I gave each of the waterski campers a squirt gun and instructed them to only shoot each other when the boat was stopped. We were, all morning, a drifting island of shrieks and giggles. Later, after each of them had had their turn to ski, I turned off the engine in the middle of the lake and let them jump overboard to pee. *Look, Cara*, they asked, *is that an eagle?* I turned my head in the direction of their pointing, and there they were, a pair of bald eagles with a nest on the south shoreline, something none of the other campers ever saw.

We were late heading in for lunch, their swimsuits dripping, fingers pruned, closed-toe shoes on, laces untied. We stood on a bench in the front of the dining hall, everyone else halfway through their grilled cheese sandwiches, and sang a song of apology for being late, none of us sorry.

In the afternoons, the counselors had thirty minutes off during rest period, and we flocked to the staff lounge to get out of the sun and the gaze of each of our twelve sets of eyes, looking at us in awe. The staff lounge was a dark, sealed-off place, furnished with basement couches from the 1970s, the back bench seats out of the camp's two fifteen-passenger vans, and a row of cubbies where each of us kept our items of value: wallets and flip phones and packs of cigarettes and piles of handwritten notes we'd written each other, warm fuzzies. Someone had bought a case of Dr Pepper, and I split a can with the counselor in the cabin next to mine, Jayne. Jayne had blonde hair sun bleached to almost white. Standing side by side, we could have been sisters, though I stood a couple inches taller, and she parted her hair on the opposite side. For two months this was our ritual: the two of us sprawled out like siblings, legs resting on each other's arms, Jayne checking her voicemail, passing the sweating can to me, our bodies like one body, sunk into the shredded upholstery of the decomposing couch.

After dinner, we had field games—capture the flag, dodge ball, capture the counselor—willing the sun to set, then, at dusk, we corralled all the kids into the bathrooms to brush their teeth. I read to my campers something my mom had read to me, *Why Mosquitoes Buzz in People's Ears* or *Harry Potter* or E. L. Konigsburg.

* * *

When I worked at the camp in 2005 and 2006, with the exception of two new cabins in Girls' Village, the 1960s cabins remained unchanged. Each cabin was named for a tribe: Zuni, Mohawk, Arapaho, Blackfoot, Iroquois, Navajo, Mohican, Commanche, Shawnee, Chippewa, Ottawa. Before every meal, we'd stand at the flagpole on the waterfront and, when called upon, shout the name of our cabin, sending it echoing out over the lake.

The entire premise of camp was built on the egotism of colonialism—that white wealthy families are entitled to be landowners, never mind that the land is already rightfully occupied by others. The camp opened in 1937 on land that was purchased by a white man from another white man. The camp's founder had a vision of building a place for young people to enjoy their summers in a Christian setting. And that mission has essentially remained the same since its founding. Like most everywhere in what is now called North America, the land camp was built on should never have been the legal property of the seller in the first place.

That first summer I worked at camp, I spent half an hour on the shared computer in the office during one of my breaks looking up facts about Shoshone that I could share with my cabin. I was distraught by the pronunciation—the town in Idaho pronounced differently than the tribe's name—and by the fact that the Shoshone were plains people, not lake people. At age nineteen, I regarded Native culture and customs with a kind of *Last of the Mohicans* reverence. *Native Americans*, I told my campers, *spent their entire lives outside and knew how to live off the land.* And for this I respected them. Never would I have considered thinking that sentence was only a partial truth, one created by the Christian church as official American policy in order to strip Indigenous people of their human rights.

In going back now to understand reservations and land cession in Michigan, I learned that the Three Fires people, in an all-too-familiar story, agreed to sign treaties under duress due to church-sanctioned genocide. Contemporary Christianity—through its nature-reverent barefoot campfire aesthetic—co-opted the sacredness of Native traditions, when it was Christianity itself that was historically used as justification for violence against Indigenous people. And, at camp, we sanctioned this revisionist way of thinking not only in the presence of young people but also for their benefit. Like a school built on a landfill, how were we supposed to pass off vespers and friendship bracelets and the mud pit as wholesome when the very foundation undergirding our entire mythology was made up of sinister omissions and erasures?

To us, the land camp was on felt like the whole point. The place was objectively beautiful, but, more than that, it was imbued with all the laughter and galloping footsteps of the thousand-some campers who spent a week there each summer. In the same way Lake Bella Vista was sacred to me, I felt a swell of ownership about the waterfront at camp. But part of the psychological gymnastics of colonialism is that assured sense of belonging is

164

self-justified because it feels like love. For me to experience a sense of ownership for a particular place, when that place, like all places in North America, has a lineage pocked with violence, is to ignore the conquer-over-the-conquered story at the very foundation of my having come to be on that land in the first place. And that kind of self-deceit, even in the heightened state of obliviousness I was in in college, made for a heart that crumbled to ash easily.

* * *

On the Friday of week six of my first summer working at camp, I became a fire tosser. Fridays were much anticipated Family Night, where the oldest campers would swim across the lake; this was followed by a spaghetti dinner, and then talent show, and then, as a kind of graduation capstone to the entire week, what we called the Indian Campfire.

As the sun dropped low, casting a glittering orange stripe across the lake, we prepared for the campfire.

Fire tossing was a four-person, choreographed stunt performed with sawed-off wooden canoe paddles, each roughly the length of a baseball bat, the ends wrapped in burlap and soaked in diesel, lit with fire. The other three fire tossers and I had practiced with the torches unlit during the afternoon rest hour all week, and we ran through our choreography one last time under the cover of darkness. The torches smelled strongly of diesel, even though they weren't lit, sharpening the adrenaline of what we had signed ourselves up for. We stood in a perfect square, five feet across from each other, swinging the heavy bats in figure eights, each of us hearing the whoosh of flames in our imaginations.

On the deck of the dining hall, four counselors were staked out painting every camper's face, two black lines across each cheek, red dots down their noses from hairline to chin, something fierce and symmetrical. Something about donning the paint transformed their affect from silly to somber. Some campers whined for rainbows, four-leaf clovers, the University of Michigan logo, mistaking this ceremony for a school carnival, and the painters would do their best rendition, giving each camper what they wanted on this last night.

The problem, it seems to me now, with a bunch of white twenty-somethings with dreads singing elegiac John Prine songs about strip mining in Muhlenberg County in an outdoor chapel with a huge wooden cross, was that the ultimate metaphor of camp—that childhood was sacred and precious—was undercut by the emptiness of our own blanched cultural identity and our belief that we could assume the cultural rites of others. We fancied ourselves gods, acting in loco parentis in our board shorts and chocolate-milk-fueled capture-the-flag mania. And, devoid of any central pole of shared common narrative to wind ourselves around, we borrowed from everyone else's. And the very real and harrowing consequences of our theft were not felt by us.

Whatever inkling I had that what we were doing was wrong, I suppressed. I looked around at the mostly older staff I worked with, none of whom were second-guessing whether we should be painting kids' faces and telling them they're warriors, and I was complicit. I saw our cabin names and borrowed customs as just another page in the photocopy of a photocopy staff handbook, a mash-up of Shel Silverstein, Cat Stevens, ridiculous secular camp songs, and contemporary worship music. I let another counselor French braid my hair into double braids, wrapped myself in burlap in an approximation of a skirt, and had my face painted alongside the other three fire tossers, something orange and yellow around the eyes, suggestive of flames, holding still and patient with my eyes closed, the brush gentle across my cheeks.

Back in Shoshone, I urged my campers to sit silent and cross-legged in a circle on the concrete floor, the lights off, waiting for the rap at the door, the Summoner's face illuminated by torchlight, their booming voice, *Women of Shoshone, you have been summoned to a sacred ceremony. Please follow in a single file line.*

The ceremony started at the end of Boys' Village, accumulating a long line of boys from oldest to youngest, all their chests bare, counselors carrying some of the smallest boys, scared of all the torches and after-dark commotion rousing them from bed.

We headed down en masse to the lakeshore, sat on tree-trunk benches around a massive fire, the flames more than five feet in the air, recited some lines in gratitude for this Great Water, and then two senior campers, wielding bow and arrow, would light the sparklers at the ends of their arrows and shoot in unison out into the water, the sparks leaving two perfect arcs of orange across all that black, summoning the Chief of Water. And from nowhere, a faint voice sang a deep song in what I would later learn is the Muscogee Creek language, slowly getting closer, like a spirit pulled from the depths of that pitch-black lake.

The Chief of Water was just the first act, though, and at the conclusion of her speech, we heard the yipping of two human voices, then felt through our log seats and the sandy soil beneath the shaking earth as two painted horses galloped up the hill, their riders bareback and wielding torches. This was our cue to follow, and we trudged, a hundred bodies in absurd face paint, up the half-mile hill to the dark fire ring at the top, the air saturated with the smell of diesel, every camper's eyes aglow in awe.

At the top of the hill, the campfire progressed through the next four acts of the six-act charade, ending finally with the fire tossers. After much waiting, it was my turn to rise with the three other counselors from Girls' Village. Somehow, in the cover of night and the adrenaline of the show, I was not nervous. The lit torches behaved no differently than they had unlit, and we ran through our whole sequence, dropping a torch only once. I thought then that I was more likely to get badly burned cooking than I was fire tossing.

Looking back now, I think I just needed to grab ahold of the nearest dangerous thing and brush up against it—flush out my synapses with the instinctual, the clarity of that burning stick rushing against the night air, nothing more than hand-eye coordination—in order to remember what it was to be alive. I was anxious at the harbinger of my dad's grand mal seizure, but that ambient din was momentarily overridden by a gush of pride. All of us stood in the glow of the fire feeling like stunt performers, like con artists for having pulled off another week with a hundred or so kids entrusted to our care. Look closely, and you could see our pulses beating in our necks, all that life contained by mere skin.

After the fire and our campers were asleep, Jayne and I would duck under the ropes delineating the waterfront, roll our jeans up to our knees, and walk barefoot through the sand onto the dock to sit on the closed bow of one of the Ski Nautiques, the fiberglass cool against our bare legs. From this vantage we could see so many stars, the boat lilting softly beneath us, tied to the dock with an old ski rope gone slack, water as black as air spreading out in all directions, the lake alive and breathing. Our two human voices suspended like ribbons within that half sphere that held us, barely whispers alongside the calls of crickets and bullfrogs, a cacophony of sound that carried for miles over the water.

Forty miles south, my parents would be sitting out on their back patio watching the lightning bugs blink on and off in synchrony in our backyard. The lake: a steely smooth blanket, lapping softly at the shore.

* * *

My second summer at camp, I was hired as a waterfront director and lived in a house full of support staff instead of in Shoshone with twelve ten-year-olds. In addition to teaching waterskiing, I was in charge of organizing the lifeguarding schedule, assessing each camper's swimming ability on opening day, and hauling the fleet of twenty kayaks from the water to their wooden racks every night just before dusk.

At camp, I began a habit of not returning my mom's phone calls, not going home on the weekends. I didn't want to be home with my family and pretend nothing was different. I was deeply unhappy that summer but tried to hide this sadness from my peers. Had my dad already died—from car crash, from stroke, from brain aneurysm—I would have felt justified in being visibly depressed. But instead, I became entangled in a web of self-censorship, unsure of whether my sulkiness was out of proportion with my circumstances, unsure if this was what loss felt like, unsure of what exactly it was that I had lost. I loathed myself for wallowing in my own maudlin sentimentalism—a self-loathing magnified by my shame in wanting attention, like a child with a skinned knee that refuses to bleed—and I worried about letting others see me unhappy.

All that summer, campers in their swimsuits sprinted through the sand up to the boathouse, brandishing garter snakes and bluegills: *Look, Cara, look what I caught.* I presided over all of this, in charge of maintaining some semblance of symbiosis between the human and the reptilian, amphibian kingdoms, caretaker of everything wet and soggy.

Camp was home to water lilies and painted turtles and a pair of swans. Cattails, taller than our campers, walled the wetland trail. I once watched a snapping turtle lay thirty-some white eggs in a hole she'd dug in the middle of a dirt path leading into the boys' bathhouse two hours before campers arrived, and I helped relocate the eggs a few yards away, just outside of camp property.

But for as much responsibility and pride I felt over that waterfront, and as many nights as I'd watched the sun set over the lake, thinking there wasn't anywhere else in the world I'd rather be, I knew camp held its appeal for me for its delusion, that Never-Never Land was in fact real, a place we could will into being if only we had enough coconspirators.

My mom resented my decision to work at camp another summer. She said my dad was getting worse, and shouldn't I be spending more time with him? They were fighting more often than they ever had, my mom confiding in me behind his back. *So much has changed,* she said, as if I weren't around enough to notice, *I don't recognize this man, and I don't think I would have married this man.* This disclosure made me uneasy. I felt it was impossible to not betray any of my mom's secret to my dad. I struggled to distinguish my own callousness toward my dad from my mom planting this seed of resentfulness in my mind. And coupled with my own teenage desire to hang out with my camp friends drinking on Saturday nights, I became furtive and distant. Instead of driving the hour and a half across corn fields and dusty farm towns to spend time with my parents on my days off, my friends and I drank cheap vodka and passed around a bong across the road from camp at the platform tents, all of us sitting on stumps in a circle around the fire pit we'd used two days earlier to cook s'mores for a group of kids.

Even though I was pretending that I wanted to be a born-again hippie, carefree and laughing, I was sick with dread that whole summer. I spent long hours daydreaming on the boathouse steps. *What if something happens to him? Would my mom call my boss? Would he come directly from his office, through the screen door and onto the H-dock, ask to speak to me in private?* I was ashamed of my own self-pity, ashamed of indulging my imagination, scolded myself for being melodramatic. I was already acutely aware of the part of me that wanted closure. I didn't know what to tell people about his condition. *Does he have epilepsy?* they would ask. *Is he mentally ill?* It seemed to me then that all of our personalities existed like the voice boxes of dolls inside us, and in his first brain surgery he'd had two and a half years earlier, they had removed his with their scalpel, along with everything else, stuffed in its place the voice box of a robot with a glitchy hard drive that would spew out phrases we'd never heard him say before, like *Okie dokie.* I imagined car wrecks and strokes and grand mals that he never woke up from.

In the years since his death, I find myself asking if it would have been better had he died in that first seizure, when he drove his car off the road. It was very well possible. He could have driven into oncoming traffic or into a cement wall or any number of other combinations. For in as many ways as a surprise death is arguably harder to grieve, he would have been freed from the six years of anxiety of waiting, and we would have been spared from watching.

Sometime early in July, I'd won enough rounds of rock, paper, scissors at the staff meeting and was slated to be the Chief of Water.

That night, I was the lead guard for lake swim, standing atop one of the Ski Nautique's inboard motor covers, watching the other guards form a corridor in their yellow kayaks, counting heads. The previous summer's waterfront director, my predecessor, was driving the boat. She was petite and wore her sandy hair in a ponytail pulled through the hole at the back of a red baseball cap that read Guard with a tiny embroidered white cross. She kept one hand on the boat's throttle and the other on the steering wheel, letting the boat idle, bumping it ahead every so often to keep up with the swimmers. With her eyes fixed on all those prone bodies, their shoulder blades heaving with each stroke, she taught me the Chief of Water's song, quiet and low. *Wichi tai tai kimurai ohwanika ohwanika hey ney hey ney no wah. Water spirit beings running round my head. Makes me feel glad that I'm not dead.* I loved the song for the repetition of the long *o* sounds, the way it made my body into a bellows, and how this handoff felt sacred and secret, away from the ever-watchful eyes and ears of campers. The song was undeniably a gratitude song but sung mournfully, and the pairing of these two emotions was an epiphany that struck me like a gong. Coupled with this realization were the acoustics of being surrounded by water, amplifying my voice. At the time, I thought the song had been made up by someone at camp. I know now that it is from Jim Pepper's 1971 album *Pepper's Pow Wow*. Pepper was a jazz saxophonist of Muscogee Creek heritage. But either way, from our mouths, it was still a rip-off.

As the sun set across the lake, the whole world caught up in rotating away, I slipped out in one of the metal canoes carrying an unlit citronella torch, the sides of the boat silent against the reeds and lily pads, the camp's program director paddling me out. We were quiet in order to stay hidden, listening to the sounds of counselors wrangling their frenzied campers into cabins, watching through the poplar branches as the camp's groundkeeper built a fire onshore, its flames the only source of light on campus. I ran my lines in my head again and again, fingering the lighter in my pocket, hyper-attuned to my own breathing, that quiet intake and expulsion of air.

At that time in my life, the song embodied the deep sadness I felt at my dad's looming diagnosis and offered a portal I could walk through and become someone else. Singing it in the range of a tenor under the cloak of night made me feel I was able to obscure my gender, that gender no longer mattered. I was just a person, flesh taking on human form, born of lake and bullfrog and blue heron and damselfly. Born of two parents who had fallen in love with water, choreographed a childhood for me that revolved around being outdoors, on the lake. And in my push to break away from them, I was homesick, self-soothing on the shores of this twin lake.

* * *

What I remember from multivariate calculus is this: The inverse of an exponential function is called a "natural logarithm," $\ln(x)$. I spent a whole semester staring uncomprehendingly at graphs with one line hugging the x-axis, moving from left to right across the page, then, abruptly, curving up, rocketing skyward, and another line hugging the y-axis, moving from the bottom to the top of the page, then abruptly curving off to the right and flattening out. The first line was meant to show exponential growth; the second, the natural log. If you held a mirror between the two curves, one was the reflection of the other. From these two lines stemmed all other calculus: derivatives, integrals, matrices, geometric figures rotating around a fixed axis.

If I could pinpoint a moment and say, *This, this is when my life took off,* it would be standing in the driver's seat of one of the camp's Ski Nautiques, broad-shouldered and squinting. This is when the line that is my life switched from being a gradual slope moving left to right across the page to being nearly vertical. Within the year, I'd admit to myself I was in love with a woman for the first time, and I would begin, in fits and starts, to live in my own truth. But the acceleration of my life was timed precisely with the beginning of my dad's failing health. Maybe, from the outset, each point along his line had a corresponding opposite point along mine.

* * *

172

During my second summer at camp, my dad had a second stroke. It was a Saturday, and I wasn't planning to go home. I was with Jayne and another camp friend, mowing his backyard in a hurry so we could finish his chores and meet up to go drinking with the rest of the staff. The phone call came like a siren—*Mom, Mom, what happened? Mom, are you there?*—her voice Dopplering in and out due to my spotty reception. I changed my ringtone after that day, on edge whenever I'd hear it in a grocery store or movie theater. In a flurry of movement around me, I was in the back seat of Jayne's car en route to the ER in downtown Grand Rapids, Tom Petty's "Wildflowers" on the radio, watching the trees blur into a watercolor of green.

My dad was released that night from the hospital after they had done some scans, and I went back to work the next day. Later that week, my dad would be diagnosed with a glioblastoma multiforme, stage 4. When I got the news in a voicemail after free swim, I stood just inside the screen door of the office and told the three program directors his prognosis, that I needed to take some time off. They said, *How are you still standing?* and I wondered if I should be sitting down.

I think a part of me knew that July was the beginning of the end, that there was no recovering from this diagnosis. The jig was up. The magic of camp was gone for me. My delusion that the outside world stood perfectly still while we were all chasing each other around with tempera paint and singing songs about fried ham was gone. My dad was given a prognosis of a year, maybe a year and a half, which would balloon into four.

* * *

A couple years ago, I met someone who was working at the camp year-round. She said they still did the campfire, that it was called the Ancient Fire Ceremony now, and that they didn't paint kids' faces anymore, that they had *some local tribal leaders*—she didn't know from which tribes—come out to camp and give them feedback. She said now, after the ceremony, the camp director, the same director as when I was there, stood in front of the crowd and *read a passage of scripture*, talked about how there are lots of times in life where you have to do something to prove yourself, *but with God you don't have to do that. He just loves you as you are. You don't have to earn anything.*

This roundabout meaning-making seems so unrecognizable to me, the opposite of what the fire meant to me when I was there: honoring the experiences and ways each camper had challenged themselves throughout their week, marking each of their transformations, each of their leveling up, however small. But I know my own propensity toward nostalgia, how reticent I am to change, how I want everything to stay frozen in time, is just the unspoken voice of my own helplessness against the biggest loss of my life.

With distance and time, I have come to believe that the campfire, the whole six-day charade, the entire summer, was built on a façade of ritual, as if in order for any of it all to be meaningful, we had to step into the costume of another people and make proprietary bids on that which was, by no stretch of the imagination, rightfully ours. And that, in co-opting pieces of Native people's cultures, we had created a cheaper Disney version, not only of the natural world but of ourselves. In all our pageantry, we had learned fraudulence, and, worse, we desensitized ourselves to it. It is the kind of ruin we will each carry inside us wherever we go.

* * *

I learned from my campers that childhood is always perforated with glimpses into the sorrows of this world, but even so, kids will themselves back into the thrall of its magic.

On our last night together, after the campfire, I would take my campers back to our cabin for lights out and read aloud to them in the darkened room until all the noise from the other cabins died down outside our screen windows. Then we'd walk silently by flashlight back up to the top of the hill and lay in the center of the playfield to look for the Perseids. For most, it was their first time seeing a shooting star, their first time even noticing the Milky Way. They'd point out airplanes and blinking satellites and ask *Cara, is that one?* and I'd say, *No, too slow.* They'd ask, *How will I know when I see one?* And I'd say, *You'll just know.*

14

The Spirograph my brother and I played with as kids came with a set of colorful mini pens and multiple gears of various sizes. The gears were made of semi-transparent plastic, each patterned with a spiral of holes. One of us would hold the outer gear in place while the other pressed a pen into a hole on the inner gear and wound the gear along, the two sets of teeth propelling the wheel forward, creating a series of loops. To complete the drawing, whoever was holding the pen would have to maintain a constant pressure pressing the inner gear hard against the outer gear, traveling three or four or five rotations. Each loop arched across the blank white page until the pen arrived back at the point where it began.

A week after my dad died, I laid in the bathtub, half submerged, only my nose and lips above the waterline, and I thought about how deafening it was, the sound of my own breathing. From the Latin, *spīrāre*, to breathe, and *graphicus*, drawing or writing.

I think I can wend my way through the labyrinth of the hospital, a sense of déjà vu snaking down my spine, the ding of the elevator, the beeping IV, everything the same, only this time I am the well one. Time, I have decided, is not a river, but a Tilt-A-Whirl. That whatever forward motion I make will inevitably contain within it backpedaling toward childhood, my dad, his life giving shape to the path I inscribe.

15

On the border between Pullman, Washington, and Moscow, Idaho, there is a museum dedicated to the Appaloosa, those mottled horses bred by the Nez Perce. The Nez Perce are renowned for their horse breeding, for their early use of gelding to weed out less-desirable characteristics from the gene pool. The horses were named by settlers for the place, Palouse, a French word for "lawn"—*pelouse*. It is easy to see how I reversed this etymology when I first moved to Idaho and thought the land was named for the horse. Out my car window, the Palouse was a prairie patchwork of green and blond rolling hills, the sky perpetually dappled with clouds, spotlighting some hillsides and leaving others in the shade.

The museum displays tell visitors that the Appaloosa were the horses some six hundred Nez Perce fled on the backs of to Montana and then Canada, a fourteen-hundred-mile exodus that took place over the span of three months in 1877. The decade preceding had seen an influx of gold miners to the region, and the Nez Perce's treaty-allotted land had been reduced by 90 percent. When Chief Joseph finally surrendered, the US Cavalry seized more than one thousand of the Nez Perce's carefully bred Appaloosas, sold a fraction of them, and shot the rest.

Inside the museum, there is a glass case with six different patented versions of barbed wire. Each rusted wire in the shadowbox is strung horizontally. The case gives the overall impression of some ancient, hellish lute. There is single twist and double twist; one that is a serrated ribbon of metal; another that has a spinning spur.

The week before Lucia started sixth grade, apropos of who knows what, she asked Ada and me why, in English, the opposite of "hard," as in "doing something hard," is "easy" instead of "soft."

Even though I did not grow up in the West, I have come to love its emptiness, the sweet smell of poplars in spring; basalt columns splitting out of the earth, evidence of some raging underground dragon; jackrabbits the size of dogs running up the tire rut of a doubletrack dirt road ahead of my headlights. At a certain point, everyone who lives in the West has to reckon with the question: What is the difference between nostalgia and grief?

Kayla and I spent that winter driving around the Palouse in my Buick. It had been eight months since my dad died. We drove to Spring Valley Reservoir and stood on the dock, her body pressed against mine. Clouds blanketed the sky. Conifers blanketed the hillsides. The water lapped against the plastic drums keeping the dock afloat, and the sound of it, coupled with the dock's gentle rocking, became a doorway back in time, one that I wanted to walk through over and over.

In November, we drove to the Dworshak Reservoir and squished through the muck down the steep bank to the water's edge. What was once a free-flowing river had been dammed into slack water. *The water level is low*, I said, and she laughed. The wind outside of the car was cold against our faces. Somewhere across the lake, a ski boat roared to life.

In the car we listened to Railroad Earth, Tea Leaf Green, Iron & Wine. Sometimes she read Raymond Carver to me. Talking was easy with her. She grew up in the arid West, California and then Arizona, but so much of our suburban childhoods had been the same. Our affair, like all affairs I suppose, was a dizzying loop of appetite and engorgement, setting arbitrary rules and then breaking them. Never before had I had this rapt attention from anyone.

We drove to Wawawai Landing on the Snake River, the road to the water's edge descending a thousand feet in elevation. The wheat fields on the hillsides had been plowed to stubble, blanched of all color, brittle with frost; the sky, a gunmetal gray, threatening rain. Lower Granite Dam was less than a mile downriver from the Landing, but like so much Western violence, it was tucked around a bend, out of sight.

We should come back here this summer and camp, I said.

Yeah, she said, her voice full of doubt.

Back in the car, it started to sleet, big pellets more water than ice, not cold enough to stick to the ground, but the static noise of it filled our field of vision, obscuring the other side of the river. She had seen snow on the ground only a handful of times in her life and never the act of snow falling, so we pulled over and got out of the car. *It's like being in a snow globe*, she said, kissing me.

The words "I love you" surfaced, like a fish jumping. Even though I never said them aloud, I am sure she heard them. Instead, I said, *Everything reminds me of him*. This was the beginning of a habit: coding every intense emotion to be somehow related to him and his dying. I would backpedal any forward-looking, romantic momentum by turning to take stock of my childhood, longing to go back. Before me, this ponytailed woman in her warmest sweater, surprised at her own giddiness at the sudden magic of snow. I was anxious that it was snowing and he was gone. I didn't want the seasons to keep progressing without him. She bore witness, unflinchingly, to my bottomless sadness.

* * *

Winter of 1998, my dad and I watched the Nagano Olympics like it was the last best TV of the twentieth century. When we couldn't watch, torn away for one of Ryan's hockey games or for meals or for school, we recorded everything on VHS, taping over the Indy 500, the Daytona 500, a post-race interview with Dale Earnhardt. I was mostly watching for the skiing events, for Picabo Street.

It was February and snowing outside our living room windows, but in Japan, temperatures kept rising to sixty degrees during the day. Snow turned to rain, cameras zoomed in on the downhill course, the mountainside sparkling with a wet glare, all that snow gone to slush. The Alpine skiing events kept being postponed, so we watched figure skating, we watched curling, we watched bob-sledding, we watched women's hockey. My dad built a fire in our fireplace, crouching on his hands and knees, each log meticulously placed over crumpled newspaper. Years later, the sound of wood crackling and the Olympic theme song remain branded so vividly

180

in my memory, every time I hear either I am back on that couch, twelve years old, my head resting against his jeans, burying my bare feet under the couch pillows.

During a commercial break, he went out to the kitchen for a snack, hollered, *Carly, how's that fire look?*

Looks like it could use another log, I reported, and I heard the door to the garage open and close behind him. While he was outside, a Chevy truck commercial came on featuring a girl, maybe my age, supposed to be a young Picabo, standing in the start gate, smiling at her dad. The ad cuts to the drive home, the intimacy of dad and daughter after the race, advertising meant to sing the song of ourselves back to us. The commercial captured the whole point of youth sports, the ritualization of dads swelling with pride at their daughters, the Olympics meant to teach us about heroes, about hope. My dad came in with an armful of logs and set them on the hearth to melt, and I raised my head from the couch to make a place for him.

When they did finally run the Alpine events, the course had turned slick. *Looks like an ice skating rink*, my dad said. *Except on a mountain*, I added. We watched in horror as Austrian skier Hermann Maier lost control of his speed during a downhill qualifying race, landed on his head, ejected from both skis, tore through three layers of snow fencing, then walked away of his own accord, went on to win gold in the super G. We held our breath while Picabo made her second run at super G, edging out the Austrians by one-tenth of a second. *This is what it comes down to in ski racing*, my dad said, *this tenth of a second.*

* * *

My mom called my dad a diehard. In the winters, we spent the weekends Ryan didn't have hockey driving the three and a half hours up to Harbor Springs to ski at Nubs Nob. We always skied first chair to last chair—opening until close. No matter how cold it was, my dad skied in a headband and windbreaker.

I loved everything about skiing: the squeak of my plastic boots walking through groomed snow, the feel of my fleece neck warmer across my upper lip, the frozen-solid Snickers bar in my pocket, the engulfing quiet on the backside, snow coating each branch and pine needle. Nubs Nob is the third biggest ski area in Michigan's Lower Peninsula, after Boyne Highlands and Boyne Mountain. It garnered its own cult following in the 1980s by branding itself as the antithesis to Boyne's ritzy resort franchise. I think my parents loved it because it was a family mountain, each of the chairlifts painted a different color. While Boyne was busy installing high-speed quad chairs, Nubs bought a fleet of snow guns and started converting five thousand gallons of water per minute into microscopic ice crystals. On the wall above Ryan's bed at home, we'd taped the Nubs Nob trail map, and we'd spend hours studying it, memorizing the names of each run and planning our next trip up north.

Most of the lifts at Nubs were either doubles or triples, and our pairings were rote: I rode with my dad. He'd take my poles and his poles together and make a kind of seat belt out of them across our laps. On the ride up, he'd quiz me on my multiplication tables, and for those five minutes, we were each other's entire world, the chairlift's mechanical buzz pulling us up the face of the mountain.

The winter I was in sixth grade, we took a family ski trip to Steamboat Springs, Colorado. I had never been out West before, never seen real mountains. Our parents tag-teamed the drive out, driving through the night, and we arrived in Steamboat just as the sun was setting. After we checked into our hotel, we rode the gondola in our street clothes up to the bar at the top of the mountain. Below us, the runs were bathed in orange. *Night skiing*, my dad said, the occasional silhouette of a skier snaking their way down. The bar was cowboy themed, deserted, country music playing on low volume, a fire in the fireplace. My dad ordered a Blue Moon, my mom an Irish coffee, and we sat in a line at the bar, Ryan's and my feet swinging off our bar stools, slurping the whipped cream off our hot chocolates. We took our cues from our parents, and they were quiet, flirting. We were happy. On the gondola ride down, the whole mountain town was lit up in twinkle lights, their light reflecting off snow, the whole valley glowing.

The next morning, the forecast was for a foot of snow in three hours. *Look at all that rail freshy,* my dad said, opening the hotel room curtain onto our snowed-in patio. We spent the first half of the day on groomers, taking breaks on the side of each mile-long run, Ryan crunching snowballs of fresh powder between his mittens and then eating them. At lunch, we stomped the snow off our boots and went into the warming hut to pop a bag of microwave popcorn.

The snow kept coming down, faster than the grooming cats could keep up with it, and by midafternoon, Ryan and I were almost waist-deep in powder. We rode the lifts out to the back bowls, the trees getting smaller as we went up in altitude. *The tree line is the elevation where trees can no longer grow,* my dad explained on the chairlift. Below us, the subalpine fir were decorated in Mardi Gras beads and colorful lacy bras. *Dad, how do people take their bras off on the ski lift?* I asked. He said he didn't know, to ask Mom. When we got off the lift, the sun had come out, and the entire mountain valley opened up around us. Skiing on an actual mountain, I decided, was far superior to skiing some hard-packed piste of manufactured snow down a clear-cut strip on the side of a twenty-degree sand dune in Michigan. I lay down on a hummock of snow, exhausted. *How you doing, Carly?* my dad said, spraying me with his hockey stop. *Good,* I said, grinning. *It feels like we're the only ones here.* He smiled and said nothing, waiting for Mom and Ryan to regroup, then he headed downhill, clicking his poles together behind him, his signal for us to follow.

That night, we skated on the outdoor ice rink in the center of town, my dad holding my hand as we made orbit after orbit around the frozen-over central plaza. That trip, the real snow, the bighorn sheep standing in the highway on Rabbit Ears Pass, our minivan switchbacking down hillsides covered in a stubble of naked aspens, wedged ajar something inside of me. Colorado, ballooned into symbol, a touchstone for where I felt most alive.

In high school I raced on my school's ski team. I was not particularly fast or technically skilled, but I loved the fluorescent, skin-tight GS suits we wore, the sound of cowbells from the huddle of parents standing around the leaderboard, and how important it made me feel carrying a second pair of skis over my shoulder on the chairlift, setting gates with a power drill and a two-foot-long drill bit, swinging my arm out in front of me to trip the clock on the finish line. I loved bombing the hill in my exaggerated parabolic slalom skis, each carve like a mathematically precise arc made with a drawing compass, the heavy skis gluing me to the surface of snow.

Starting in November, before the snow came, we had practice two nights a week out at our local hill. Dryland practice was basically calisthenics: hike the hill five times, then see who can do wall sits the longest, our legs making perfect right angles at the knees, our backs pressed against the lodge siding.

My teammates and I all dreamed of living in Colorado someday. Our coach used to torture us with the snow report in Summit County. *Three feet last night*, she'd say while we'd drip warm-weather wax into our skis, watching the fog set in under the dingy fluorescent lights of our hometown hill. Our coach was an ex–ski bum who lived through the 1970s in a van in Colorado, wearing huge sunglasses and knit headbands. She called us all "chicks," and I adored her.

She was also my first boss. She had moved to Michigan and started the ski school at Cannonsburg in the late 1980s. Cannonsburg was 250 feet, or the equivalent of thirty seconds, of pure skiing bliss. It had three chairlifts and as many rope tows, a lodge that perpetually smelled like hamburgers, a maintenance shed, and a rental building. I'd been in her ski school as a kid, and I worked weekends for her as a ski instructor all through high school. For the team poster she hung in the lodge dining room, she'd dug up ten-year-old photos of me from Small World World Cup, the ski school's annual kids' race. In my photo on the poster, I am wearing a pink-and-teal one-piece ski suit, goggles over my hood, pre-parabolic skis with Mickey Mouse on them. This was a joke

184

among my teammates. All of their photos were recent, each of them in their helmets and racing suits, patterned with spiderwebs. Then there was me, making a pizza with my skis, the photo fading, washed out by sun.

* * *

The summer after I graduated from college, I moved to Colorado. An education professor of mine had arranged for me to student teach in Fort Collins that fall, and I found a summer job working as a backpacking guide in Durango.

My grandma volunteered to drive out to Durango with me, a one-way road trip. She said she needed to see the West again. It was the summer Obama eked ahead of Hillary in the Democratic primaries. We sat on the plasticky bedspread in our motel in Walsenburg, Colorado, watching CNN on the TV in the corner of the room.

". . . we owe it to our children to invest in early-childhood education; and recruit an army of new teachers and give them better pay and more support; and finally decide that, in this global economy, the chance to get a college education should not be a privilege for the few, but a birthright of every American. That's the change we need in America. That's why I'm running for president of the United States."

My grandma taught first grade for forty years through the height of Michigan's so-called school desegregation. She was a staunch Republican. I had been the one to turn on the TV. She said, *He's a good public speaker. Young people like you want a good public speaker.*

After the speech, she took me out to Pizza Hut. We had traveled thirteen hundred miles together in two days. I had done all the driving while she figured out our miles per gallon, longhand, in the margin of my Rand McNally map. We slurped our Pepsis through straws without lifting the giant red plastic cups from our grease-smudged table. I had that homesick feeling I got whenever my grandparents had taken Ryan and me out for junk food. Our parents never let us eat at Pizza Hut.

The next morning, in the cool violet predawn, she bought my last tank of gas. I sped twenty miles per hour over the speed limit most of the day, and she never told me to slow down. Outside, the grain elevators and irrigation systems of eastern Colorado disappeared, replaced by whole hillsides of aspens. I thought then of my college roommate Jessie's undergraduate thesis, which she had had me read drafts of before she submitted it. It was about Deleuze and Guattari and their idea of rhizomes. She'd written about Pando, an aspen grove in the Fishlake National Forest in southern Utah, over one hundred acres in size and more than 14 million pounds in total, the entire grove a single organism. It is the largest known living being on the planet, each individual tree branching off from a root network underground. Jessie had moved to Florida after college, and I took comfort in metaphorical thinking, knowing that even though we were so far apart that we might be connected by something invisible, rhizomatic. At Wolf Creek Pass, my grandma and I rolled down the car windows at the sight of snow still on the ground in June and felt the icy fresh blast of change. At the Continental Divide, she spotted a doe and her fawn on the side of the road, and they looked exotic to us with their huge mule ears.

When I dropped her at the airport in Durango, she told me these three days were the longest she had been away from my grandpa since they'd been married, and I couldn't fathom that kind of companionship.

Back in the Buick, the car she'd given me, she'd left her wildflower field guide and sudoku book on the front passenger's seat. Gifts. All I could think about were the thousands of times I had ignored her when she had offered me a penny for my thoughts.

* * *

The first gay bar I went to was in Fort Collins. I was twenty-one and student teaching at a middle school. I lived alone in a one-bedroom apartment subsidized by my parents, who I still was not out to.

That fall, I ate bean and cheese quesadillas three meals a day,

186

bike commuted across town to work, and listened to Ani DiFranco's "You Had Time" on repeat. The song is atypical for DiFranco, quiet, epistolary, a slow D-G-A major chord progression. It's about the distinction between the impersonal adoration of fans and the intimate adoration of a lover. DiFranco sings about coming home to her lover after a tour, after they had been on some kind of break. There's a two-minute, thirty-second piano intro before she switches to acoustic guitar and starts in with the lyrics, "How can I go home / With nothing to say / I know you're going to look at me that way / And say what did you do out there? / And what did you decide? / You said you needed time / And you had time."

I was single and not dating, fantasizing about a specific future life where I might come home and be looked at in a specific future way. I spent the four months I lived in Fort Collins reading 1980s gay and lesbian fiction from the library—*Annie on My Mind*, *The Price of Salt*, *The Object of My Affection*, *People in Trouble*—and I was thrilled at the coded language, the practiced restraint, the private affirmation of self. But the protagonists were all closeted to their families, the plots fueled by spies finding them out. It was 2008 and marriage was illegal everywhere except Massachusetts and California. I'd spent all the weekends in October canvassing for Obama, then watched California approve Prop 8 on the same night Obama was elected to office. In a country that couldn't make up its mind, I was unmoored by my own flimsiness about who I was, prone to frequent misgivings. I harbored a smug, self-important hatred of Katy Perry's song "I Kissed a Girl." Who was she to break this particular ground? Why did pop radio insist on playing this inane garbage every fourth song? But really I hated her because she made gayness—this huge, inflated, clandestine thing to me—so flippant. I was cultivating a self-imposed otherness born out of the belief that the world, namely my parents, would be revolted by me for who I was. And, stagnating in the queer literature of the 1980s, I read book after book that confirmed that belief. California voters confirmed that belief.

As the polls closed on the West Coast, I drank a Fat Tire and ate a quesadilla, then curled up with my dog on the loveseat my mom had purchased from Goodwill.

I was in the business of secret keeping all that year, and for two years after that, and by then the secret had become so deep-seated, all my attempts at lovemaking turned into affairs.

The gay bar was a dive. Empty save for the male bartender and two men in their sixties wearing acid-washed jeans and tucked-in jean shirts, dancing to the jukebox.

I don't know what I expected. Fort Collins, the "Vanilla Valley," is a family-friendly, Moral Majority town. I think I expected to walk into the Life Café straight out of *Rent* and enter into some kind of narrow hallway where patrons waited in line for the bathroom, something to facilitate close proximity to strangers, the intimacy that comes from shouting into people's necks to be heard. Maybe I thought there would be a bored, tattooed bartender in black jeans and a black T-shirt who I could ask about when her shifts were and come back and become one of her regulars.

I ordered a PBR, drank it over the span of two songs, then pedaled my way home, my headlamp, its elastic band coiled around my bike's handlebars, blinking across wet asphalt like a strobe.

* * *

In November, I finished my student teaching and moved to Breckenridge for a ski instructing job. This had been the plan all along, chasing some fantasy idea of leisure and living "the good life" that I had inherited from my dad.

It was the second week of January, Breckenridge's annual Ullr Fest sponsored by Bud Light. There was a parade up Main Street. Tourists came out of their hotels in complete bewilderment. I came out of the T-shirt shop where I was working second shift after my day teaching on the slopes. There were nearly naked men wearing Viking hats and faux-fur shawls riding atop a blue, inflated NRS raft, holding a spray-painted bedsheet that said BIG SNOW = BIG WATER. The raft was not on wheels; instead, it was being towed up Main Street by a four-wheeler, the street completely iced over. There were floats on runners pulled by dogsled teams, women in bikinis cross-country skiing up Main Street, tossing candy to children and condoms to adults. There was a mother, dressed as a Viking, towing her young kid, dressed as a Viking, in a red plastic sled. There were coed Vikings tossing sample-sized sunblock SPF 15 from atop their floats. There was a float with a fort built out of pine branches and a spray-painted sign ULLRS SHACK with a bunch of twenty-year-olds drinking Bud Light and standing around a bonfire, also atop the float. There was a truck towing a hot tub on wheels. The hot tub was steaming, full to capacity with men and women, no one wearing any clothes. Someone else's Ford 4x4 was towing a trailer with a snow gun hooked up to a water tank shooting snow above the heads of the crowd that had gathered.

I smirked at my coworker, here on a work visa from Brazil. In this resort town, where becoming a Local took over a decade, we were in the middle tier, Seasonal Employees, ranking barely above Tourists. Despite our best efforts to appear unfazed, to adopt the knowing look of Locals, we too were entertained by the spectacle. We knew that every supposedly original thought we had—from our fashion sense, to our taking of second jobs, to our sudden perfunctory climate-consciousness—had been clichéd by the other thousands of young people who had moved to this town for a season and who would all eventually leave when the snow melted.

I lived in a house five miles outside of town, ten thousand feet above sea level, at the first switchback heading up Hoosier Pass. In the mornings, I would shovel my Buick out from under the new snow and drive on my studded tires into town. I didn't have cell service at my house, but I could get a signal after the last curve on the way into work, and I used that stretch of my commute to call home.

On a morning like any other morning, I drove the snowplowed road into town, parked my car in one of the city lots, pulled up my windshield wipers until they locked pointed toward the sky, and hopped a bus into the resort. I wore my red snow pants and red Ski and Ride School jacket, my work uniform, and stood in the aisle of the bus with a gloved hand holding on to the bus's grab bar.

The bus lurched in and out of stops through town, and I was still on the phone with my mom, watching a dad help his young daughter with her skis. *Here*, he said, putting them in the PVC pipes. The bus had a built-in ski rack on the outside to make room for more people inside. He held her hand as she climbed the bus steps, wobbly in her ski boots.

How's Dad? I asked my mom. That month, he had started Avastin, a clinical trial drug that made him fatigued, headachy, sick to his stomach with bowel incontinence. My mom was relaying the change in his condition over the phone, said, *You should have come home for Christmas.* Said, *I think it was his last one.*

Seven years after he died, Avastin would gain FDA approval for glioblastoma treatment. The trial my dad had been a part of didn't show any difference in the overall survival rate of patients compared to the control group. However, Avastin had been demonstrated to "delay disease progression" and decrease the need for corticosteroids, the anti-nausea meds used in conjunction with conventional chemotherapy and radiation. My mom had signed the paperwork, gave the go-ahead for the trial, and now was watching him suffer on it, second-guessing her decision. What was there left to say? I said, *I'm sorry*, then unloaded from the bus and headed into work.

Up until the last few months of my dad's life, I never questioned whether "delaying disease progression" was a good idea. I think part of me was still hopeful, even if skeptical, that the terminal diagnosis could be wrong, that this new drug could surprise us in its effectiveness. The drug companies prey on this human gullibility, our illogical sense of hope. During the time I lived in Breckenridge, I had a child's sense of time, that more was always better, that there was no gradient of quality. The worst possible thing would be the day he died, so keeping him alive, in whatever state, was preferable to that. People talk about death as the single Great Mystery, but I think there are states of being alive that are tunnels of unknowable torment, and I am certain, now, are not worth prolonging.

Teaching three-to-six-year-olds how to ski is easy. *Make a pizza, get a Skittle.* I was assigned to teach Level 3s that day, the kids who could turn and stop on their own but who hadn't yet been on a chairlift. After suiting everyone up and zipping their Ski and Ride School red vests over their ski coats, I piled all their skis into a wagon. We sang "The Ants Go Marching" and practiced high-stepping in our ski boots all the way over to the base of the Quicksilver Super6. I brought all seven of them to meet the liftie's attendant who was scanning passes. She taught the kids to watch the huge metal chairs go around and around inside the terminal and to study how the other people were loading safely, then we walked back over to the wagon to get our skis. *Squish the bug,* I chanted, trying to get them to clamp their heels into their bindings themselves, but the four-year-olds still needed my help, and I crouched in the snow to clean all the snow off their boots and click them into their bindings by hand, my snowpants soaking through in the knees. According to strict Ski and Ride School policy, each kid under age seven had to be paired with an adult, and I could take two. I picked my two most apprehensive kids to ride with me—we would go last—and then I pawned off the rest of them. I introduced each kid by name to the tourist they would ride with and reminded them to wait for me at the top. The liftie knew by their red vests that this was their first ride and slowed down the lift for us, and all seven of them got off the ground with little incident.

On my lunch break on some sunny slow day in February, a twenty-one-year-old girl fell off the Quicksilver lift and died. There were rumors it was premeditated, that she jumped. I watched as the Ski Patrol wrapped her up in a blue tarp and laid her into one of their orange toboggans. When I asked my boss the next morning if she knew the whole story, she said she didn't know, told me to put the *E-i-E-i Yoga* tape in the VCR for the kids.

I played I Spy with my two on our ride up until they got distracted. Up on the summit of Peak 8, they were shooting off avalanche cannons, triggering avalanches on purpose before opening

191

the area to the public. One of my kids, who was from Florida, said, *Uh oh, Miss Cara, it's gonna storm. We better go inside.*

At the top, it started snowing big flakes, and they were giggling, loving this big wide world adventure I had brought them on.

* * *

Mark and I had signed up together for the Ski and Ride Race League. Mark was a coworker from the East Coast, preppy and quiet. Looking at him was like looking at what I would have been had I been born a boy. We were the same height and weight, the same Mondo-point boot size, and sometimes we traded skis because we wouldn't have to adjust the bindings. The courses were set as mirror images of each other, one red and one blue. In the lift line, I traded my goggles for his, said, *Let me try them out for one run*, flirting. He told me he just bought some powder skis off eBay, one-tens underfoot, and skied them on his day off. *You should borrow them*, he said.

We need more snow before they'd be worth it, I said.

Somewhere halfway up the lift, in a moment bulging with anticipation, he reached to hold my hand, the tenderness of skin on skin muted through our Gore-Tex gloves, and I felt fifteen again, back on the chairlift with my first boyfriend. But this time, something in me was hiding secrets from itself. The conflation of being gutsy and a good athlete and male solidified so deep inside my psyche, I worried my entire façade of being an "outdoorsy chick," a so-called badass woman, my entire identity built on the thought process that "woman" needed that adjective, was rooted in misogyny. I was nervous at the suggestion that this was more than a friendship for Mark, that my wanting to *be* him was standing in as a proxy for having any sort of authentic crush on him.

On the course, we went head-to-head, and he finished 0.6 seconds ahead of me. Whatever competitive nerve I'd once had had been dulled, muted, frozen over in the five years my dad had been sick. I wanted nothing more than to be a carefree ski bum, but his illness had made me feel out of control of the basic premise of my life. I'd become rigid, calculated, wanting to convince everyone, namely myself, that nothing had changed. I was racked with indecision about whether or not to move home, full of self-doubt.

That night, I worked second shift at the T-shirt shop, and Mark came to visit in his acid-washed jeans, his backward baseball hat. He sat with me behind the register and worked out the day's sudoku in the *Summit Daily*.

When I got off at ten, we stood out back while my coworkers smoked cigarettes. Neither Mark nor I smoked, and it had to have been below zero degrees Fahrenheit, but we didn't mind. The snowcats were grooming up on the mountain, and we watched their orange headlights angled toward the sky, like rockets, ready for liftoff.

We all went to the only club in town, a cement basement that reeked of booze, and danced, a sort of halfhearted, not-really-drunk-enough spectacle of two tired bodies. When it was over, we all split a cab, a Dodge Caravan like my mom used to drive, and because I lived too far outside of town, I got out at Mark's stop.

He was unassuming, shy even, and turned on the TV to something ESPN, and we sat side by side on the edge of his unmade bed, the only seating in his whole apartment, and talked and talked and talked. And then we were kissing and taking off each other's layers and neither of us was really all that pervy or frantic, but there was something hugely nice about the whole thing. Like we were doing each other a favor, and maybe this was all there was in that freezing, lonely mountain town.

At some point, as was to be expected, he wanted sex, or maybe I made him think I wanted sex, or maybe neither of us wanted anything, and we were going through the motions.

The next morning, I woke up to the sound of Mark's body moving in and out from under the spray of the shower and then his electric razor buzzing behind the closed door of the bathroom. He complained about how strict our boss was, that she'd send him home for showing up to work with one-day's growth. I watched him move around his apartment in his boxers, and as he stepped into wind pants and then into his red snowpants, the same size as mine, I wanted his body, wanted to stand upright in the shower without hunching my shoulders out of an impulse to hide my breasts, wanted to feel the vibration of his razor against my cheek. The morning was sunny, and we walked to his bus stop together, sitting in the back holding hands as the bus wound around and then down the mountain into town.

Breckenridge looked like some Dickens Christmas Village all winter long: twinkling, frosted-over shop windows, glowing old-fashioned streetlamps coiled in real blue-spruce garlands, red velveteen bows tied around every shop sign, the scene complete with daily new snow indistinguishable from quilter's batting. I had moved to Colorado chasing a fantasy—to become a ski bum and live a life of carefree debauchery. All of Breck was tinged with beauty in my eyes. And yet, it was meaningless. The person who had shown me how to live the good life was dying.

A year and a half later, when we moved my dad into the hospice home, my mom offered to give Ryan and me each some time to say what we wanted to him in private, but we declined her offer. He had mostly lost the ability to communicate at that point, though the doctors told us he was able to hear us just fine. I felt like it was too late for apologies or gratitude, that it didn't matter, nothing I could have said to him would have had any consequence in the land of the living, and it would have just been a sentimental gesture for my own benefit, a waste. I never gave my dad any indication that I was queer, though it loomed large in my thoughts toward the end of his life. I didn't think he would have been able to understand had I told him. The emotional locus of his brain was too far frazzled. And anyway, I had no girlfriend to introduce to him. In the years leading up to his death, my own coming to terms with my sexuality had been secondary to me trying to conceive of a life without him. This was something, the first thing, in the long series of major life events that I would have to deal with without him.

* * *

194

One of my dad's journal entries to me began:

November 19, 1994
I just left you guys at home, and I'm again on my way to Erie. I
am lonely.

This line, more than anything else from his diary, is a window into who he was as an adult, stripped of the put-together façade he donned for my sake when I was a kid.

I was twenty-three when he died. I had paid attention to him only through the lens of a parent-child relationship. Now, with Ada, I ached for the adult friendship he and I never got to have, that I might have been able to call him up and ask him how he'd made his marriage last. That I could ask him about loneliness, about how you can feel such a deep sense of belonging and still, at times, feel so completely alone.

On the ten-year anniversary of my dad's death, Ada and I drove to a lake near our house to light a candle and try to name something specific about how grief had come to define the last decade of my life, how his influence was still very much a live wire, a defining force in all of my decisions, vital to how I moved through the world. In the car on the way to the lake, I played John Mellencamp's song "Your Life Is Now." He lived by that motto.

A pair of ducks at the water's edge preened each other, settling in for the night, each tucking its beak under a wing. I've come to take a great deal of comfort in knowing that his legacy is not some finished, hermetically sealed thing but rather that it is alive inside of me, through the ways I am him inevitably and the ways I try to live more like he did so that Ada and Lucia and everyone I encounter can know a bit of what he was like.

16

n 1947, behavioral psychologist B. F. Skinner published a paper titled "'Superstition' in the Pigeon." Skinner, then a graduate student at Harvard, starved a group of eight pigeons to 75 percent of their ideal body weight and then placed each one in a cage. He had his undergrads set up machines that would feed each pigeon at regular repeating intervals fifteen seconds apart, and then they observed the pigeons' behaviors. Six of the eight pigeons developed a strong correlation—what Skinner called "operant conditioning"—with whatever bodily movement they were doing right before the first feeding came. One pigeon was turning her body counterclockwise when the food appeared, so fervently continued doing so between feedings. One was thrusting her head into an upper corner of the cage. One kept phantom pecking toward, but not touching, the floor.

It's easy to laugh at the pigeons for their naive egotism, their adamant belief in the efficacy of their own agency. It's harder to turn that sense of humor on oneself. Even as a kid, I worried about the cause: I had eaten Pop-Tarts at my babysitter's every morning before school, a snack my mom had strictly forbidden. I suspected the carpet cleaner. Weeks prior to my diagnosis, I was watching *Animaniacs* at my babysitter's house. I had rubbed my cheek against the carpet's coarse shag, noted the chemical smell, and kept rubbing.

My family was deeply superstitious about cancer; we'd fallen hard for the gambler's fallacy. We thought one catastrophe had protected us from others, believing all those weeks I'd spent on the ninth floor of the children's hospital to be our penance, that we'd served our time. After my dad's diagnosis, I replaced one superstition with another. I believed that my cancer and my dad's cancer were manifestations of the same malevolent agent, correlation equaling causation.

* * *

In 2016, the Rogue River running through my hometown was declared a Superfund site by the EPA. It had been six years since my dad died. *This is my answer*, I thought then. Wolverine Worldwide, the parent company of popular footwear lines like Hush Puppies, Merrell, Chaco, Saucony, and CAT work boots, operated their leather tannery for forty years, from 1958 to 2000, in downtown Rockford. In middle school, my cross-country team had practice on the paved bike path that ran along the river through the site that is now gated off for cleanup. The tannery smell—ammonia and burning flesh and rotten eggs—was so pungent then, it stung in the backs of our throats.

Throughout those forty years, the tannery used Scotchgard to waterproof their leather. In 2000, Scotchgard's parent company, 3M, was forced to change its formula when an EPA investigation showed a positive correlation between PFAS, a class of per- and polyfluoroalkyl compounds developed by 3M, and human health risks, including cancers. But internal documents from 3M released as a part of their $850 million settlement with the state of Minnesota showed that the company's scientists knew of the toxic, accumulative, and persistent nature of their PFAS compounds as far back as 1970.

Rockford is a company town, one that breeds local allegiance. The main drag that runs through downtown is called Wolverine. The public library is named for Wolverine's founder. Rockford is where people from across West Michigan come to antique shop, fly-fish, eat a hot dog, and walk along the river taking pictures of fall colors. It's a middle-class town with a Not in My Backyard obliviousness. Ignorance is its own kind of wishful thinking. But in my thirteen years in public schools there, I learned critical thinking. In eleventh-grade language arts, we read Aldous Huxley's *Brave New World*. The town's air might as well have been laced with Huxley's happiness-inducing, coup-quelling drug, soma.

I read about the unfolding Wolverine scandal in 2017 from my loft apartment in Seattle. I took breaks from grading papers to listen to town halls broadcasted live over YouTube by high schoolers enrolled in a video production studio class. Not only did the tannery site itself leach into the Rogue River for forty years, less than a quarter mile upstream from the city's wastewater treatment plant, but the township confirmed more than thirty unlined dump sites that were used, starting in the 1950s, to dispose of tannery waste, which continue to leach into wells across the county. Tannery waste, in the 1950s and 1960s, was classified as nontoxic, and Wolverine's dump sites were apparently legal. But when their main House Street site was rezoned for housing in 1966, the township and the Michigan Health Department both knew of the former waste disposal site and still permitted houses, each with their own individual wells, to be built there. In 2016, one of the wells from that neighborhood tested for PFAS at 37,800 parts per trillion, more than five hundred times the EPA's maximum limit for human exposure. The woman whose house draws from that well? Her husband died from liver cancer.

Watching the drama unfold from afar, I grew increasingly wary of Wolverine's malfeasance. Their public statement on their website was factually inaccurate and came across as defensive and fragile. Like a teenager unskilled at lying, they simultaneously said "there is no evidence of PFAS at the tannery" and denied that they ever used PFAS in any stages of their processing plant. Their lack of PFAS evidence at the tannery was because they never tested for it, and they claimed all memos sent to them from 3M during those forty years to have been lost. It seemed absurd to me that they would try to claim that 3M didn't inform them that Scotchgard contained PFAS, which was potentially harmful to the environment and to human health. The Minnesota lawsuit against 3M gained international news attention in 2000. In 2017, after Wolverine's culpability became increasingly clear to the public, Wolverine tried to place the blame on 3M, to which 3M swiftly countered by publicly releasing documentation they had sent to Wolverine in 1999 that explicitly informed them of their plan to discontinue their patented Scotchgard formula and reformulate it because of its environmental persistence and toxicity.

198

Ada, Lucia, and I went to the movie theater in our neighborhood to see Todd Haynes's *Dark Waters* when it came out. The film tells the true story of corporate defense lawyer Robert Bilott, who represents a dairy farmer in Parkersburg, West Virginia, whose cattle, and later himself and his wife, all died of cancer. Parkersburg, like Rockford, is also a company town. Its biggest employer: DuPont's Washington Works plant, manufacturer of Teflon nonstick. In the 1980s, DuPont purchased a piece of land from the dairy farmer to use as a landfill for liquid waste product from the plant. The waste was piped directly into Dry Run Creek, which ran across the swath of land purchased by DuPont, through the farmer's grazing pastures, and then dumped into the Ohio River. The case ballooned into a class action lawsuit, which ended in 2017 with a $671 million settlement, but the water contamination, and subsequent lawsuits against DuPont, persist.

After the movie, we went home and looked at the bottom of our Teflon pan, inspecting it for nicks, knowing we were missing the point. Lucia dubbed it our Dead Cow Pan, and within weeks we retired it, learned how to cook pancakes and eggs in cast iron. I tell Lucia that it's okay that we ate out of Teflon before, not to worry, that exposure to PFAS is accumulative, that there are regular dosages that we can all be exposed to and then there are towns like Parkersburg, where the dosages are concentrated. But, of course, it is more complicated than that. All cancers are genetic—that is, mutations happen at the level of genes—even though only certain cancers are passed from parent to offspring. There are basically two types of tumors: ones that spring from sporadic mutations—mutations that happen randomly, in a single cell—and hereditary mutations that pass, inevitably, from parent to offspring. My mom explained cancer to me like this: *Every human is genetically predisposed to varying degrees of susceptibility. Our cells are inundated with insults every day, but most immune systems can fight them off. When the right conditions exist, based on any number of factors, cell growth has a heyday. Then: cancer.* Sometimes I worry about the frequency of cellular "insults" and how some tissues divide more often and are therefore more prone to mutation, like rolling the dice more. And how, in this country, the burden of proof is on us regular people, that it is our job to be ever-vigilant.

The winter of 2017, I was all-consumed by following the scandal developing in my hometown. I set a Google Alert to automatically email me every time a headline came out about Wolverine and PFAS. I set up phone interviews with local health officials and members of a concerned citizens group. I desperately wanted an epidemiology study to show a correlation between glioblastomas and germ cell tumors and PFAS. But that wasn't what the research showed. Instead, it showed exposure to high levels of PFAS to be associated with non-Hodgkin's lymphoma; liver, kidney, testicular, prostate, and breast cancers; birth defects, early-childhood developmental defects; increased cholesterol; ulcerative colitis; and other autoimmune diseases. Although the research is still emerging, and all too often couched in battalions of qualifiers, it didn't confirm any of my suspicions. The infamous Parkersburg, West Virginia, epidemiology study, for example, focused only on cancer incidence in patients over twenty years old. The type of germ cell tumor I had is only a pediatric cancer. There is no analog adult version of it.

Of the ongoing PFAS studies in my hometown, Brian Hartl, an epidemiologist spearheading a cancer cluster study for the Kent County Department of Health, told me, *We're never going to identify something that's causative. None of these studies that have been done are going to prove causality. They're going to show an association. That's all that data can show.*

Corporations capitalize on these scientists' qualifiers. The precautionary principle, which places the burden of proof on chemical corporations instead of on regulators, is the legal law of the land in the European Union as of 2006. US legislation passed in the 1970s reflected much of this same sentiment—heightened regulation in the case of a product's uncertain safety. In one of the virtual town halls I attended, I learned it was in fact our hometown hero, Gerald R. Ford, who signed the Safe Drinking Water

200

Act into law in 1974. Since the 1970s, however, these pieces of environmental legislation have been weakened with amendment after amendment, undermining the precautionary principle in favor of more risk acceptability and cost-benefit balancing that points to burdensome and expensive testing as reason for making testing optional instead of compulsory. Under current US chemical substance laws, if a company finds a known toxin in any of their products or footprint, they have to do something about it, which, in practice, disincentivizes companies from looking for toxins in their product. It is voluntary after all. And this, in turn, disincentivizes our governing bodies from classifying any new substances as toxic.

During Trump's first presidency, the Office of Chemical Safety and Pollution Prevention was led by chief chemical industry lobbyist Nancy Beck. Prior to her tyranny on Capitol Hill, she had worked for the American Chemistry Council. While there, she criticized the Obama-era EPA for erring on the side of too much caution. She blamed universities and their publish-or-perish research cultures for churning out what she called an everything-causes-cancer hysteria.

But in spite of the political indignation and big-corporation distrust all of this stirred in me, the Lake Bella Vista neighborhood water came back with only trace levels of PFAS. It was a dead end.

* * *

I learned in tenth-grade pre-calculus that the probability of B given A, written $P(B|A)$, is the probability of event B occurring knowing that event A has already occurred. *Three blue and two red marbles are in a bag. What are the chances of getting a red marble on the first draw? What are the chances of drawing two red marbles in a row?* I made neat charts in my notebook of all the possible combinations, and I began to find comfort in the way every combination has a given probability. Then, on a sunny morning in October, my math teacher dumped a coffee cup full of pennies across his desk. *Pick a partner and grab a penny*, he said. We were to flip the penny a hundred times and record each flip on a piece of paper. My partner flipped the coin; I kept the tally. *Heads*, my partner said. *Heads again*, he said. *Tails*, he said. For each flip I wrote the number of the flip and an uppercase *H* or *T* next to it. We oscillated back and forth like this until the thirty-fifth flip. *Heads*, he called. *Heads again. Heads* again. We flipped heads nine times in a row.

Let me flip for a while, I said.

At the end of the class period, my teacher turned on his overhead projector and wrote in blue pen across the screen "nCr." *Does the probability of flipping heads change given the previous flip?* he asked. We sat there, silent. *No*, he said. *It's fifty-fifty every time. A one in two probability.*

* * *

I know that in my superstitions about cancer and my frenzy for knowing the etiology, I am just playing out my child self's exacting sense of justice. This past year, I read a handful of half-sensible scientific papers about pediatric germ cell tumors. I read a series of papers published in 2004 about the AE22 study, which were the culmination of over fifteen years of mailing questionnaires to the parents of 274 pediatric germ cell tumor patients and 421 control group (non-cancer) parents. My parents participated in that study. *Did you use hair dye in the six months before pregnancy, during pregnancy, or during breastfeeding? Did you smoke? Did you drink alcohol? Did you drink diet soda? Did you use any indoor insecticides like flypaper? Did you have exposure to any paints or lacquers? Did you burn incense? Were you or your child exposed to any engine exhaust fumes? To industrial dust? To raw or unfinished metals? To any petroleum products? Did you receive treatment for a urinary tract infection? Did you receive any infertility treatments? Did you use any exogenous hormones in the six months prior to your pregnancy?* By the time they filled out this questionnaire, ten years had passed since my parents had been pregnant with me. My mom had been on birth control prior to getting pregnant. I suspect they answered "yes" to the questions about paint and exhaust fumes and diet soda. For some of the other questions, they couldn't remember. This is a well-known flaw in these kinds of retrospective epidemiology studies. The results of almost all the AE22 questions were inconclusive. All but one: There was a weak association shown between maternal exposure to herbicides during the postnatal period and risk of germ cell tumors in girls. But my mom only breastfed me for less than a month. And they couldn't remember if they had used any herbicides when I was an infant.

Looking back now, I wonder how much the questionnaire itself was a kind of ambient torture for my parents? To what extent did it plant the seed of self-blame?

Throughout my childhood, my mom worried aloud that my cancer might have been something she could have prevented. She looked out our kitchen window, her brow furrowed, whenever the aquatic weed control boats came through our cove, spraying wide fans of teal-green sludge out of huge fire hoses and then leaving a yellow warning sign stapled to our neighbor's poplar tree, warning us not to swim for seven to ten days because of the copper sulfate they sprayed in the lake.

In a home video from my second birthday, I am making sand castles with my dad while my mom films from the deck, commenting on how my dad lets me wear my best dress in the sand, how I am unfazed getting it dirty. The tape cuts to me in a bathing suit, pink with tiny white hearts and a bow in the back. I squat in the lake, slurping it. My dad is filming, and the camera zooms in on my mom, sunning herself on the dock. I take the sand castle bucket, fill it with water and muck from the shallows, and dump it on my head. In the video, the lake might as well be a bathtub. I'm lying in the water, flailing, gulping, gurgling, pretending I know how to swim even though it's only two inches deep. I watch this video now looking for evidence, some kind of foreshadowing, but all I learn is that I have always been a creature of the water, a nymph.

In an email exchange with an epidemiologist this past year, I found out that endodermal sinus tumors, the type of tumor I had, are latent at birth. She had recently published a paper that looked at family history of cancers in relatives of children with germ cell tumors. But out of the 780 children in her study, none had relatives with glioblastomas. She said researchers still don't know what causes germ cell tumors, but the DNA mutation happens in utero, or maybe pre-conception, possibly in the egg or sperm pre-pregnancy, or possibly in the fetus itself post-conception.

I think of tenth-grade biology, when we each had to pick a part of the cell to study in depth and then present our findings to the class. I picked the mitochondria, the power plant of the cell. *Cells*, our teacher said, *are the building blocks of life, built with coded instructions to divide and multiply.* The mitochondria are in charge of producing the cell's chemical energy. They control cell life, cell growth, cell metabolism, cell proliferation. This is how blood replenishes itself, by creating new cells, and this is how it clots, by damming up the break in flesh. A healthy body produces 300 billion new cells a day. It is mitochondria that are responsible for telling a cell when it is time to die, a preprogrammed death, apoptosis. It makes sense that the part of the cell that causes cells to be self-perpetuating is the same part capable of destruction. Tumors are formed from a glitch in DNA transcription, when apoptosis fails to happen as it's supposed to. Cancer is just the body, full of life, performing its most basic function in excess. Now, looking back, it is unnerving to think, even as a zygote in the womb, my cells knew this would happen.

The type of tumor I had originated from a primordial germ cell—the cells that precede sperm or egg cells—and then, later in childhood, something led it to begin dividing again, unchecked. But my parents lived in Marne during my mom's pregnancy with me. We didn't move to Lake Bella Vista until I was two. Environmental exposure from something in Rockford was ruled out.

For glioblastomas, the cell-dividing glitch that leads to cancer happens later in life, increasing the time and amount of environmental exposures possible. From an epigenetic standpoint, as we age and move into new towns and new homes and change jobs, the more complicated the retrospective line of questioning becomes. Multiple studies have linked glioblastomas to disproportionate exposure to polluted air, atomic bomb fallout, magnetic fields, cell phone use, and, most notably, ionizing radiation from x-rays and CAT scans.

I think about holding my dad's hand while the CAT scan machine raged above me, his torso covered in a lead tunic the technician had given him, his head uncovered. When I emailed an epidemiologist in Seattle to ask about this, he was surprised that my dad would have been allowed in the CAT scan room at all, even in the early 1990s. He said the ambient exposure risks then were known.

* * *

Reading all these articles and talking to epidemiologists, I felt I'd traveled nowhere, that I was no closer to having a satisfactory answer. It is difficult now for me to remember who he was before he was sick, difficult to remember that this illness was never the most important thing about him, about any of us. For a while, it seemed that in order for my connection to him to continue beyond his death, I had to find solace in knowing the thing that killed him—that in the story of genetic heritability, both of us suffering from a familial curse, we could be forever intertwined, our fates contingencies of each other. But in this mythology, my sense of self would inevitably be rooted in illness, in my dad's and in mine. Maybe, for me, finding something to blame was never the end goal but rather wanting to feel connected. The epidemiologists I reached out to, total strangers, were willing to reply to my emails because I served as a reminder that behind the data points on their tables and graphs were people's lives, and their family's lives, and their family's family's lives, and that we are all connected to each other in this way. Asking the impossible question *Why twice?* then searching endlessly for an unknowable answer feels, to me, the only way to be alive.

17

have memories of napping, face down, on the floor of our Glastron outboard. I am wrapped in the snug grasp of a yellow life jacket, my cheek pressed against the gold Astroturf carpeting. I can hear the sound of ripples beneath the boat glug-glugging against the hull and the sounds of my parents' voices, and I am content.

The Glastron was a dream boat for my dad. The boat was the 1980s version of the one James Bond drove in the 1974 movie *Live and Let Die*. Its fiberglass was sparkling gold, the driver's and passenger's seats were upholstered in gold vinyl with white piping, and the windshield was tinted and curved, like a boat-sized version of aviators. Nearly half the boat's length was just its needle-nose closed bow. That triangle of fiberglass glinting in the sun was smooth and flat, like the top of a pelican's bill, designed to make the boat quick to plane. The boat was svelte and light, its wake nearly nonexistent.

My mom says the day they came home from the hospital after I was born, they strapped me into a car seat, dropped the Glastron into Murray Lake, and drove me around for a *tour of the lake*. When I had insomnia in high school, I would sometimes walk out on the dock, peel the cover back on the back half of the boat, and arrange my sleeping bag on the floor, the boat still tied to the dock. This was what I knew of rocking.

I took a boater's safety class when I was twelve. The class was offered at the boat show inside the DeVos Place convention center in downtown Grand Rapids. While I sat in a folding chair in a makeshift classroom and watched the instructor demonstrate the proper ways to wear a variety of life vests, my dad peered under the engine covers of MasterCrafts, Ski Nautiques, Malibus, and Moombas, taking notes. I'd been driving the Glastron on his lap since I was three, knew to drive counterclockwise around our lake,

206

knew the boater ahead of you always had the right of way, and to never follow closely behind a boat with a skier. At the end of the day, the instructor gave me a small blue square of cardstock paper to sign, and he signed, and then I was a certified boat driver. My dad was puffed with pride when I came out of the classroom holding my new license. He folded it into the bright green cylindrical keychain attached to the boat keys, meant to keep the keys afloat if they were to ever get tossed overboard.

The next summer, my dad sold our gold Glastron outboard and bought a Malibu inboard. He said we had outgrown the Glastron, though I think the rectifier was going out, and he had spent too many hours lugging the boat's battery up to the garage and waiting for it to charge. In the twenty years since he had purchased it, the Glastron had become a kind of trendy retro model, made valuable by people's nostalgia for the 1980s. The day my dad pulled the Glastron out of the lake and hooked it up to a man's Chevy Tahoe, my mom watched from the driveway, sobbing. In recounting that day to me later, she said, *We had so many memories in that boat. It was just so hard to see it go.*

* * *

The August before my dad died, I moved from Colorado back to Michigan. My mom had already made up her mind to sell the house. I was too late to convince her otherwise. When we were alone, she said to me, *The lake is too much work for me to keep up with alone*, and *I don't want to live here without him.* She and my dad had remodeled the house ten years earlier, retiled their bathroom with hundreds of tiny black-and-white hexagons like something out a 1950s drugstore, laid all the bricks for a backyard patio, redone all the landscaping, turned half the yard into flower beds for her perennials, trained a wisteria up a trellis that had bloomed for the first time the summer prior. My dad was sulking, staunchly opposed to selling the house. I attributed his mood to his old stubbornness, which had been accentuated by his two surgeries and anti-seizure meds, but I wonder now how much of his defiance was just base instinct, the mind's inability

207

to fully admit one's own mortality. I intuited that my mom needed an ally. I said, *Okay. Whatever you think is best.*

In October, my parents took the Malibu out for the last time. My dad had been tinkering around the beach, cleaning the boat for us to sell it, and had asked our neighbor with a truck to meet him at the launch with our trailer. My mom had allowed him to drive the boat a few times that fall, as long as she was with him. His vision had degenerated, and as much as she wanted to think nothing could happen on all that open water, she'd learned to expect the worst. So, when she saw him backing away from the dock alone to take the boat across the lake to the launch to meet our neighbor, she hollered from the deck, *Hey, wait for me. I want one last color tour of the lake.*

Where was I? Maybe at work? Maybe sitting at the desk in the windowless basement, reading everything on Craigslist, education jobs, food/bev/hosp jobs, women seeking women, women seeking men, men seeking men, missed connections. I paid little attention to my parents in those first months after I moved home. I had made the decision to move home because I was worried about my dad's declining health. A part of me found watching him unbearable, but a louder part of me felt guilty for having moved to Colorado in the first place. I couldn't bear the idea of not being there at the end, and I knew my mom could use the help. But even knowing I had made the decision myself, I was full of childish resentment. Mustering the poise to mark our last fall together on the lake with any intentionality would have meant admitting to my dad and to myself that he was dying. All I know is my dad and mom drove that boat for the last time together on the lake, and I wasn't there.

The day they took the boat out, it was already late in the fall. There were only two other boats out on the lake, fishermen. My dad didn't see them. They were on his left side, and even though my mom was coaxing him to turn the wheel, he didn't hear her. In the story my mom told me later that night, he missed both boats, but just barely, cutting the fishing lines from one of the boats. The fishermen yelled, and my mom yelled back, *I'm sorry*, and let my

208

dad complete that last circuit around the lake. But the fishermen weren't finished yelling and sped their tiny gray boat over to the launch, continuing to shout at my dad, chewing him out.

The following week, she wrote in her journal:

> *10-27-2009*
>
> *It is the NOT knowing that is the hardest for us both. Fall feels like it is the beginning of the end of something every year anyway and now it is hard to take since we both know it could be our last anniversary together or our last fall to enjoy together. That makes it all the more critical to make the most of it and brings on guilt when we stay home and don't do something special to celebrate. This year it seems that the fall leaf show has gone overboard to prove that it is worthy of notice. This forces me to contemplate on the craziness of my job and our house sale, and I question if it is what I should be doing right now. But we have shared 28+ of these seasons together in somewhere and with someone special already and we have missed nothing as a result, even if it is not repeated.*

My mom said that she knew at that moment at the boat launch that it was good they were selling the house and the boat and leaving behind this place where we had been a family. That there was no way we would have been able to live there without him. And she was probably right.

* * *

A friend of mine from Colorado, Jason, drove out to Michigan to visit right before we moved. He was five feet eleven and clean-shaven, his dark hair kept messy on purpose, a military haircut grown too long. He and I had worked together one summer at the backpacking camp in Colorado. He wore a different plaid flannel every day of his visit. He brought his giant dog, Jack, a Great Dane–black Lab mix, and the dog kept knocking things off my mom's shelves with his tail. My parents' dog, Maggie, was beside

209

herself with jealousy, first at my dog, Scout, and now at this gangly boy dog.

It's easy to see why my parents assumed that Jason and I were a couple. He had driven from St. Louis, where he was living with his parents, to Michigan. Neither of us was out to our Midwestern parents. Both of us had twenty years of practice calculating a façade for whomever our audience wanted us to be.

Jason helped me take the dock out that last time, standing in the lake in my dad's brown rubber waders. It was cold already, the lake freezing around the edges in the mornings. All the leaves had come off the trees and the lake looked brown; the sky, gray. I wore the dry suit my dad bought me the summer I learned to ski barefoot, now several sizes too small, and waterski gloves I'd soaked in a cooler of warm water, as my dad had taught me to do before we'd ski on cold mornings. Although my dad wouldn't admit it, he was too weak to be much help with the dock, and my mom said she didn't want him getting in that water. *It's too cold*, she said, so he sat on a lawn chair in the sand and gave us instructions, wearing jeans and a sweatshirt, boat shoes with no socks. *You want to take that section off last*, he said, pointing. *Start from the back.* Jason knew how to use a ratchet wrench better than I did, and I knew how to stack the sections of the dock.

Are you selling the dock before you move? Jason asked my dad.

No, my dad said. *The family that bought the house said they'd accept the price if we threw in the dock.*

Do you think they'll know how to put it together in the spring? I asked.

No, my dad said. He'd cut the top off a milk jug, and we were to put all the bolts and clamps for the dock in the jug, leave it in the garage somewhere for them to figure out in April. Jason's dog kept wanting to swim, kept extending his paw toward the water's cold surface and then pulling back.

When we had the dock out, we waded out to where the end of the dock had been and searched with our feet for the weights we'd strung to Maggie's electric fence. The weights were two plastic ice cream tubs my dad had punched holes in, strung the wire through, then filled with sand. I found the one on my corner, reached down with my hand, the freezing water up to my armpit, and handed the tub to Jason, then went to find the one on his corner. When we had both corners, we walked together toward the shore, set the tubs in the sand, straightened out the wire.

Do these people even have a dog? I asked.

I don't know, my dad said. *Maybe they'll get one after they see we have the fence already set up.*

Jason and I drove out to Lake Michigan that afternoon, let the dogs run off leash on the beach. The gray waves were pounding on the wet sand, and we had to shout to call the dogs back, two black dots bolting up the perimeter of Michigan's western edge, kicking up sand. Jason said, *I'm glad I got to meet your dad. You're just like him, you know.*

* * *

The day before Thanksgiving, a week away from moving, my mom and I took a trip to Best Buy and bought my dad a giant flat-screen TV.

The TV was meant to be a consolation prize for selling the house. He was becoming less and less mobile by the day, growing more and more tired, and we figured he might as well enjoy this one last remaining thing, propped up on pillows in front of a TV.

My mom had just finished packing the entire contents of the house into boxes, the house where she had lived for most of her marriage and nearly all of her motherhood. I had been offered a job coordinating an after-school program in a Montessori school in downtown Grand Rapids. We walked through the automatic sliding doors under that giant off-kilter yellow sign on a mission. We knew nothing about TVs—just that we needed one, a big one.

One of my mom's college students had previously had a job at Best Buy, and she asked him to write down all the latest features—what to look for, what to avoid—on a piece of paper, which my mom clutched in her right hand. A football game flashed on over fifty screens across the back wall, an exhibit of the surplus of inventory more than a realistic mode of visual comparison. All that green made me dizzy.

We had left my dad home alone and driven to Best Buy, just the two of us. In the store, we felt unburdened, like we had just come through some great adversity together. We were slap happy, laughing at the idiocy of buying a new TV. Everything seemed futile and absurd. *Hey, Mom*, I said sarcastically. *Check this one out. It has a V-chip. You can block certain channels you don't want your kids to watch, then override the block with your secret code.*

Or this one, she said, raising one eyebrow. *This one says Smart Capable.*

We went back and forth with the salesclerk for a while, until he sold us the forty-two-inch Sony my mom wanted. We didn't care what model he sold us, just that it came in a big box and that we could take it home that day.

When we moved into the house a week later, we unpacked the TV first, sat it up in the new living room, positioned the couch across from it, and turned it to ESPN. My dad fell asleep there, the new remote in his hand, while my mom unpacked box after box in the kitchen, unwrapping all the twenty-year-old appliances and kitchenware they'd received at their wedding and placing them gently into the cabinets.

That winter, my dad and I watched pledge-a-thons for Haiti relief. We watched the opening ceremonies to the Winter Olympics in Vancouver. We watched Lindsey Vonn crash out of the course in the women's slalom finals. We watched the Daytona 500, all those stock cars low to the ground, tracing oval after tedious oval, feeling the Doppler roar of their engines somewhere deep in our chests. I thought then: *What else is there?* I felt as if we'd been tracing that same stretch of track around and around, five hundred miles and traveling nowhere.

We watched *Rent* on repeat, my head on his lap, Maggie at his feet. Whatever callousness I felt toward my family that winter, fiction still undid me. I felt more watching Roger and Mimi confess their mortality to each other in the courtyard behind the Life Café than I did about any of my dad's incremental deteriorations. I began to crave that movie, if not for its depiction of sexual plurality, then certainly for the way it stirred some ache inside me, all of these twenty-somethings living in the face of chronic illness. In the decade after my dad died, I would clean my apartment and grade papers with *Rent* on in the background. I watched it twenty, maybe thirty, times a year until I wore out the DVD. Each time, I wondered what my dad thought about the scenes with Angel and Collins going to life support meetings, when they sang, "reason says I should have died three years ago." But I never asked him when he was alive. Part of me felt it would have been cruel to ask him, forcing him to give voice to his terminal diagnosis when I knew he wanted nothing more than to go back in time, to a time when none of this was happening. And part of me knew he knew, at some subconscious level, why I loved the movie so much.

* * *

I didn't help much with the move. I packed a few boxes, labeled them "kitchen," "dining room," "storage," in slanting lowercase letters. I mostly made myself scarce while my mom did all the packing. I didn't have the self-awareness to notice or name my own sulkiness for what it was—misplaced remorse—but I know that I too am stubborn, resistant to change. When I moved home, I reverted to the teenager I had been the last time I had lived under the same roof as my parents. Some part of me felt shame that my dad was dying, for the mornings in high school when I'd rolled over and gone back to sleep instead of getting up to ski with him, for the hundred times he'd asked me to put the cover on the boat and I'd forgotten. In college and in Colorado, I had been surrounded by friends who were profuse with their affection. I wanted to be able to say something honest and sentimental to both my parents about all the memories they'd curated for me in that house, what it meant to me, but be it pride or embarrassment or cowardice, I never said anything.

The day the moving vans came, I helped assemble tall boxes, placing the metal rods the movers gave me across the width of the boxes while my mom carried down armfuls of dresses and suits and pants, twenty years' worth of clothes from their closet, all of them still on hangers. I watched as the movers hauled furniture out of one house and into another, told them which room was which. My mom recounts that day as a *sad, sad day*. When we finally emptied that house of everything and she pulled out of the driveway for the last time, she was alone. My dad was at work, and I was already at the new house directing traffic. That afternoon, while she was putting away china in the new dining room, I watched TV with my dad. She hollered from the other room, *Hey, Cara, where are the shelves to the china cabinet?* and I said I didn't know. She said, *I think I left them on the curb back at Belinda for the trash pickup.* I said I would drive back and check.

It was still light out, and the drive was only twenty minutes. When I arrived at the curb of our old house, the garage doors were shut and the house looked cold and forlorn, as if a person seeking shelter could hole up inside it for days and never get warm. I rummaged through the debris on the side of the road, found the shelves she was talking about, threw them in the back seat of my car, and drove away.

Years later, I asked my mom, *Where are those red-and-white skis you bought Dad the day you found out you were pregnant with me?* She said she didn't know, to look downstairs. I said, *I've looked already. They're not there.* She said, *I don't know then. I don't have them.* She never asked why I was looking for them. She said she lost her mind the day we moved, started chucking things in that trash pile by the side of the road. She said, *Who knows what got put in that pile. I was cleaning out the back room, and I couldn't bear it.*

* * *

I miss that lake nearly every day. I read online that mayflies lay their eggs on the surface of lakes and streams, let them sink to the bottom, and their nymph forms are born from the depths. Mayflies

214

are the only winged creatures to shed a skin of themselves, all those crunchy exoskeletons littering the railing of our back deck, leaving behind their blueprints of flight.

On the one-year anniversary of my dad's death, I drove an hour and a half from my apartment in Moscow, Idaho, to Lake Coeur d'Alene. It was the nearest lake, and I was compelled to go even though I had no ritual planned. I just drove.

When I got to the lake, it was snowing. It was April, and my dog was sleeping in the back seat, so I let her sleep. I got out of the car and walked down the white dock all the way to its end without looking down. When I did finally look into the water, I saw nothing, not even my reflection, just a steel-gray surface, and beneath it, ripples of sand. Maybe this was the biggest loss of all. I stood there for a minute, horrified, then walked back to the car, turned the ignition, and drove home.

* * *

Two summers after my dad died, I moved home for a few months to live with my mom. I was in grad school, and she was still teaching microbiology. Both of us were on academic calendars and lonely, needing the company.

I emailed a local university waterski team. I asked if I could ski with them a few days a week. They emailed me back within minutes. They said practice was at three and they would see me there. I found my ski and life jacket in the basement, grabbed a pair of worn-out ski gloves, and piled everything into the back seat of my car. I drove barefoot with the windows down, Tracy Chapman on the radio. From a mile away, I spotted those red and yellow buoys laid out in a pattern across the water's surface, and I knew whatever spirit of my dad's that remained wasn't left behind on the curb at the Lake Bella Vista house. The sun glinted off the surface of the water, and I stood on the end of the dock, my ski under one arm, as the boat whipped into shore, slingshotting the skier in behind it.

18

In the four months we lived in that new home together, my mom, grandparents, and me tiptoed around my dad, not wanting him to catch on that it was almost the end. Ryan was in Chicago at school.

The new house was a part of the Heritage Hill Historic District that covers more than five square miles of neighborhoods in Grand Rapids—all the homes built at the turn of the twentieth century, meant to house the furniture CEOs and doctors and lumber barons who built the city. Our house was a Craftsman style, built in 1912, with eve brackets and a big porch, where, in the spring, my mom hung the white wicker swing that used to face the lake in the backyard at our old house. Across the street was a Dutch Reformed church where, every Sunday, all the women wore dressy hats and stood in the parking lot chatting with each other. Next to the church was another Craftsman with a north-facing widow's watch. My mom joked that you could sit up there all day and not see any ships coming or going—all you would see from up there was I-196. But we both didn't say what we were really thinking, that in our house, you wouldn't have to climb into an alcove in the attic to watch in vain for your spouse's return.

My mom went to work every morning at nine, and I spent most of my days on the couch with my dad while my grandpa alternated between the financial news network and Fox News, muting the commercials, and my grandma knit pastel-green and pastel-pink and pastel-blue baby hats for the hospital's neonatal unit.

I was hired for a part-time job as an after-school program coordinator, and every day at two o'clock, I walked the two blocks north of our house to a gas station and bought a sixteen-ounce coffee. Then I walked south on Michigan Avenue to the Montessori school and laid out fifty-five state-mandated healthy snacks and fifty-five chocolate milks.

216

My office was a closet at the back of the cafeteria with a filing cabinet full of basketballs that didn't hold air and plastic jump ropes and bins of crayons and markers and pony beads. I was issued a work cell phone by the YMCA when they offered me the job, and it was broken at the hinge, so when I flipped it open, the screen was black and dead until I shoved the socket back in. Sometimes parents would call me to tell me they were running late to pick up their kids, and I would say, *Okay*, and stay late with their kids.

* * *

The week before Christmas, some of my parents' friends from Lake Bella Vista came over for dinner. My mom made a three-layer white cake with coconut frosting and raspberry jam in between the layers and decorated it with fresh raspberries. While she was in the kitchen with her guests, washing dishes after the meal, Maggie the dog stood, all four feet on the dining room table, and ate the cake right off the crystal cake tray. My dad sat on the couch, looking straight at the table, at the dog, not registering any of it.

I hid out in the attic during their dinner, watching the Olympics. I feigned a story in my head, that my parents' friends would think of me as a washed-up twenty-something, unemployable with a degree in English and in debt from spending a year living in Colorado pretending to be a ski bum, come to live with my parents as a part of some twenty-first-century trend—a whole generation of young people graduating from college as the economy tanked. But after the dinner, one of my mom's friends climbed the stairs up to the attic, on a self-guided tour of the house, and sat down next to me on the couch. *I know this must be hard for you*, she said. *Seeing your dad like this*. I bristled, resisting her sympathy, and didn't take my eyes off the TV. She went into a soliloquy about watching us ski all the time off their back deck, my dad and me out there every Sunday morning, as regular as the sun rising, and I gave in a little to her sentiment. She talked about how hard it had been on my dad to see me sick, and how her husband had made a point to come visit us every day in the hospital. I remembered him coming. My dad had acknowledged his visits in the journal he kept for me. She said, finally, *It's gonna be okay, Cara, you're gonna be okay,* and I didn't know if she was saying it for her own sake, just because it was something to say, or if she was saying it because she genuinely thought it would comfort me, but I realized in that moment, with this neighbor I hardly knew putting her hand on my knee, a part of me had been craving an onlooker, someone to acknowledge the tragedy our household had come to. The tragedy of moving off the lake and living in a city surrounded by strangers, and the tragedy of acknowledging in the private spaces of ourselves that my dad didn't have much longer to live but never speaking it in the daylight. And her words—*Cara, you're gonna be okay*—struck something in me that I hadn't yet considered: that I would continue living after he died, that I would have to assemble a life for myself, that this was what every one of my parents' friends saw when they looked at me.

* * *

That winter break, I took an Amtrak to Breckenridge for a New Year's Eve reunion. My friends picked me up from Union Station at eight in the morning, all four of them, still drunk and in their pj's. The sun was the kind of blinding white that happens only close to the winter solstice at five thousand feet above sea level during the dog-walking hours of the morning.

We drove up to Breckenridge and met up with a friend of ours who still worked for the resort and gave us half-price lift passes. I called home before dinner to check in with my mom. When she answered, I asked, *How's Dad?* and she said, *Oh, the usual.* Then I asked what they did that day, and she said, *Watched a documentary about Henry Ford with Grandma and Grandpa.* I read disapproval in between her lines, that she was upset I had left, that I had thought that even though he wasn't doing well, that it was okay to go on this trip. I asked her what their plans were for New Year's Eve. She said, *Probably just go to bed. I don't think we're going to stay up like we usually do to watch the ball drop,* and I said, *Okay. Tell Dad hi from me,* and hung up the phone.

That night we took mushrooms and played a drinking game called land mines, where you have to spin a quarter and take two shots of beer and then pick the quarter up before it stops spinning. We drank through an entire case of PBR and then gathered ourselves to walk to the bus station to hitch a ride into town to see a jam band at the New Year's Eve party. I sat on the rug by the front door and took great care tying my gray New Balances in double knots, slow and methodical, like a kindergartener. On the driveway, I skated circles around everyone in my bald sneakers, my hands deep in my jean pockets.

We steamed up the plastic windows of the bus stop, all nine of us crammed in there, breathing like ferns in a terrarium. A friend I had a crush on buried her hands in my pockets, full now with both sets of hands, and I pulled her close with interlocked fingers until we were thigh to thigh.

Somebody asked *Who has the tickets?* and we all searched through our coats. No tickets. Dustin and I volunteered to walk back up to the house to search for them. Back inside, I laid on the rug in the entryway while the whole room spun. The rafters in the ceiling seemed to split apart from the rest of the roofing and kept plummeting to the earth, over and over. Dustin found the tickets on the fridge and we walked back down to the bus stop, but the bus had come and gone, taking our entourage with it. The night was cloudless, and suddenly Dustin and I were sober and quiet, the stars a mess across the sky.

We walked side by side for nearly a mile, sticking out our thumbs for every westbound car that passed, but we didn't get picked up until we were nearly to town. The driver of the van scolded us for loitering in the street, like he was trying to be our dad.

When we finally made it to the venue, the band was on its second set. Inside, the lights were crazy. I walked outside to the bathroom in pursuit of a drinking fountain. There was no drinking fountain. I stuck my head under the bathroom sink, soaking one side of my hair, lapping water like a dog. At midnight, the band played "Auld Lang Syne," and everyone around me coupled off, kissing.

After the show, we tried to call a taxi, but it never came, and we ended up hitching to my friend's house in two separate cars. Back at the house, each of our bodies throbbed with significance. Full to the brim with beer and strobe lights and bass line, all our touching became bloated, limbs draped over each other, lingering, as if love were not a scarce or finite thing. I dangled my feet from the barstool and sipped water from a dirty wineglass. I wanted, in that way a child craves to be held, for all of us to curl up in some gigantic nest of a bed together, but when Dustin and his girlfriend invited me to come to bed with them, I said, *No thanks.* I put all the dirty dishes in the sink and the cans in the recycling and thought about my dad.

* * *

On my return trip home, it dumped snow. My train was delayed in Chicago for ten hours before they decided to put us all in a van and drive around the bottom of Lake Michigan and then north to Grand Rapids. My parents both came to the Amtrak station to pick me up at midnight, and, in the five-minute drive back to the house on Crescent Street, my dad fell asleep and was snoring. My mom said, *The Buick is in the shop*, and I said, *What?* She said that he tried to move it one night from the south side of the street to the north, in compliance with a citywide law for snow plowing that said between November and April you could only park on one side of the streets on odd-numbered days and the other side on even-numbered days, but that he didn't see a parked car and smashed into it. She said, *He was just trying to help, Cara*, and explained that she had fallen asleep on the couch watching TV, and when they went up to bed, he had said, *Shouldn't someone move Cara's car?* My dad didn't say anything about hitting anything when he came in that night, so my mom didn't find out until the next day, when she saw my car parked on an angle and smashed on one side. The other car that he'd hit was gone, with no note or attempted contact. She said, *You know he can't see very well out his right side.*

Back inside the house, I stood in front of the fridge, considering

220

its contents. The light from inside the fridge was the only light on in the house, and it cast a ghostly glow across my silhouette and onto the kitchen floor. *I'm so sorry, Cara*, my dad said, and I lost it completely, starting to sob, crumpling into a ball at the base of the fridge, the door still cocked open, hitting against my leg.

Maybe I was just relieved. I'd been coiled into a tightly wound ball the whole five days I'd been gone, half expecting something to happen to my dad while I was in Colorado. Now that I was home and everyone was relatively okay, I was able to let go of all of that. But in that moment, I knew my dad was watching and that I had failed at keeping it a secret from him that he was dying and that all of us were worried sick about it. Our interiority is never fully our own. I knew in his words, *I'm so sorry*, that he understood every bit of what that meant to me.

* * *

In the months that followed, every day or so, my mom emailed me from her office six blocks away to find out how my dad was doing. I would email her back that he was fine, that he was sleeping, or that he had incontinence again, but I'd put the couch cushion cover in the wash on the sanitary cycle and not to worry. One day she emailed me a link to a website that outlined the timeline of a glioblastoma patient with signs and symptoms for three to six weeks prior to death, two to three weeks, one to two weeks, five to seven days, two to five days, final hours. The symptoms for three to six weeks included "increased weakness on affected side," "urinary and bowel incontinence," "may say some odd things that make you think 'where did *that* come from,'" and I knew we were already there, but I said in an email reply, *He's been like this for more than two months. How are we supposed to know?*

* * *

There will be casseroles. I will eat enchiladas, cold, out of someone else's glass pan, peeling back the foil and standing, fork in hand, in front of the fridge. We will have a parade of old neighbors with chilies and quiche and meat loaf and endless store-bought pastries. My mom will go to KFC for the first time ever and bring back a bucket, will sit it in the middle of the dining room table and we will eat from it without plates. I will go to the Wendy's drive-through at two in the morning one night for Frosties. There will be Chinese takeout moldering in the back of the fridge. A whole case of Caffeine Free Diet Cokes down in the basement for five years after he dies that no one else will drink.

My mom and I will drink too much together. Pinot grigio and swiss cheese. Gin and tonics, in the morning, on a Tuesday. She will begin to say "shit" in front of me, and then "fuck," and later, while trying to use the self-service photo kiosk in Walgreens to enlarge the best photo we have of him for the memorial service, she will say "this fucking piece of shit." And the photo specialist will glare at us.

He will lose the ability to support his own weight, and my mom and I will try, one Sunday night, to help him back up the stairs to bed. My mom will want more than anything else for him to die at home, in their bed upstairs. And I will say, *We can do this. I can carry him.* But he was nearing 170 pounds, and we will all three of us fall hard on the landing, panting like dogs, and he will never walk again.

They will bring a metal hospital bed that night and set it up in my mom's office. We will need to move furniture, my mom and I, to make room for the bed, and my back will ache for weeks after he's gone from all the heavy lifting. I will text Ryan to get his work for the week from his professors. That things are getting exponentially worse.

We will stay like that, three days in my mom's office. Maggie won't get off the end of his makeshift bed, will growl when you try to lure her with treats. I will sit with him while my mom goes to work to try to get her lesson plans in the hands of the other faculty who will step in and teach for her. I will have tons of time alone with him, when he is still understanding words, still speaking a few of his own. But I will file my taxes on TurboTax.com and watch episodes of *The Mary Tyler Moore Show* on my laptop and he will ask to see, but I will tell him he can't, that the screen is too small. And those will be the last words he'll say to just me.

Mom will take an emergency leave from work, and I will drive around the bottom of the lake from Grand Rapids to Chicago to get Ryan. To make sure he's okay, that he remembers to bring home his dress shoes and black sport jacket, so he doesn't have to do the train alone this time.

The hospice nurses will explain that our insurance only covers one visit a day, but he will piss himself more times than that and will need to be rolled, will need to have new sheets and diapers put on. And Mom will need more help than she has. We will talk about options, whether we want him to die here in the office, if we can handle that kind of haunting on the main floor. And we will decide to move him to the end-of-life home where all the plants are fake.

* * *

In the hospice hell home we took him to for those last few days, there was a player piano set to play hymns in the lobby. Ryan sat down on the piano's bench and pretended to be playing, his facial expressions exaggerations of what an energetic Sunday pianist might have looked like, making me smile. The place had a communal coffeepot in the lobby with Styrofoam cups in a stack next to it, suggestions. We found the staff's mug stash instead, in a cupboard somewhere in the dining room, a collection of thrift store purchases, each with a rainbow or a baby bunny or some kind of birds in flight, a Hallmark message on a banner in their beaks, and it was our competition to find the most inappropriate mug, one steeped in irony, to bring to our mom. Happiness Depends on Ourselves. God's Love Endures Forever. Life Is for the Brave. She kept giving us dollar bills, sending us down to the vending machine in the basement to bring her back Chili Cheese Fritos, the only food she would eat.

We played bridge, my grandma teaching me to count cards, teaching Ryan to keep score. We assembled one-thousand-piece puzzles. We played Clue until we ran out of blank sheets to keep track on. We smuggled in wine and sipped out of our inspirational mugs. We listened to music on our laptops, our faces illuminated by our backlit screens, doing time together, each of us in our private versions of elsewhere. Our mom was applying to present at a health sciences conference on a cruise ship, working on her proposal. Ryan said, *A bunch of microbiologists on a boat?* smirking. He pulled up YouTube, played "I'm on a Boat" by the Lonely Island and T-Pain for her. When the nurses came in to check on us, we were cracking up.

What we thought would be a day, maybe two, turned into eleven. Ryan and I commuted the thirty minutes home each night. Before leaving the hospice home each night, we asked our mom if we should stay, if she wanted us to stay with her, our question loaded with euphemism. On the last night, we stalled. We went out to Blockbuster and rented *Kiss Kiss Bang Bang* and *The Men Who Stare at Goats* and watched them with our mom with the volume down low. When the movies were over, he was wheezing and we left anyway. I tried to sleep with both dogs in my parents' bed, but Maggie whined all night and refused to get up on the bed. My mom called the landline at four in the morning and said maybe we should come, then called back and said forget it, he's fine. And then at seven she called again and said he was gone. I was asleep when she called. Real, untormented sleep. I woke up Ryan and my grandparents, and we drove the thirty minutes not saying anything, Joe Pug playing in my CD player.

* * *

The morning he died, it hailed. Big shooter-marble sized. We watched the hail accumulate at the bottom of the glass sliding door in the space between the edge of the curtain and the floor.

In the lobby, the player piano was still playing the same hymn, the notes laid out like a barcode, each perforation a premonition of its sound—that suck of air, the way a choir holds its breath just before beginning, the way a father leaves his daughter filled with holes.

19

Drowning is death by water. A lack of oxygen to the brain. Asphyxiation.

In the lifeguarding course I took before my first summer working at summer camp, I learned there is typically no gasping for air, no flailing of arms and splashing about, but rather a glassing-over of eyes, general unresponsiveness, then sudden sinking. Those who are drowning are usually unable to speak, unable to notify anyone nearby of their state of emergency. Their heads bob, tilt back, and, eventually, the weight of their unconscious body dips them below the surface. Then: hypoxia. Brain death.

I pulled plenty of kids out of that lake the summer I worked as a waterfront director. Kids in over their heads. Panicky kids. Kids with blue lips and skinny arms and wrinkled finger pads. No one drowned on my watch.

Once a week we practiced Lost Swimmer Dives. The camp director would blow the air horn, unannounced, and we never knew if it was a drill or the real thing. I was assigned to the green area, the deep end of the roped-off swim area, twelve feet down, and more than that with the muck. All twenty or so guards searching the shallows, their legs making uniform sweeps under the dock, churning up sediments, blurring my view. The other three guards and I were taught to dive straight down—one of us on each side of the square Astroturf-carpeted swim platform—then make neat zippers along the lake bottom, propelling only with our feet, keeping our arms outstretched like a T, high-fiving the diver next to us. We'd hold our breath as long as we could stand and then some, not leaving any time to resurface. They made us search until someone found the object planted earlier, when none of us were looking. Usually, it'd be a bowling ball or a coffee can full of cement or something equally inanimate.

Afterward, I took long showers, rinsing the algae and muck out

226

of my hair, my suit, every crevice. There was a kind of whole-body exhaustion following adrenaline that had run its course. My arms and legs became loose bags of bones and muscle and nerve, my flesh down to the core, completely wrung out with fear, anticipating the worst.

* * *

According to its surface area, Lake Superior is the largest freshwater lake in the world. The summer we vacationed in the UP, I learned about all the shipwrecks on that lake, learned that some say the lake is haunted, that the Witch of November will never be satisfied. She takes bodies, cargo, tons of ore, and, eventually, the heavy iron ships themselves.

The southern shoreline that traces the outline of Michigan's UP is known as the "Graveyard of the Great Lakes" for all the ships that have gone down there. Local legend says the lake never gives up her dead. Year-round, the water is too cold for the bacterial growth that typically brings a drowned body to the surface, leaving families to mourn lost husbands and fathers with empty caskets.

During the booming industrial surge from the turn of the twentieth century to the mid-1970s, huge freighter ships hauled loads of grains and iron ore across Lake Superior, through the Soo Locks to shipping ports in Detroit, Toledo, and Buffalo. Historians point to the winter of 1913 as part of the progress of humankind, that it took hurricane-force winds, thirty-foot waves, four days of snow, two hundred fifty people dead, and nineteen boats swallowed whole to teach Michiganders to build stronger ships, better infrastructure, more accurate weather-predicting instruments. But in 1975, when the same weather pattern brought down the *Edmund Fitzgerald* and all twenty-nine of her crew members, perhaps we submitted to the fact that there are some forces of nature too great for human preparedness. That nothing could have prevented those crew members' bodies from sinking.

* * *

Canadian musician Gordon Lightfoot memorialized the wreck of the *Edmund Fitzgerald* in his ballad of regret. I listen to the song now with Lucia, playing all six minutes over and over on repeat, a mnemonic for the family vacation we took the summer I turned ten, when, holding my dad's hand in the Great Lakes Shipwreck Museum on Whitefish Point, I stood looking at the green glowing screen of a ship underwater: rusted deck railing, intact windows looking in on the darkened captain's cabin, the blades of the propeller as large as the fins of an orca, motionless, forever frozen in time.

Twenty years after the wreck, two divers set out on Lake Superior to be the first to descend the 530 feet down to the ship's resting place without the assistance of a submersible.

It is said the divers took six minutes to descend, six minutes to survey the wreck, and three hours to resurface. They found, next to the bow of the ship, the remains of a crew member fully clothed and wearing his life jacket, lying face down in the mud.

* * *

It is said we die of old age. We die in our sleep. We die peacefully, surrounded by those we love. But nurses know all these are euphemisms. That no one's "lights" simply "go out." The body's ability to sustain life is built on three main systems: the circulatory, respiratory, and nervous. When one system shuts down, the whole body goes into total system failure.

When we asked the nurses *How long?* they said, *He has a strong heart.* When we asked, *How will we know?* they said, *Listen to his breathing.*

In *How We Die*, Dr. Sherwin Nuland describes acute pulmonary edema as "Severe air hunger rapidly supervenes, the gurgling, wheezing respirations begin, and finally the poor oxygenation of the blood causes either brain death or ventricular fibrillation and other rhythm disturbances, from which there is no return."

My dad didn't die of a brain tumor. He died when his lungs gave up. He died by drowning, an anchor heaving into the muck and murk at the bottom of a lake.

Six minutes of "rhythm disturbances."
Six minutes for the blood to pool, turning him yellow.
A decade later, and I'm still trying to resurface.

* * *

Four days after he died, my mom and brother and I drove 170 miles north to Glen Lake. It was early spring and the snow was mostly finished melting, leaving behind brown fields, naked deciduous trees, the medians of the highway outlined by piles of gravel and rims of white residual salt. None of us had ever made this trip without him, and we got lost twice on the back roads, my brother folding and unfolding the ten-year-old accordion map labeled *Michigan* with a sailboat on the cover.

I sat in the back with my dad's ashes in a white cardstock box on the seat next to me. The box was smaller than a brick and weighed nearly nothing, and when my mom parked the car in the pullout for Glen Lake, I tucked the box in the bottom of my backpack next to a Nalgene of water and shoved a sweatshirt in overtop.

Overlooking the water, I recalled ten summers earlier when my dad taught me to ski the slalom course here. I could still see the six red buoys and sixteen yellow boat balls set in a neat corridor, bobbing like ghosts on the horizon, even though the lake's superintendent hadn't yet installed the course for the season.

In this sacred place, my dad was alive again, in the Glastron's driver's seat, pulling me up and back through that corridor until I got the timing right. When I finally made it around that sixth buoy and tossed up the rope in celebration, gliding to a stop, he U-turned the boat to come back for me. Standing now, with his hair whipping above the windshield and grinning widely out over that sparkling blue lake.

The hike down to the shoreline was steep, and there was no trail, but none of us doubted that this was the right place, the right thing to do.

20

t was May, six weeks after my dad died, and I was ten thousand feet above sea level, back in Colorado working at the same backpacking camp I'd worked at the previous two summers. The sunrise glowed orange on the peaks in front of us. Wyatt and I were down in the shadows, our boots crunching through the frost-crusted meadow on the west shore of Little Molas Lake. We were quiet, trudging uphill.

For the two weeks before the camp opened, we had staff training, and my coworker, Wyatt, and I were given the morning off to prepare for a two o'clock presentation on preventing and responding to backcountry emergencies. *We're gonna bag Sultan and Turk*, we told our boss the night before, casting our eyes toward the buttress across the highway, unable to hide the excitement the limestone and granite rock faces incited in us. Wyatt and I were hired to work with the oldest campers: high school juniors and seniors. In a week, we would begin leading twenty-six-day backpacking trips up and over these thirteen-thousand-foot peaks with eight or so teenagers in tow. That night, we dispersed camped off the south slope of the highway connecting Durango to Silverton. A thousand feet below us, the Animas River carved its path south to Durango. Above us stood a cirque of thirteeners striped with snowfields.

That night, we were giddy, anticipating getting up at dawn, lacing up boots around frozen toes and strapping on day packs, packing the bare essentials: a loaf of pumpkin bread, block of cheese, prepackaged Oh Boy! Oberto beef jerky, GORP, the streamlined first aid kit, a full liter of water each, gloves, rain jacket, ice axe.

Sometime before six in the morning, we were up and moving, our conversation picking up where we left off the night before, filling in the quiet corners of a new friendship. He was a plant biology major, so I asked him the name of every plant we passed. *The green buds barely poking through the ground are skunk cabbage.*

230

Awesome for toilet paper, he said. *The tiny yellow flowers are dogtooth violets, also known as snow lilies. They bloom right after the snow melts out.* I wanted to ask him what kind of plant flourishes instead of withers in below-freezing temperatures. What kind of world is this that invents adversity and then evolves a whole category of flora and fauna to be resilient?

We passed an adult elk skeleton, all of its bones in their original arrangement on the ground, as if the flesh had been stripped away midstride. The skull was white as a wall mount, boiled by the sun, and antlers rested against ribs, too heavy to hold, puncturing that cavern where a heart once pumped blood, pumped warmth. Vertebrae as large as my two clasped hands interlocked still. The pelvis, built for running, convex instead of concave, lay crooked, toppled. The bones: a stark-white grave marker in this green alpine tundra. A few minutes later we spotted a circle of twelve other skeletons, and I felt as if we were standing in a museum exhibit, that maybe the mastodon extinction happened just months ago, their massive bodies submitting to some predetermined date. Wyatt said, *They must have frozen; it was a hard winter here this year.*

I wanted to tell him then about what bones looked like when they've been incinerated, how a living thing can be reduced to clumps of dust and shards. I wanted to tell him what weariness looks like, what it meant to be fifty-two years old and completely worn out, bone tired. A part of me wanted to lie down and stay here with the elk; I, too, was bone tired, didn't want to keep having to carry on without him. But I kept quiet, willing one foot in front of the other.

We were above tree line now, our boots crunching through alternating fields of talus and mud, the earth soggy and yielding beneath us. That morning, sometime before dawn, we'd climbed through the thick subalpine region where Wyatt pointed out the differences between lodgepole pines and mountain hemlocks. Letting me catch my breath, letting me remember my mom, whom I had left widowed and alone fifteen hundred miles away, where she was still making whole pots of coffee, then dumping most of it out. *See their cones,* he'd said. *The lodgepole's fat and rigid, splayed open, and the hemlock's small and long, its scales flexible, soft to the touch. See the angle of the branches,* he'd said. *The hemlock's branches are tapered down at the tips, the lodgepole's crown is conical-shaped, reaching skyward.* At about seven in the morning, up at twelve thousand feet, the forest started to thin, and soon we were taller than any of the trees around us. *The krummholz,* Wyatt called these stunted trees, named by the Germans. The trees that still tried to grow at that elevation were windbeaten and dwarfed, their branches gnarly and twisted. I could tell, for Wyatt, there was a kind of security in knowing the names of each plant, knowing weather patterns, seasonal trends. Even though we could control so few of the factors out here, we could count on all observable phenomenon to be explainable. When we looked at these defiant trees, we could know they were slouching from all the wind and weather at this elevation, and when we looked at a May creek crossing, we could know it was raging because of the snowmelt. Wyatt's naming was, in a way, a kind of acknowledgment of causal relationships. The more you looked, the more sense it all made.

I saw myself then as a part of that same string of cause and effect, that my coming back to Colorado was just gravity rushing snowmelt downhill, and all this ever was about was running away.

Out there, breathing that thin air, I was torn. I kept oscillating between grief and liberation. I felt I should not have been allowed to be out there with Wyatt, surrounded by mountains, feeling alive and in awe.

But, more than survivor's guilt, I had grown tired of my own solemnity, my self-imposed constraints, that everything I said out loud kept coming back to his illness, this loss. I wished I could just go on a hike, be in the present moment, enjoy how invigorating it felt.

When I first came to Colorado three summers earlier, freshly graduated with a liberal arts degree, bored and antsy and full of ideas about what living in the backcountry would be like, I remembered how exhilarated I had felt on our family ski trip to Steamboat, seeing the mountains for the first time, hanging my head upside down in the back seat of our minivan to try to view the tops of the peaks. I imagined a kind of daily rejuvenation basking in the shadows of an awe-inspiring landscape. Instead, I found that my own shadow followed me, that I was stalked by guilt for having left my mom alone. My anguish kept me awake those freezing nights, under so many stars.

My first summer working at the camp, I learned the wilderness was not some sort of sanctuary where it was easy to forget where you came from. I thought maybe if I took on external responsibility, keeping kids safe, keeping their morale high enough to pound out fifteen miles a day, maybe if I made a living out of getting up at sunrise to boil water for oatmeal, I would feel useful. But instead, I spent all those hours walking at the back of the line, like we were taught to do, running worst-case scenarios inside my head, wondering if my mom called the camp, how long it'd take my boss to hike out here and find us, to tell me my dad had died. At night, I sat under the tarps with my headlamp pointed at our USGS quads, using the red string from my compass to measure mileage from the nearest trailhead. Thirty miles would be something like ten hours until I would know. Ten hours between my mom's phone call and my receiving the message. Ten hours of ignorance.

Now that my dad was gone, I thought I would feel relieved. But I'd just replaced all that worrying about my dad with wondering how my mom was holding up without me. I imagined her walking the dog for hours just to fill her days, mowing the lawn, pulling the blinds in the front window so no one would know she was alone in her house.

* * *

By nine o'clock, Wyatt and I were almost to the crux of our ascent, and we found a faint climber's trail, beaten-down grass and scree in the shape of a Z, switchbacking toward the lowest point on the buttress. I'd been over this saddle before with a group of campers two summers prior, so I warned Wyatt this was a false summit. We were trying to avoid the snowfields, because it was steep, and one slip could cost us our summer jobs, so we were sticking to the trail most of the time, sidestepping from grass tuft to grass tuft, where the scree was held in place by shallow roots from vegetation.

It was slow going up to the saddle for Wyatt and me, but we knew in a week there would be so much more at stake, so much more verbal encouragement, coaching our campers through every step. I kept thinking the past two summers we'd been lucky that no one had been seriously injured climbing these mountains, and I wondered how I would cope if something were to happen to one of our group. In that moment, I noticed a shift inside of me taking hold. The previous two summers, I had thought nothing of the risk. But in the span of a year, the risk-taking had become so unpalatable. Having just watched my dad die, I felt all of us stood on a thin precipice between life and non-life, that anything could happen at any moment, that there was nothing inherent about staying alive, no momentum to it.

I was breaking in new hiking boots, and my heels had blisters, but we didn't have time for moleskin or athletic tape. We took risks that day because we were only responsible for ourselves, so we left behind the bulky items from our first aid kit like the SAM splint and the instant ice packs and the huge bag of bandages, but soon we would be carrying all of the first aid kit, so we were calculating how much space we had in our day packs. Possibility Packs, we called them, in honor of the first rule of Leave No Trace: plan ahead and prepare. The name was laughable.

I was watching my feet, calculating each step, not looking ahead, when Wyatt sidestepped a marmot carcass in the middle of the trail. Its fur brown and gray, fiercely baring buckteeth even in death. Wyatt said it must be recently dead, that easy game like this wouldn't last long up here. We stepped nonchalantly around it, knowing it was just nature running its course, and everything living was preprogrammed to die. As we plunged ahead, Wyatt wondered aloud if the marmot froze too, like the elk, and I say, *Yeah, probably*.

A few minutes of short breaths and lunge stepping, using our

234

hands to grab clods of earth, and we were on top of the saddle. The white world opened up to us on this ridge, and we could see the peaks that were hidden to us down in the valley below. I had been up on this saddle before but had run out of time to climb to the tops of Sultan or Turk. I pointed them out to Wyatt, orienting our topo map to the shape of the road, my best guess at north. Silverton was right over that ridge, two miles downhill, and it felt useful knowing things Wyatt didn't, like we would be able to be a team this summer, dependent upon each other in a familial way. I broke off one piece of the pumpkin bread for him and one for me, and we sipped from our cold Nalgenes.

After our break, we followed the ridgeline, skirting a cornice, and soon we were on top of Turk. The feeling of standing on top of a thirteen-thousand-foot peak, being the tallest thing around, was a familiar one to us both but hadn't lost its thrill. The wind was still a surprise, and I shivered, pulled my down jacket out of my pack. The sun was blinding and we could see forever, the whole summer, our whole lives, stretched out in front of us. I pointed across the highway to the Twilight Mountains, and I said, *I hope we're going there with our campers.* We could see the Needles, Chicago Basin, Vestal Basin, seemingly all of the western half of the Weminuche Wilderness. Forgetting for a moment to be somber, I said what I knew Wyatt was already thinking: *This is where we'll be living for the next two months. This is our job.*

We goofed around in the snow with our ice axes for a few minutes on the spacious peak, and then I set my camera on a cairn and pressed the timer, and we took a picture of ourselves smirking and wielding our menacing red and yellow ice axes, like we were young and capable and there was no one out here but us, no one else so certain of what it meant to be alive.

Wyatt and I summitted Sultan and another unnamed thirteener all before noon, keeping to our schedule, then scampered back to the saddle, back toward our base camp, retracing our footprints in the snow. We plunge-stepped downhill, leading with our heels, a technique we would teach our campers to build their confidence on

235

steep snow descents. I'd once excelled at this kind of off-piste walking, trusting my body to hold me upright. But everything seemed more precarious now, my assurance wasn't what it had been just one summer earlier, and I wondered how I would teach my campers all these things I lacked in myself.

After a short break to fill our water bottles in the snow runoff, it was one thirty, and we were practically running back to our base camp, not wanting to make the rest of the staff wait for our return. When we wrapped around the corner of a switchback, I grabbed Wyatt's shoulder and pointed. *Look.* A bird of prey swooped down toward the shadows of the tree line, the dead marmot in its right talon. *It's a golden eagle*, I said.

Down below the krummholz, we were windburned and tired, hiking on autopilot, propelled by the nearness of our destination and the knowing this, too, would soon be over. At the first stand of trees we stopped midstride, in sync with each other. Not even thirty yards away, we'd startled two eagles out from under a lodgepole pine, its branches angled toward the sky. On the ground beneath the pine, they'd abandoned the marmot, red and bloody. Its carcass, evidence that out here, the living kept on living in spite of the dead. The eagles circled back above us, their wings wide, like hands splayed, displacing the air and casting shadows resembling our own.

21

I n the few sluggish days between when my dad died and his memorial service, Ryan and I played Risk with our mom, coaxing her into game after game, each one taking several hours to play, filling the infinite space between waking and sleep. Risk is a game of probability. Each player has forty tiny plastic figurines: metaphors for battalions. The board is a color-coded map of the world. The goal: to annihilate the other players, occupy every country on the map. Each player rolls dice over and over, three dice for the attacker, two for the defender, and whenever the attacker's sum of numbers exceeds the defender's, the defender loses a figurine. Ryan is able to look at the figurine populations of two neighboring countries and know the probability, weigh the risk of an attack. It had been like this since he was seven, when my mom sat us down at the kitchen table, taught us the moves of each chess piece, and he beat her at the first game he ever played.

So, when our mom refused to play another game, Ryan and I re-rationed the countries and played two-player Risk. The game devolved into mindless dice rolling, and we were bored with each other's company, left wanting a third player. Ryan called his girlfriend, said, *Come over*. But the girlfriend had never known a family member to die, walked into our mom's kitchen and said nothing to her. After hardly five minutes, my mom said to my brother, *I think she should go*.

When the girlfriend left, my mom and brother fought loudly in the kitchen. They were an equal match, my brother, stubborn in his right to see his girlfriend after his dad died, my mom, hot with rage, unbridled. She had been quiet, seething over the last few days, existing in a state of the surreal, something that must have felt uncontrollable, and she found an outlet for her anger, however small and unsatisfying, in Ryan's girlfriend and, by default, in him. I cowered. They would fight, say whatever they needed to say to each

238

other, and then be fine, forget they were ever angry, feeling better that whatever was welling inside them had finally been released. I had never been like that. My dad had never been like that. We carried the imprint of anger or disappointment or guilt around for days, for months sometimes, felt the fog hang in that house long after a fight.

I went down to the unfinished basement and hid under my dad's work saw. We had moved it with all his other toolboxes only a few months before, and he hadn't used it, hadn't even plugged it into the wall, but still there were piles of sawdust under it, knocked out from when the movers set it down on the concrete in the back corner of the room. Bereft of a parent, I was overcome by the desire to be held. In search of fulfilling that desire led me to sit in the most enclosed space in the house, to return to the womb.

The whole basement was full of my dad's tools—drawers of wrenches and drill bits and screws—and I felt safe contained in that small, dark space, surrounded by everything that had been his.

My mom came down after twenty minutes, asked what was wrong. *Cara, why are you under the saw?* I took the question as condescension: this isn't how a person is supposed to grieve, to behave. I ran the words over and over in my mind, *Mom, I'm gay*, certain she could read minds. But I said nothing, stared at the concrete floor, the secret like a hard candy pressed against the roof of my mouth.

Ashamed of my avoidance, my muteness, I hated that in a moment when I should be grieving my dad, my mind kept jumping to this secret, my whole identity forged around being private. The grief at the loss of a parent was compounded by the grief of my inability to communicate with my one remaining parent. My arms, wrapped around my knees; my fingers, etching circles into the pile of sawdust on the floor.

I was offended by her cooing, struck suddenly by the huge vacancy my dad left behind, the realization that I might spend the rest of my life misunderstood by my mom. I left the isolation of the basement for the even-more-private cab of my car sitting in

239

the driveway. I wasn't planning to go anywhere—I had nowhere to go—but the car served as a kind of escape, a latent freedom.

I sent a text to Sloan, the woman I had a crush on: *What you up to?* She was the friend of a friend. We had met two months earlier in a bar. The bar was dark and she was wearing mascara, big earrings, and a teal 1980s headband, her hair like Medusa's. She lived a mile across town and was finishing her undergrad thesis. Over the past two months, I had read bits and pieces of her thesis that were still in progress, offering what I'd hoped was the same level of attention she had given me when I talked about my dad's declining health. That winter, she and I started running together, meeting up on the cement steps in front of her apartment, lacing long loops through city parks over frozen sidewalks, the breath of our conversations hanging in midair. She was who I talked to the most during his last weeks.

A few weeks before my dad went into hospice, in bumper-to-bumper traffic south of Chicago, driving home from a friend's wedding, I discovered that time was bendable. That if I was thinking about Sloan—getting chased by the geese in front of the zoo entrance, her stretching her quad by holding onto her porch railing with one hand and her foot with her other, her palm on my forearm after drinking unfiltered porters in a pub—time was a sort of accordion I could speed up or slow down with only the power of my imagination, that all of Indiana could pass by outside the window of the Buick without me registering.

After he died, I wanted badly for her to come to his memorial service, to have someone there who wasn't related to me, who hadn't known my dad but who had come anyway, for me. She responded to my *What you up to?* text the next morning, but I never invited her to the service.

The day before I left Grand Rapids to move back to Colorado, she came over to help me pack boxes and then load them into the back seat of the Buick. After, we went out to a brewery. It was May and starting to stay warm after the sun set. We stayed out until last call. In the hollow dark shadows of the parking lot, she took my hand, interlocking her fingers with mine. I wanted to kiss her there, under the honey locust, to fill in the colossal silence of everything I'd left unsaid, but I let the moment pass, afraid of what it might mean to confuse her compassion with attraction.

Then, six months after I moved, I came home to visit my mom for a week during the holidays. During my visit, I drove three hours through lake-effect snow coming in off Lake Michigan to see Sloan at her mom's house. We made tomato, basil, and mozzarella baguettes and sat in front of the hearth feeding each other, her mom refilling our wineglasses until sometime after midnight.

In bed that night, she reached her hand across the sheets until her fingers were inside mine, her legs entwined with mine, and then we were kissing, hands under T-shirts, unhooking bras one-handedly, as easy as undoing our own. We were nervous lovers, quiet and breathy with our pleasure, not wanting her mom and stepdad to hear, like high schoolers seven years overdue.

After, she brought me a glass of water, and we stayed naked that way until morning. I woke up to a silent house, alone in a bed that was never her childhood bed, and put on my clothes. In the kitchen, she had made coffee, and even though her mom and stepdad had left for work, she wouldn't kiss me in the daylight. I took her reticence as more secrecy than regret, that she did not want to name what had transpired. I finished my coffee and drove back to my mom's house over snowplowed roads, numb with sadness.

* * *

My impulse to connect the dots—to say my dad's cancer is somehow related to my own cancer, and my grieving him is somehow related to my search for a lover—is an attempt to stave off meaninglessness, to line up all the events of my life and regard them in gestalt, in accumulation, and decide they add up to something logical. I know that each time I go back over each of these memories, it is always, inevitably, a reduction, glossing over him, rounding his sharp edges. But what else is memory if not a map of cause and

241

effect, something to carry in your pocket for reassurance, wearing bare the seams of its folds?

* * *

Lucia tells Ada and me that she doesn't like hiking, but whenever we take her to the mountains with us, she rallies. Content to be with us wherever we are, she coaxes us into playing word games with her, and when that runs out, she pretends to be an F1 race announcer, her right foot versus her left. That day, we went on a hike up on Snoqualmie Pass an hour east of Seattle, one Ada and Lucia had done in part before when Lucia was younger, but one I had never been to. The experience of hiking, for me, has always served as a kind of kinesthetic memory trigger. The patterns of geological forces that shaped each place I'd been were repetitive, enough so that each new place reminded me of some other place. Like the red View Master toy my babysitter had, the landscape around me in present time presented to one eye, and the landscape of some previous time and place presented to my other, converging to form something sepia and 3D.

All of Washington's hikes west of the Cascade Crest are predictable. We would start down low, in the trees, wherever the road dead-ended into trailhead. Then we walked, typically steeply uphill, through a dense canopy of Douglas fir and western red cedar and hemlock, until we broke out of the trees, on a ridgeline or a basin or a talus field, and then the valley we'd walked through would open up all around. This hike was no different. Lucia hiked between us, more focused on talking than walking. At the first clearing, we paused on a rock to eat a snack.

The place felt hauntingly familiar. It made sense to me, the way the land was shaped here, each mile or so marked by another tributary where the hills parted, each tributary draining into the main valley below. We looked across the valley at a couloir Ada and I had ski-toured the previous winter, and I used an app on my phone to identify and name each peak. Lucia asked how mountains get their names, and I said something about white men mountaineers

242

having a penchant for naming things after themselves. Two of the high points were unnamed on my app, and Lucia decided, tongue in cheek, that they should be called Sig and Ringo. She wore her hair in a ponytail, tucked through the gap at the back of her red-and-white trucker's hat, like Ash Ketchum's from Pokémon, a hot pink Under Armour sun shirt, and her purple dance pants. We crossed over from one side of the drainage to the other, picking our way gingerly across a wide bench of a waterfall, Ada reminding Lucia in Portuguese to be careful, to watch her step, and then, abruptly, we left the dense forest behind, and an alpine basin opened up around us, green everywhere, striped with snowfields. Lucia was giddy at the sight of snow in July, and the whole experience—traipsing through an hour or two of homogenous salmonberry and slide alder and vine maple and then popping out into some gorgeous place—was made novel again, witnessing her surprise.

A marmot stood on a rock outcropping above us and whistled, and Lucia whistled back, their two shrill voices indistinguishable from each other's. The trail petered out, or we lost it somewhere, and I tried to skirt the main flow of the creek, sidehilling through clumps of grass and loose mud. Lucia, unfazed, followed my boot path, Ada coaching her on how to put her trekking pole in her uphill hand and lean into the hill, passing down an animal intuition: this is how to move in the mountains.

At the top of the ridge, we sat on some glacially smoothed rock and ate chicken and pesto sandwiches. Lucia didn't want to get her pants dirty and sat, instead, on my lap, picking the lettuce off her sandwich and putting it on mine, then declaring it to be the best sandwich she'd ever had. When she finished eating, she skipped off to a nearby snow pile and started spinning, forehead to trekking pole planted in the snow. *Look I'm Big Bertha!* she said, a reference to the massive tunnel boring machine used to build a new viaduct in downtown Seattle. I sprawled out on the rock, soaking up its warmth, and Lucia came and laid out starfish on top of me, making up for lost time.

I believe that every hallowed place we move through with our bodies is imbued with an imprint, and that we are encoded with more than just genes, playing out some prewritten cellular destiny. That our bodies touch rock and therefore touch each other, in ways we can never fully know. And in this way, Lucia can know something of my dad and the lake where I grew up because I carry him, it, inside of me.

On the way back down, Lucia asked to borrow my rain jacket so she could glissade down the snow and keep her pants dry. I told her she could borrow it but that the snow might not be steep enough to get up enough speed for sledding. Undeterred, she laid out my coat at the top of the next snowfield, and then, suddenly nervous, asked her mom if she would go first. Ada rustled around in her pack for her rain jacket, then laid it out next to Lucia's, and, using her trekking pole as a kind of paddle, she propelled herself down the gentle slope. I thought then of the home video from when I was two, my dad trying to convince me to slide down my Little Tikes red slide into the water, his long legs hurdling the slide as he situated himself into the tiny seat and pantomimed sliding down into the water, egging me on. When we reached the bottom of the last snowfield, Lucia turned to us and asked, *Can we go back up and do it again?*

Maybe our human impulse to map out the past as a way of explaining cause and effect is just an affectation, a tic, our active imaginations running on overdrive. In reality, our bodies are merely permutations of the land that holds us.

We funneled back into the elbow of the valley, which was just a trickle here at the headwaters, and I pointed out to Lucia where to place each step, that the dark rocks were algae-covered and to be avoided, but the lighter gray rocks were less slick, and she could get some purchase there. I took one last look out across the valley, toward Sig and Ringo, and then turned back to Lucia and smiled.

22

Three years after my dad died, I convinced my mom to come with me to the Grand Rapids Public Museum. I hadn't been since I was a kid, and it was only seven blocks from where my mom lived now, built on the banks of the Grand River. The museum in its current location opened in 1994 when I was eight, and its opening was much anticipated in my family because of a children's book my mom had read to us, *Eliza's Carousel Lion*, written by a Grand Rapids author. My mom took Ryan and me to the museum's grand opening, and I sat perched atop the lion from the book, disappointed that it was one of the stationary pieces, watching as my brother rode up and down on his ordinary horse next to me.

Nearly twenty years later, my mom and I walked into the lobby, and we studied the piece of the Berlin Wall preserved inside a Plexiglas case near the ticket booth. It was a three-foot-wide slice, standing ten feet tall, and my mom remembered that last time we were there there wasn't a Plexiglas case. Frederik Meijer, a local billionaire and sculpture collector, obtained the piece when the wall was taken down in 1989. On a plaque in front of the slab was a photo of the section of wall this piece was taken from, the words Long Live Dalai spray-painted near the top of the wall, although the piece we have in our museum only had the letters "Lon."

Inside the entryway, past the ticket counter, the room opened into a huge foyer, and the skeleton of a fin whale hung from the rafters three stories above it. Two huge bones formed the shape of the head, conjoined by a white putty representation of cartilage at the snout, followed by a rib cage that looked almost human, save for its girth. Two stunted arms—rendered meaningless without their flesh—hung from where shoulders might have been, limp and posed. Beyond the rib cage was just spine, vertebra after vertebra after vertebra, tapering off into a plastic blue tail fastened at the end. *Does the tail of a fin whale have bones?* I wondered. Not here, in this representation, but perhaps they were lost. The looming presence of it begs the question of assembly. Where did these bones come from? And how did a human come to possess the entire skeleton of a whale, an animal that is born, lives, and dies at sea? The artifact was a stand-in for the living being that once was, poised in a moment of stillness, its plastic tail cocked, as if in an instant the whole of it would swim away.

Beyond the whale was a small anteroom, Plexiglas cases on three walls: the Doll Room, packed with over five hundred dolls. My mom commented that she owned several of these dolls as a girl: the apple head doll, the cornhusk doll.

Beyond the Doll Room was an exhibit honoring the old city hall clock tower that was destroyed in 1969 and photos of a Mrs. Mary Stiles Kimmel hitched to the wrecking ball in protest. The museum still owned pieces of the city hall, including the inner workings of the clock apparatus itself, but the plaque in front of the exhibit read, "Mere pieces cannot replace an entire building."

Then, leading up the stairs were 3D topographic maps, one of Kent County and another of Michigan, mounted to the wall. I ran my hands along the topography, remembering making salt-dough maps of Michigan in art class during fourth grade. We learned then the names for topographic features: an isthmus—that narrow strip of land between two bodies of water—an archipelago, a butte, a buttress. *Michigan is a peninsula,* our teacher told us, *surrounded on three sides by water.* In the sand down by our dock, teaching my brother everything I knew, *Look, Ryan, this is an isthmus.*

Upstairs were the dioramas, what we had come to see. In the hallway leading into the Habitats exhibit was a primer for what was to come: a taxidermied cougar, black bear, wolverine, baby bison, muskrat, and fawn the size of a house cat, each stuffed into the same case, with nondescript deciduous trees painted on the backdrop. Some of the seams in the animal hides were showing, looking raised and raw. My own seam was nearly twenty-years healed, white and prominent below my belly button, stretching hip bone to hip bone, sunken now instead of raised, but I remembered its being puffy once, my mom worrying about infection. My skin cells' mitochondria triggering the cells to heal.

I was transfixed with questions about this tiny deer, its hooves pressed up against the glass. How could a deer ever be so small? How did the museum come to own this newborn, its spots so vivid they looked fake? The art of taxidermy so far beyond my imagination's reach, I wanted to know what of the insides were taken out and what was stuffed back in in their place. The glass suggesting there is a firm partition between past and present, real and not real.

My mom said, *Do you remember Muskrat Susie and Muskrat Sam?* and I said *No*, but then she started singing a song, and I was instantly back with my dad, watching as a muskrat scampered out of its den under our paddleboat. *What is that, a song or something?* I asked. She said it was one they had made up.

Beyond the initial case of mammals, we entered a small room of seemingly unrelated exhibits. There was a case of birds pinned beak-up to a corkboard, redundant displays, four of the same species in a line, supine, their bodies packed tightly like colored pencils, two male and two female of each species. There were meadowlarks and flickers, rose-breasted grosbeaks—all four males—five bluebirds instead of four, Baltimore orioles, a whole caseful of color. I thought then of sitting on my grandma's lap in the dining room of our house on the lake, watching the sun rise over the water, listening as she named the bird that went with each song.

On the backside of the bird display was a snake skeleton curved into a perfect *S*, all of its ribs intact, as fragile as potato chips underfoot. Above the snake, a monarch butterfly was pinned next to a viceroy, but this was a room designed more for aesthetics than instruction. There was no plaque explaining the animal habit of mimicry, just these two winged insects with small identifying tags. The butterflies triggered a memory of a student's essay, that millisecond it takes for synapses to fire, like opening a window, caught in the brief thrill of recognition, that inward gust of meaning. My student had been making an argument about straight-acting gay men, comparing himself to the viceroy, a self-implication, for sure, but also a compulsion to examine what is personal, familiar. A scientist's first subject is always himself. I was surprised by the metaphor, fascinated actually, immediately penned "yes!" in the margin because of the precision of the comparison.

The craving for these associations, I thought, was what had compelled me to visit my hometown museum in the middle of July. The self-reification of seeing an object—here a refinished doll bed, here a topographic map, here a fierce-looking muskrat—and investing in it a slew of personal significance was made easy in this building brimming with stuff. I thought if I could piece together enough memories, prompted by the objects in this museum, which remained unchanged from when I was a kid, the impression of our family as whole would congeal in my mind.

There was the shell of a giant clam in the hearth. *It's really real*, a teenager announced to no one in particular, dragging out the "real" in "really." A young boy crouched to touch the smooth inside of the shell, one of the only things left uncased.

Beyond the room with the birds and the shell was a darkened hallway with two long, opposing dioramas on the north and south walls. This was the aquatic habitat display. The fish in here were not real specimens, subject to the art of a taxidermist, but rather plastic look-alikes hung from real fishing line, each with an authentic lure—one you could buy at Walmart—stuck in its mouth. The backdrops were painted blue-green, an expectation, even though there were no windows, no sky to reflect. Those two mirrors and our existence between them, all that blue, a trick of sunlight and air.

When we entered the main habitat exhibition, a drafty room with a real breeze rustling through fake trees, I was caught off guard by the sharpness of remembering. There were bird sounds coming from the next habitat, one room over, and I was undone by their familiarity. The moment seemed to collide with a previous one from many years ago, when I had stood in front of these same Plexiglas cases in a much smaller body. I had the feeling then that

I had completed a full revolution, was beginning again, retracing the past with the ever-unfolding present.

The dune exhibit looked exactly as it did when I was eight: the position of the barn owl overhead, the beady gaze of the two deer staring offstage somewhere, as if startled by some unseen predator in the distance, each grain of sand unmoved. The same red Coleman cooler was still sitting in the sand, two tattered hiking boots propped against it, their tongues lolling out as if, only moments ago, the boots were filled with human feet.

In front of the dunescape was a transparent wheel filled with sand. The plaque here was instructional. "Tilt this wheel and see how the angle of the dune becomes too steep—the sand slips and slides to a rest. For dry Michigan sand, this angle is approximately 32 degrees. This is the angle of repose." I kept spinning and spinning the wheel, flinging the sand in circles on itself, hoping for what? An angle steeper than thirty-two degrees? A slippage of granules against each other that never stopped? For recursiveness to reveal some sort of meaning, that if I came again and again to the altar of these memories, they might be preserved instead of eroded into tinier and tinier fragments?

When I was eight years old, I ran down a sand dune with my dad, both of us barefoot and falling. It was dusk at Sleeping Bear Dunes, Lake Michigan spreading out behind us, Glen Lake teal and sparkling before us. The sand giving way beneath our feet, each stride elongated by gravity, *Like walking on the moon*, I think I said then. At the bottom, he looked at me and asked: *Do you want to do it again?*

Acknowledgments

I wrote much of the first draft of this book in one summer, but it took another thirteen years to bring it to fruition. If not for the enduring belief in the viability of this project from those named here, I would have given up on it long ago.

Thank you to the editors and various literary magazines that gave space to my writing when I was a very young and very new writer. Early excerpts from this memoir appeared in *Flyway: Journal of Writing and Environment* ("Krummholz," Fall 2011), *The Gettysburg Review* ("Lake People," Winter 2012), and *Ninth Letter* ("To a Player Piano, Grand Rapids, MI, 2010," 2013).

Thank you to Banashee Cadreau of the Sault Ste. Marie Tribe of Chippewa Indians, and Kristen Green, Jade Green, and Janice Dewey from Bimose Ode, for your careful reading of my camp chapter and for generously providing resources, context, and suggestions for revision based on your lived experiences and inherited knowledge.

To my teachers, Christa Craven, Jessica Jones, Sean Prentiss, Alexandra Teague, Kim Barnes, Mary Ann Judge, and Joy Passanante. Thank you for all your time and attention to my writing, for curating reading lists, for coaching me on how to improve, and, most of all, for showing me the kind of adult I wanted to be, how to lead a "life of the mind" and what it looks like when you treat students with the utmost dignity, making them feel beloved.

To Karl Woelz, for the gifts of Alison Bechdel, Sarah Schulman, bell hooks, Audre Lorde, Dorothy Allison, and Kate Millett; for the epiphany of seeing myself reflected in print for the first time; and for giving me the language to finally name for myself how it felt to move through the world in my body. For your tongue-in-cheek benediction, writing in my graduation card, "go West young man!" And for all the Lisa Frank snail mail over the years.

And especially to Mary Blew, for your Long Form class that incubated this book, for giving me direction in a directionless void, for inspiring me to believe I was capable of something I previously thought completely insurmountable, and for your always frank and kind feedback.

To my readers, Eric Hayes, Sonya Dunning, Katie Lee Ellison, Jeff Jones, and Matt Sullivan, for reading the whole manuscript through multiple times, for being generous of your time and ear and spirit, for seeing what this book could be instead of what it was. To Marla Koberstein, for believing in me and this book when I couldn't. And to my writing group, Amy Whitcomb, Kelly Smoot, Emily Benson, and Tom Pamperin, for fifteen years of friendship, camaraderie, and always knowing what my essay is about before I do.

To Marie Sweetman, for championing this book, and to the whole team at Wayne State University Press, for your warmth, humanity, and attention to detail.

To Erika Rader, for reminding me again and again that the world needs more nature books authored by queer people, and for convening a once a week Zoom writing hour during the pandemic, during which the bulk of the revisions on this manuscript were made.

To Jayne, for living through all of this with me, for never wanting to miss a sunset, for always picking up the phone.

To Danny Caine, for being the best first person to come out to, for seeing me when no one else did, and for your fraternal friendship. I am forever indebted to you for convincing me to move home the year before my dad died.

To Jason Riebold, for bearing witness to my family on the brink of our darkest hour, for figuring out how to fix the goddamn Coleman stove, and for always knowing exactly what to say after a heartbreak.

To Julia Resnick, for corroborating so, so many of my patterns of thought that I assumed were just superstitions I'd made up. Our conversations about illness and serendipity became the blueprint for all of what is here.

To all the summer of 2012 baristas at Sparrows Coffee in Grand Rapids, for your queer haircuts and rainbow pins and always saving the last trail bar for me.

To Sloan, for holding taut the tender barbed world beneath me when I thought that I'd be swallowed whole.

To Kristen, for accompanying me everywhere across the Palouse in the Buick, and for your bottomless adoration.

To Amanda, for teaching me what it feels like to be loved without shame. So much of the first draft of this book I wrote to and for you.

To Ryan, for the army men on the overhead fan, for naming all the purple triangle and orange octagon runs on the end-of-cul-de-sac snow pile, for a pinch of lettuce to satisfy the mind. For your discretion and fierce integrity. For turning your body into a bellows and making music from all this sadness, and for reminding me that Dad is always with us, on the wind.

And most of all, to Lucia, for the wormhole in time, for resurrecting so many memories of my dad I didn't know I had forgotten, for Skronkball and "Despacito" and all the late night 1v1 at Parkwood Elementary. For teaching me your quiet seething confidence, and that there is a big difference between a hobby and a passion. Thank you for this light. Thank you for this life. Thank you for this love.

About the Author

CARA STODDARD is a creative nonfiction writer and poet, who grew up on a lake in Michigan. Their poems and essays have appeared in *Fourth Genre*, *The Gettysburg Review*, *Terrain.org*, and *Ninth Letter*. Currently, they live in Seattle with their stepdaughter.